Returning to Normal

A Cry For Revival
and
Reformation

Peter Whitehouse

"Revival is always born in prevailing prayer. This is the one, the basic unalterable central principle of awakenings." Drummond

To the Glory and Honor of Our Lord Jesus Christ!

Returning to Normal

A Cry for Revival
and
Reformation

First Edition Oct 2005

ISBN 1-59975-058-9

CONTENTS

About Revival... 9
*The Need for Revival, Revival Accounts,
Prevailing Prayer, Hunger for God and much more.*

Personal Awakening... 66
*Abiding in Christ, Living in the Spirit
Walking in Humility, Loving God
The Depths of Jesus*

Reformation ... 191
*A fresh look at our doctrines
and the ways of doing church*

Introduction

"Return, we beseech You, O God of hosts; look down from heaven and see, and visit this vine and the vineyard which Your right hand has planted, and the branch that You made strong for Yourself. It is burned with fire, it is cut down; they perish at the rebuke of Your countenance. Revive us, and we will call upon Your name. Restore us, O Lord God of hosts; cause Your face to shine, and we shall be saved!" Psalm 80:14-16, 18-19

We are usually so consumed with the affairs of daily living that we seldom consider the big picture. Nevertheless, most can realize there is something wrong... in the Church and in the world. Clearly, unrighteousness abounds throughout the land and it is getting worse. One can hardly turn without hearing of murderous violence, child molestation or seeing some indecent thing. And as far as the Church is concerned, we have grown lukewarm... trying to do the work of God without the power of His Spirit. We have plans and programs for just about everything, but there is little fruit that remains. And the decisions made during this generation by some of the clergy to endorse abortion and divorce... and to ordain active homosexuals really puts it over the top. In addition, we love our toys, lusting after the bigger and more expensive. Surely the Church has become like the world, rather than influencing it for the better. And then there are the usual divisions and doctrinal things. God help us!

On a personal level, sometimes it seems as though you are simply going through the motions, doesn't it? Your zeal has diminished, the fire has dwindled, complacency is setting in. Worldly activities are much more appealing than when you first started the race. Does any of this sound familiar? No one likes to quote these verses anymore but what did Jesus say to the Laodicean Church? *"I know your works, that you are neither cold nor hot. I could wish you were cold or hot. So then, because you are lukewarm, and neither cold nor hot, I will vomit you out of My mouth"* (Rev. 3:15-16). We had better pay attention!

At times like this it is worth reviewing a bit of history to gain some insight and direction. There have been numerous instances through-out the ages when the people of God have lost their first love... and evil has increased. There is definitely a cyclical pattern to be seen: The children of God turn away from Him, they disobey. This is followed by a season of suffering from the consequences of sin. Then they cry to the Almighty with heart felt desperation and He sends His deliverance. The entire book of Judges reveals six consecutive periods like this. These spiritual revivals in Israel lasted for approximately one generation... about forty years. There is a fresh zeal for righteousness with an accompanying season of prosperity... and rest from their oppressors. Again unrighteousness increases, the nation declines, falling prey to it's enemies for extended periods of between one to four decades. The people cry out, and God sends a new judge who establishes righteousness in the land... bringing forth a fresh season of fruitfulness and blessing.

You can also see this pattern throughout the history of the Church. The Bride forsakes her First Love (intimacy with God and the daily guidance of His Spirit) and substitutes with mere religion... ecclesiastical and ceremonial. This has happened ad nauseam since the time of the early Church fathers. Thank God for His mercy and grace. He has revived His Bride time and time again. There have been four revival periods in the "modern" Church age: The Great Awakening (1735), the Second Great Awakening (1800) The Prayer Revival of 1857 and the Welsh Revival including Azusa Street in 1904 and 1906 respectively. I realize that some may disagree, but these are well documented and it would be worth your while to investigate them with an open mind. Just because they did not occur within your particular denomination does not render them invalid. One side note: There is an obvious correlation between the Church turning from the Lord (and His ways) and the moral decline of any given society. Check it out! The Church declined first... then the society. You thought it was the other way around, didn't you?

At the risk of redundancy, here is the cycle again: the church declined, then society declined with a myriad of social ills made manifest. The Church (usually beginning with a faithful few) began to cry out for a spiritual revival. This season of "desperate" prayer would last for months or even years... and then God would answer with His supernatural reviving power. Something like mouth to mouth resuscitation, He breathes life into His emaciated Bride, nourishing her with His own body and blood. She repents of her sins under His strong conviction, and now filled with His Holy Spirit, she falls in love with Him all over again... and worships Him. She joyfully serves her Bridegroom with all of her heart.

During such seasons of revival the work of evangelism begins to flow like a river, at home and abroad, with signs and wonders following. Conviction of sin and the gift of repentance sovereignly falls upon entire communities. Thousands, if not millions, are swept into the Kingdom. Glory to God! This makes me want to shout! And best of all, there was fruit that remained: Many works of mercy were established (Salvation Army, Red Cross, etc.) and social issues like slavery and child labor were abolished. Hospitals, orphanages and numerous colleges were opened and industrial and agricultural productivity increased. Entire cities have been transformed; police and judges had little work to do because the crime rate dropped dramatically ... all as the result of a glorious spiritual revival!

It is so obvious, dear Christian: we need a spiritual awakening right now! We need Jesus to resuscitate His bride now. Oh that God would demonstrate His mighty power in our day! ... that He would convict us of our sins and confront our cities and our nation with a glorious manifestation of His presence... including signs and wonders that are so awesome they could not be explained away. *Many will see and fear and place their trust in the Lord....* falling to their knees in heartfelt repentance, worshipping the King of Glory!

Pray, beloved, and continue to pray. We are not speaking of some pie in the sky fantasy. Revival has occurred numerous times throughout history... and we need it again, before it is too late. Our sins are great, beloved. Even now the judgment of God is occurring to a lesser or greater degree. Make no mistake; His glory will be revealed in the midst of darkness, yes, gross darkness (Isaiah 60:1-2). We MUST realize the lateness of the hour! This is the season for fervent, effectual prayer for revival. This should be one of your very highest priorities.

Much of the Church has been satisfied with superficiality and when exhorted to go farther into the things of God, even into God Himself, we think it to be too much, too radical. Who wants to pay the price anyway? In fact, our form of Christianity has become so diluted that when hearing of death to self, complete abandonment or sacrificial

6

giving, we consider it to pertain to the "deeper" Christian life. Dear child, these things are not deep; they are merely normal Christianity, thus the title: *Returning to Normal*. The Lord would have you understand that there is so much more to the Christian faith than what you are presently experiencing, much more than your doctrine and particular method of service.

Hopefully, this book will be a useful tool in your pursuit of a personal awakening and encourages you to diligently pray for revival and transformation in your region and your nation ...a challenge to you personally and to the Church collectively. Page by page, day by day, the Lord will lead you another step forward as He reveals your heart. These lingering questions are intricately woven throughout this simple offering: *Are you willing to love God above all things? Will you humble yourself? Will you take the time to pray?* I trust that you will see the dire need in this hour and receive this loving exhortation to be conformed to His image... and will be strengthened and encouraged to press on for the Magnificent Prize.

When you read, invite the Holy Spirit to unveil the truth. Use this as a primer for repentance. When you see yourself in this mirror do not justify or excuse; simply admit your sins and turn from them. There is no condemnation here, only love that heals and revives. It is well known that religion has done much to expose sin, but very little to mend and restore the sinner. It has often been said that Christianity is the only army that shoots it's wounded. Not so with our God, His plan for your life hasn't been diminished because of your sins. If you will respond to His grace, He will use your failures to refine you and make you all the more effective.

The joy and fulfillment of intimacy awaits you, dear one. Your revival is at the door. God loves you so very much. He desires to give Himself completely to you and will do so according to your capacity to receive Him. In other words, you can have as much of God as you want. Needless to say, a life filled with self has a lesser capacity for God. However, in His mercy and great love, the Holy One will arrange circumstances to bring your self-life to destruction. He empties you out, so that He can fill you with more of Himself! You can rest assured that this work of sanctification is His work, not yours; simply cooperate. You are a sweet fragrance to your Lord; He desires you! This is your destiny: to be the eternal Bride of Christ!

The insights expressed here are certainly not meant to be an indictment or an all-inclusive addendum to your catechism. Nor is it to be considered sectarian: denominational, evangelical or pentecostal. But hopefully you will be encouraged to live your life in the Spirit, void of legalism and other empty ways... and that you will be filled with fire, fresh zeal and Holy Spirit power with authority to do mighty exploits in His name. Remember, the whole earth groans, awaiting the revealing of the sons of God! One thing though, please hold your peripheral doctrines loosely. Clinging too tightly can prevent you from receiving new understanding.

This is the hour, servant of God, for an absolute transformation, a reformation. Nothing less will do. Much of the Church has become sinfully complacent; we have lost our first love. Our many ways of "doing" church have failed. It requires but a glance at the news to realize the magnitude of that failure. Wake up Church; this mess is our fault! What will it take for us to become resolute, to fully submit to the purposes of God? Make no mistake, much has been given to us, much is also required. Dear Christian, only by His amazing grace will we turn from our selfish ways and love God with all of our hearts. Let us encourage one another to surrender once again, and to follow the leading of the Holy Spirit. He is calling us to pray for Revival. Don't quit; don't settle for less. We must have revival now! Can you feel the wind of the Spirit blowing? His holy fire is getting hotter. There is a cloud rising, the size of a man's hand... Keep praying; don't stop. It's about to rain!

"Come, and let us return to the Lord; for He has torn, but He will heal us; He has stricken, but He will bind us up. After two days He will revive us; on the third day He will raise us up, that we may live in His sight. Let us know, let us pursue the knowledge of the Lord. His going forth is established as the morning; He will come to us like the rain, like the latter and former rain to the earth." Hos. 6:1-3

A special thanks to all of my brothers and sisters who have spilled out their lives in intercession for the sake of Revival. Your prayers will soon be answered! Together we will behold with awe and wonder those things that we have longed to see!

About Revival

The Need for Revival, Revival Accounts,
Prevailing Prayer, Hunger for God and much more.

Normal Christianity

"...and you are not your own? For you were bought at a price; therefore glorify God in your body and in your spirit, which are God's." *1 Corinthians 6:19-20*

What is often described, as the "deeper Christian life" is nothing more than normal. The Church doesn't realize how watered down and aberrant our form of Christianity has become. This is why some call normal, deep. Giving yourself wholeheartedly to God, without reservation, this is normal Christianity. You are not your own.

Soon after the church was birthed at Pentecost, complete abandonment, total commitment and Spirit-led living were commonplace; read the Book of Acts. They were in one accord and in awe of His glory. These early saints loved God and loved one another. Holy fear and a deep reverence for truth permeated the Body of Christ. They walked in faith and experienced mighty miracles. This is your reference point. This is normal Christianity.

Some might say there is no mandate to emulate the activities of the 1st century Church... and this is absolutely correct. Your form and format of prayer, worship and ministry should change according to the culture and the leading of the Holy Spirit. However, the very centerpiece of normalcy is not ecclesiastical; it is a matter of the heart, a deep love for God, a surrender of will, humility, childlike faith, commitment, reverence and awe. How far the Bride has fallen.

Be encouraged, dear disciple, our God is love. He has shamelessly pursued mankind for six millennium; He will not give up on us now. He is calling us once again to come closer. Will you abandon all else and draw near? There is no striving or religious activity needed in His loving presence, only surrender.

What is Revival?

"It is time for You to act, O Lord, for they have regarded Your law as void." Psalm 119:126

We have all heard about revival meetings... a church or group comes together for a protracted period, having daily meetings for a week or more... to reinvigorate the faithful (and the not so faithful). Usually repentance is preached and the people are blessed and encouraged. These types of meetings are good, however, this is not what we are speaking of here.

R.A. Torrey, in his book *How to Pray,* defined "Revival" in the year 1900: "A Revival is a time of quickening or impartation of life. Since God alone can give life, a Revival is a time when God visits His people and by the power of the Holy Spirit imparts new life to them, and through them imparts life to sinners dead in trespasses and sins. *New Life from God* - that is a Revival. A general Revival is a time when this new life is not confined to anyone locality but is general throughout Christendom and the earth." Torrey sensed that God wanted to do this, sometime soon, and strongly exhorted his readers to earnestly pray for a general Revival (In 1902, Revival did breakout in Australia, then in Wales, 1904 and in 1906, Los Angeles!)

Some of the obvious effects: A Revival revives the minister. He or she falls in love with God all over again. They receive a fresh love for the Word of God and a renewed love for souls. Their preaching becomes filled with power... the power to convict of sin and to clearly portray Christ; the listener is transformed. Christians of all persuasions are touched in various ways, but all feel the need to step away from the lusts of the flesh and other worldly pursuits. They actually desire to pray and want to spend extended periods with God and with other believers. They also begin to do the work of evangelism, not by compulsion but with burning passion. Works of mercy begin to flow like a river. Revival days are filled with great joy.

Revival also affects the unsaved. Strong conviction of sin comes upon a region as the Holy One draws near. Jesus told us that the Spirit would convince the world of sin (John 16:7,8). We should expect every Revival to begin with this conviction. During these seasons, thousands are converted. As on the day of Pentecost, first the church is filled (the 120 in the upper room) and then the multitudes in the streets were converted. All praise and glory to our Lord; He makes everything new. Just when all appears to be lost, He shows Himself strong and rescues His people. *"It is time for You to act, O Lord..."* Send Your Holy Spirit; revive us again!

The Revelation of the Need for Revival

"Because you say, `I am rich, have become wealthy, and have need of nothing'--and do not know that you are wretched, miserable, poor, blind, and naked-- I counsel you to buy from Me gold refined in the fire, that you may be rich; and white garments, that you may be clothed, that the shame of your nakedness may not be revealed; and anoint your eyes with eye salve, that you may see." Rev 3:17-18

There are yet so many within the body of Christ that do not perceive the need for a spiritual revival. Dear intercessor, allow this to be a strategic prayer: Beseech our God to reveal the need for revival.

Do you understand? Things have been going along just fine for them. They have a good-sized congregation with regular attendance; the offerings are consistent. Participation in church activities is fairly good too... a lot of nice people doing nice things. Some would only hope to have a congregation like this.

I trust that you have not been taken in by our little set-up. We have been describing the lukewarm Laodicean church. They were not wicked sinners and yet the Lord warned them quite sternly. *"I know your works, that you are neither cold nor hot. I could wish you were cold or hot. So then, because you are lukewarm, and neither cold nor hot, I will vomit you out of My mouth"* (Rev. 3:15).

It is only when we admit our sinfulness that we can truly repent... and we must recognize the depth of our spiritual poverty if we are to cry out for revival. Let us revisit the definition of normal Christianity: 1) A deep love for God with complete abandonment to His purposes. 2) A self-sacrificing love for others while flowing in the Spirit with child-like faith and lowliness of heart.

How we need Revival... personally and corporately. How we need God to help us now. *Dear Lord, we choose to buy from You, gold refined in the fire, that we may be rich; and white garments, that we may be clothed, that the shame of our nakedness may not be revealed; and anoint our eyes with eye salve, that we may see.*

The First Great Awakening 1735

The following historical accounts of past Revivals as documented by Mary Relfe in her book Cure Of All Ills:

As you read these vignettes note the deplorable conditions, the seasons of extraordinary prayer and the abundant fruit produced. Our God is faithful! He stirs us to pray, prays through us by His Holy Spirit and then answers. He is truly all in all! This should cause you to pray, dear saint. Pray for revival!

Jonathan Edwards, while stirring the colonies to pray for a spiritual revival, lamented the deterioration of society. "Children were given to night walking and tavern haunting." In England and western Europe, the "gin craze" found every third to sixth house a tavern. The slogan was "get drunk for a penny." The drunkenness caused an increase in gambling and prostitution. "The masses were neglected, lived in poverty, were uneducated, and calloused from youth." Hangings were a daily gala event. The hangman was applauded by men, women and children.

Meanwhile, a faithful band of persecuted Christians know as the Moravians sought the Lord with fervent, effectual prayer. The Holy Spirit descended upon them in 1727, a glorious outpouring that changed the world. Many renowned men of God could trace their roots to this movement, among them George Whitefield and John and Charles Wesley. In fact, the rebirth of western Christian culture can be traced back to the Moravian prayers. (These faithful saints agreed to pray for one hour each, round the clock... 24/7. This meeting went on, non-stop, for over 100 years!

"The Revival of 1735 brought about a transformation which reversed the social, moral and political declines. The brilliant historian Elie Halevy attributed to this great revival: 1) the stability of 18th century England, 2) the absence of riots and bloodshed which characterized the continent and 3) her avoidance of a French style revolution. Multitudes of new Christians addressed social sins with such compassion and mercy that enemies of the state were unable to incite unrest among the poor. The Christian conscience permeated society after this great revival as yeast does dough. An observer said that a "psychological earthquake has reshaped the human landscape." *Lord let it be so in our day! Revive You Church, Lord!*

The Second Great Awakening 1800

The revival fires that ignited the First Great Awakening and transformed western society had subsided. The Revival had lasted about 40 years. "Again, the salt of the earth lost it's savor. Problems of unbelievable proportions began to plague America once more." The revival historian Edwin Orr wrote, "There was an unprecedented moral slump following the American Revolution. Drunkenness was epidemic. Out of a population of 5 million, 300,000 were confirmed drunkards. For the first time in American history, women were afraid to go out at night. Bank robberies were a daily occurrence." The famous atheist, Voltaire was adamantly declaring: "Christianity will be forgotten in 30 years." Tom Paine was echoing these sentiments all across America.

In 1794, Isaac Backus, known for his praying and his exhorting had an encounter with the Holy Spirit. As a result, he initiated concerts of prayer among several denominations. Soon, America was interlaced with a network of organized prayer meetings. "As the people humbled themselves and began to cry unto the Lord, God poured upon them a Spirit of Supplication. This is a prerequisite for burning, believing, prevailing, persuading, persevering Revival praying!"

In 1798, Revival fires began to burn in New England. Churches couldn't accommodate those enquiring about salvation. Multitudes were won to the Lord! Then the revival spread westward. Consider this eye witness account of a meeting in Cane Ridge, Kentucky where 25,000 attended: *"I counted seven ministers preaching at one time, some on stumps, others on wagons. Some of the people were singing, others praying, some crying for mercy. The noise was like the roar of the Niagara. At one time, I saw 500 swept down in a moment as if a battery of a thousand guns had opened upon them, and then immediately followed shrieks and shouts that rent the very heavens."* Thousands were mightily converted at Cane Ridge. Some received visions of Jesus; others received a call to the ministry!

"Out of this second great awakening, came a sustained missionary movement, the roots of the abolition of slavery and the initiation of popular education. Over 600 colleges were founded by these revivalists! The Church began to influence the world once again! Chastity was in vogue; honesty and integrity were the rule rather than the exception. Decreased crime, drunkenness and gambling provided the backdrop for a period of genuine national prosperity." *Lord, let it be so in our day! Revive you Church; Revive Your Bride!*

The Prayer Revival of 1857

"Revival is always born in prevailing prayer. This is the one, the basic unalterable central principle of awakenings" Drummond

By the late 1840's the Church had seriously declined again. The full churches had grown lukewarm, even dead... and some churches began to empty. The population of the United States at that time was about 30 million.. Yes, there were many Catholics and Protestants but in their emaciated spiritual condition, they surely weren't influencing society. Dr. Lewis Drummond describes that era: "Absolute authority of the Bible was questioned; dullness and lethargy pervaded God's people. Many fell into open sin as compromise set in. Worldliness took over; the Church sank into a Laodicean syndrome. The programs went on, often with greater fervor, but spiritual power was missing." Sure sounds like our generation doesn't it?

In 1857, a businessman named Jeremiah Lamphier heard the Lord tell him, "Take your lunch hour and start praying for Revival." Although his first meeting drew only six men, soon there were thousands throughout New York City meeting for prayer at lunchtime, and then every hour of the day and night. According to Dr. Edwin Orr, this revival went up the Hudson and down the Mohawk Rivers. They had to cut holes in the ice to baptize the many new converts. The Revival quickly spread across America; every community was touched. There were one million new converts from outside the Church, and at least another million who already occupied the pews were converted. A typical church of that day had a few hundred members... Some were now bulging with over 1,000.

"The Revival of 1857 restored integrity to government and business in America once again. There was renewed obedience to the social commandments. An intense sympathy was created for the poor and needy; a compassionate society was rebirthed. The reins of America were returned to the godly. Yet another time, Revival became the solution to the problems, the remedy for the evils."

This glorious work of God spread to England where one million new converts were added to church roles... and to Ireland in 1859. Multitudes of Irish Catholics and Protestants stood together in the fields as the Holy Spirit moved them, under strong conviction, to heart-felt repentance with sighs and groans and crying out to God. The Rev. Magill writes, "The multitude heaves to and fro like a ship in a storm; and like drunken men in the streets, the men stagger and fall with a deep sigh or a shout. Tears are shed and groans are heard. Prayer and praise, tears and smiles, mingle together. Husbands and wives are locked in each others arms weeping and praying together; while those who came to scoff, stand still, and in fear and trembling contemplate this strange thing that is going on before their eyes."

The Revival of 1904

The period between 1902 and 1912 was perhaps one of the most exciting in Church history since the days of Pentecost. This Revival truly had a global impact... And all of this is well documented.

Mary Relfe states, "Spiritual decadence pervaded society in the late 1890's. Corruption, immorality, drunkenness, cults, gambling and agnosticism rose in proportion to the Churches ineptness. By the turn of the 20th century, the glory had departed, the saints had defected, the salt had lost its savor, the world had lost its light and deep moral darkness prevailed."

It seems that during the early days of the 20th century, a Spirit of Supplication was poured out simultaneously around the world. Missionaries in remote regions, having no contact with the happenings of the hour, reported the Holy Spirit was stirring them to pray for a world-wide Revival. Others in Australia, Britain and the United States were hearing the same thing. When R.A. Torrey traveled to Melbourne in 1902, he found 1,700 neighborhood prayer meetings being held every week. Revival swept Melbourne, then all of Australia , then flowing to England and Whales.

In 1904, a young Welshman, Evan Roberts, had an encounter with God and He was given a word for his generation. At first, he addressed only seventeen people... and his message was concise:

1) You must confess every know sin to God and make every wrong done to man right.
2) You must remove every doubtful habit from your life
3) You must obey the Spirit promptly.
4) You must go public with your witness of Christ. Christ said, "If I be lifted up, I will draw all men unto Me."

"All seventeen responded... and the Holy Spirit descended with awesome power. Within weeks every church building was packed with hundreds standing outside unable to get in. The nation's atmosphere was suddenly electrified by the presence of God. General conversation turned to the things which are eternal." This four point message was repeated time and time again.

George Davis of the New York Witness, a few weeks into the Revival, printed: "It is sweeping over hundreds of hamlets and cities emptying saloons, theaters and dance halls and filling the churches night after night with praying multitudes. The policeman are almost idle and in many cases, the magistrates have few trials on hand. Debts are being paid and the character of entire communities are being transformed almost in a day."

By 1905 the Revival was spreading around the globe. Ministers in America were meeting to plan how they would accommodate this move of God when it hit our shores. And their anticipation was not unfounded...throughout the land the fear of God fell. A somber God-consciousness settled upon the United States. Atlantic City with a population of 60,000 was wonderfully overshadowed by the Most High. Only 50 people remained unconverted! In Portland, Oregon 240 stores signed an agreement to close from 11A.M. to 2 P.M. daily to permit everyone to attend prayer meetings. The Mayor of Denver declared a day of prayer and by 10:30 A.M. the churches were filled and by 11:30 almost every store closed. Even the Colorado legislature shut down. More than 7 million were drawn to Christ during the 2 year period between 1905 and 1907! All praise and glory to our merciful Lord!

Azusa Street 1906

"And when they had prayed, the place where they were assembled together was shaken; and they were all filled with the Holy Spirit, and they spoke the word of God with boldness." Acts 4:31

William J. Seymour and Frank Bartleman are the two names most often recognized as those who were used to start the Azusa Street Revival. They were different in many ways, but they were both young men who had an uncommon desire to know the Lord and see His power restored to the church. Seymour was the unquestioned leader of the revival, and he had the authority on earth, but Bartleman was the intercessor who had authority with God.

Seymour, who was ousted from his first ministry assignment because he continued to speak of a new Pentecost, recognized the hand of God in his rejection and was content to form a little home prayer group which met regularly for several months. While in the middle of a ten day fast, Seymour and the others in this little group were dramatically baptized in the Holy Spirit, receiving the gift of tongues as well as other charismatic gifts.

Word spread "like fire in a dry wood" about what had happened at Seymour's little prayer group. This was probably caused by the remarkable ministry of Frank Bartleman, who had written a stream of articles and tracts, and constantly moved about the city exhorting churches and prayer groups to seek the Lord for a Revival. He longed to see the Lord do in Los Angeles what He had recently done in Wales. After a time, Bartleman began to sense that what was to come to Lost Angeles would be different from what was happening in Wales, and began to boldly prophesy the coming of "another Pentecost." Bartleman's zeal for the Lord at this time was so great that his wife and friends began to fear for his life. He missed so much sleep and so many meals in order to pray that they did not think that he could last much longer. His response to their pleas for moderation was that he would rather die than not see Revival.

As soon as word got out about the experience that came upon Seymour's little prayer group, large crowds (black and white) descended on them. To accommodate the large numbers of people, they were forced to rent a rundown old barn-like building in the middle of a black ghetto. One of the most remarkable characteristics of this revival from the very beginning was the diversity of the people who were drawn to it. Some considered it unprecedented in church history. Within a week even a prominent Jewish rabbi announced his full support. Soon astounding healings and dramatic conversions were taking place almost daily.

Within weeks a steady stream of missionaries were coming from every continent on earth. Those who were on the front lines of the battle against the forces of darkness were the most acutely aware that they needed more power. Just as the Lord's own disciples were told that they would receive power to be His witnesses when the Holy Spirit came upon them, this had become the only hope for effective ministry that many of the missionaries had. They seized it like a drowning man grasps a lifesaver. They left Azusa with the power they needed, and soon gospel fires were burning brightly all over the world. In just two years the movement had taken root in over 50 nations, and was thought to have penetrated every U.S. town with a population of more than 3,000. Millions came to Christ!

There is another aspect to Seymour's remarkable leadership at Azusa... it was his ability to discern and trust the Holy Spirit's leadership, and give Him the freedom that He requires. In spite of almost constant pressure from world-renowned church leaders, who came from around the globe to impose what they perceived to be needed order and direction on the Revival, for over two years Seymour held the course and allowed the Holy Spirit to move in His own, often mysterious, ways. Like Evan Roberts, who was at the same time leading the great Welsh Revival, Seymour's greatest leadership quality was his ability to follow the Holy Spirit.

Seymour and Roberts both believed that the Holy Spirit required the freedom to move through whomever He chose. They both resolved to allow anyone to be used by the Lord, even the most humble believers. This sometimes brought embarrassment, but more often it allowed the Holy Spirit to do marvelous things among them. (Excerpts from *Azuza Street... The Fire that could not Die* by Rick Joyner)

Prayer and Fruitfulness

"Now it came to pass in those days that He went out to the mountain to pray, and continued all night in prayer to God." Luke 6:12

"Verily, verily I say unto you" isn't this how Jesus prefaced His weighted words? *"Please believe Me, I'm telling you the truth."* There are few things as important. This is purely fact, not conjecture... absolutely, positively proven throughout the ages. Here it is, beloved: **There is a clear correlation between the amount of time you spend with the Lord, and the consistent fruitfulness of your life.** There is no way around it. Prayer, meditation, worship or simply laying before Him in silence... you must spend time with God if you are to become like the Master. There are times Jesus would spend all night in prayer. If the Son of God needed to commune with His Father, how much more do we! Haven't you heard this before?

You may be very busy - who isn't? If you desire to bear fruit that remains you must spend time with the Lord. Rearrange your priorities, make the time. Go to bed earlier, arise earlier. Pray as you commute, at your job, whenever you can. Pray in the spirit and with your understanding. Ask God to invigorate you; He will help you. Those who spend time with God are far more likely to proceed with accuracy, hearing His voice and then do what He is doing.

Yes, you can and probably have had God use you in meaningful ways without much prayer. Surely He will use any willing vessel to accomplish His purposes... even the unsaved, even a donkey! Nonetheless, the glorious Father of lights is looking for true sons and daughters who will take the time to be with Him, those who truly want to be with Him. It is they who will receive the choicest assignments (not the easiest), and the greatest blessing. They are trusted with the secret things.

True disciples of Jesus Christ take note. You have earnestly desired to bear much fruit... and to see lives changed by the power of the Holy Spirit. This is your key, faithful servant; this is your answer. Spend more time with God. Believe that He hears and will answer. *Don't grow weary in well doing, in due season you will reap the harvest!* Press in, He will help you. Whatever you do, don't feel condemned or defeated because you don't spend time with God. Actually, those thoughts are nothing more than an excuse. You can begin today, right now. Will you spend a few minutes right now?

Diligence

"I have fought the good fight. I have finished the race, I have kept the faith." 2 Timothy 4:7

Did you realize when Jesus said to ask, seek and knock (Matthew 7) that the Greek present tense for these words emphasizes continuous action? You are to continue to knock, like the persistent man asking for bread at midnight. Keep knocking until the door opens. The Master wants to teach His servants to be diligent and persistent.

God has given each one of us an assigned task. He provides guidance, grace, and anointing to all. He encourages, forgives, and picks us up when we fall. With God being no respecter of persons, there is equal opportunity for each runner to win their race. Why then do some remain less fruitful? Diligence is the key. Dear disciple, only the diligent and persevering will win the highest prize. Those who are faint-hearted and faltering will not fulfill God's best.

The Master requires you to reach high for the best things. This stretches you beyond yourself and makes you more dependent upon Him, His strength and grace. Because of this, only a few will press on past the good, and the better, all the way to the best. Why can't you be one of these? His grace is sufficient for you. Those who keep going in spite of problems, pain and difficulty will eventually break through. We will see Revival; keep praying! Don't stop now; you're almost there. *"Do you not know that those who run in a race all run, but one receives the prize? Run in such a way that you may obtain it"* (1Cor. 9:24).

An Open Heaven

"No one can enter a strong man's house and plunder his goods, unless he first binds the strong man. And then he will plunder his house." Mark 3:27

It was rough going. The well-seasoned preacher clearly proclaimed Christ to the 1,500 or so Hindus, Muslims and Christians in attendance, but when the invitation was given only a few came forward to accept salvation. Even these needed to be wrestled from the demons who held them back. The intercessors on the platform fought diligently for each soul. Powerful preaching, but little fruit. And when the sick received prayer you could only trust that God was answering because there was no apparent manifestation of healing. It continued like this for 5 nights... in northern India. But there is more to this story, dear believer. (I witnessed this with my own eyes.) God gave His strategy, the Church broke the strongholds of darkness... and then. Well, hold on a minute.

During the daytime we were teaching about 300 Christian leaders. In the evening, open-air evangelistic meetings were conducted. And as mentioned, these evening meetings were not bearing much fruit even though the preaching was quite powerful. (The well known evangelist had preached in over 60 countries.) Nevertheless, on the morning of the 6th day, the teacher spoke of spiritual warfare and the need to pierce the veil of darkness that canopied the region. The leaders were taught that the long entrenched spiritual powers and principalities needed to be uprooted before the blessings of God could be received by the people... the heavens must be opened!

And then came the strategy, unveiled by God Himself, and it was implemented with little instruction. The 300 stood to their feet and began to shout into the heavens **Hallelujah! Hallelujah! Hallelujah!** Over and over again, the eternal praise word was declared into the heavenlies for about 10 or 15 minutes! The sense of authority was profound. I felt as though I was brandishing a 10 foot sword. Let me reiterate, this was not orchestrated by any man but a spontaneous act of God. It stopped as suddenly as it had begun... and we were exhausted. We knew something of significance had occurred; we could sense something had changed in the atmosphere. Were the heavens now open?

That evening the air was charged with electricity. The same evangelist preached with the same anointing but when the invitation was given many people rushed forward to repent of their sins. When it was time to pray for the sick all heaven broke loose! Let me remind you, this was not a pumped up emotional format. The gospel was preached and the sick were prayed for - per tradition. But this night, the power of God descended like a flood, overwhelming many people. There were no ministry lines with people waiting to catch those who might be overcome, as is customary in some Spirit-filled churches, but the people were falling on top of one another. Children were on the ground weeping and prophesying and seeing visions of angels and Jesus. Glory to God in the Highest! The heavens remained open for another night, a different preacher, but the same results. Even a notorious criminal fell to the ground weeping and repenting of his sins.

What has been described here is not unique. This type of warfare and subsequent victory is commonplace around the world. And although the methods may vary, the stories are quite similar: Where the strongman is bound the fruit is abundant; where he is not, it is minimal. We must learn this lesson. Spiritual darkness is pervasive... over our region as well. Ask for God's strategy, and then implement it with all diligence. It will cost you a great deal to break the strongholds. Are you willing to pay the price of fervent prayer, worship, fasting, travail... warfare? Prevailing prayer requires your time! We are not playing games any longer. We must dislodge the enemy and plunder his holdings. With God's help... and with His holy angels we can do this. We must wage war!

"...Do not fear, Daniel, for from the first day that you set your heart to understand, and to humble yourself before your God, your words were heard; and I have come because of your words. But the prince of the kingdom of Persia withstood me twenty-one days; and behold, Michael, one of the chief princes, came to help me, for I had been left alone there with the kings of Persia." Daniel 10:12-13

Desperation: Revival Prerequisite

"Yet I am poor and needy; come quickly to me, O God. You are my help and my deliverer; O LORD, do not delay." Psalm 70:5 "For this is what the high and lofty One says-- he who lives forever, whose name is holy: 'I live in a high and holy place, but also with him who is contrite and lowly in spirit, to revive the spirit of the lowly and to revive the heart of the contrite.'" Isaiah 57:15 (NIV)

Have you heard it said: "If we just had Christian unity, we would experience revival." "If we would simply do the work of evangelism, then revival would come." "If we would walk in holiness and repentance... etc., etc?" Dear saint, when will we realize that our best efforts to do any of these things have failed time and again? We have had countless meetings and have been taught 7 steps to this and 10 to that. Do you really think this presently complacent Church will finally get it all right and somehow entice God to visit our region?

In saying this, I'm not suggesting that we should not diligently work toward unity and do evangelism. But fervent prevailing prayer is the only golden thread that has run through every revival, the only common denominator. Nevertheless beloved, Revival will be made manifest when we finally realize that we are not capable of doing any of these things adequately. Only then will we cry out with prayers of humble desperation. Israel was in bondage for 400 years; did Yahweh deliver them because they got it right? No...but because they cried out in utter helplessness. In His perfect timing, the Merciful One sent a deliverer. How we need Him now!

Our Lord is at work among us. Through revelation and difficult circumstances He is bringing you to the place of humility and desperation. Do not despise this work in you, dear one; embrace it! From the depths of spiritual poverty you can truly cry: *Revive me Jesus, I need You; forgive me for my sins. I can do nothing without You. Revive Your Church; have mercy on us; transform our city by the power of Your Spirit. Amen.*

Fresh Vision for Intercession

"Then He taught, saying to them, "Is it not written, `My house shall be called a house of prayer for all nations?'" Mark 11:17

Our old ways have not worked for years. We keep doing things the same way and the results remain the same. We think that we possess the truth and yet we are not winning souls. In fact, we are not even maintaining them. There is very little healing and deliverance offered in our churches; and when we do missions, we carry the same ineffective ways somewhere else. When will we learn?

Intercession is considered less, while doing is considered more... and many regard it a waste of time to pray and wait in the presence of the Lord. Some may even view it to be an escape from reality. However, if you are patiently observant, you will learn that the *pray-er* will out do the *do-er* every time. Those who spend time with the Lord will hear from the Lord; and at the proper time will arise from their knees to do God's will with stunning accuracy, accomplishing His purposes. The *do-er* (usually very busy) has many ideas, tries many doors, and makes many mistakes. Eventually, he will fulfill God's purpose. Accomplishing the desired results reinforces the use of this "broad brush" method and the cycle continues, sometimes leading to burnout or compromising short cuts.

Dear Christian, the enemy has brought murder, violence, divorce, division, addictions and poverty. The children are far from God and terror is knocking at the door... we are at the crossroads of human history. What will it take to stir you to frequent, fervent prayer? Church history is replete with examples of national revivals and personal transformations resulting from fervent, effectual prayer. When will you spend time with the Lord today? The Great Intercessor is now in the process of correcting church leaders because of prayerlessness; much shaking is in progress. Intimacy, humility and fervent prayer are what He really desires.

Adding Weight to Your Prayers

*"So He said to them, "This kind can come out by nothing but prayer and fasting." Mark 9:29

For your discernment: While praying, I saw a clear image of an apothecary scale. You know, the one that hangs in the balance. You put the item to be weighed on one side and a measured weight is placed on the other. Anyway, on the right, various problems: sickness, the need for salvation, etc. On the left, prayers were added until the scales were tipped. Do you see it?

And then the Lord impressed on my spirit: "Although God receives every prayer prayed according to His will, certain things add weight to prayer: 1)Faith 2) Fervency and 3) Fasting. It may be worth briefly reflecting on this. It appeared that He was collecting the prayers in a bowl (on the left side of the scale) and when there was a sufficent amount, the scales would tip. I assumed this meant the problem was solved, the prayer answered. Obviously some problems required only minimal prayer while others needed more.

When faced with the need for a general revival, one would assume that much prayer is needed. I mean we are not talking about an individual's need, but the needs of tens of thousands, or millions. This will require much prayer, beloved. Some have already been praying for two or three decades or longer. These prayers have not been wasted; God has been collecting them. Will you add some weighted prayers soon?

Prayer with Fasting

"Moreover, when you fast, do not be like the hypocrites, with a sad countenance. For they disfigure their faces that they may appear to men to be fasting. Assuredly, I say to you, they have their reward. But you, when you fast, anoint your head and wash your face, so that you do not appear to men to be fasting, but to your Father who is in the secret place; and your Father who sees in secret will reward you openly." Matthew 6:16-18

Have you ever considered fasting? Many Christians are beginning to understand the need to pray, but few have explored the "secret place" of fasting. What is fasting? It is the voluntary abstaning from food for a certain period of time… hours, days or weeks for the purpose of focused prayer. A fast can be partial or complete, with liquids or without. Daniel fasted from "pleasant things" for 21 days. Jesus (and others throughout history) embraced a complete fast for 40 days. As you can see from our text, fasting is to be done in secret as an act of worship unto the Almighty. It is not to be demonstrated before men to reveal your piety.

So why fast? First of all, fasting subdues the flesh. You are actually humbling yourself in a very practical way. From this place of weakness, your prayers are empowered…you gain faith and spiritual confidence. In the very depths of your being you realize that you are laying it all down for the fullfillment of God's purposes. Let us point out you are not trying to earn something from the Lord. You are simply cooperating with Him as He leads you beyond your flesh into the realm of the Spirit. Nonetheless, self-denial is a very normal part of Christianity. *"If anyone come after Me, let him deny himself..."*

Be sure that God is leading you to do this, beloved; and check your heart motives. All through the scriptures you will see God's people fasting for very specific reasons. *"As they ministered to the Lord and fasted, the Holy Spirit said, 'Now separate to Me Barnabas and Saul for the work to which I have called them.' Then, having fasted and prayed, and laid hands on them, they sent them away."* (Acts 13:2,3)

Remember, you're not trying to lose weight, you're seeking God. Don't forget to pray and worship... ministering unto the Lord. During your time of fasting, approach the throne of grace with all boldness and confidence. Press in! God is listening.

Just prior to the Revivals of the past, some faithful intercessors were called to extended periods of fasting and prayer.

The Spirit of Supplication

"And I will pour on the house of David and on the inhabitants of Jerusalem the Spirit of grace and supplication..." Zechariah 12:10

Because the challenge is so enormous and our request so BIG, it should be obvious that it will take many people and many prayers to accomplish the purposes of God in bringing forth a regional or national Revival. Surely one individual or a few prayer groups will not be able to "pray in" a glorious Revival that returns the Bride to her first love, saves untold multitudes and transforms our society.

I encourage you to review the history of the various Revivals and you will find that it was God who actually initiated the prayer. Yes, the saints came to a realization that they were unable to fix the mess that they were in... and then they became desperate for God's help. But it is the Holy One who pours out a Spirit of Supplication.

Prior to any Revival, our merciful God stirs the saints to pray. He pours out a Spirit of Supplication. At first, only a few hear the call;

then more are added over a period of months or years. Prayer for Revival truly becomes the burden of their hearts. One of the Hebrew meanings for *supplication* is *to be weak or make oneself sick*, clearly indicating the intensity of such prayer. (Some were born for this very purpose!)

Soon thousands of men, women and children are praying in small groups and larger corporate gatherings. And these fervent prayers continue as the manifest presence of God descends. A word to the wise: When the Revival arrives don't be so enamored by its manifestations that you diminish in prayer. Pray all the more! Keep stoking the furnace as the Spirit leads...

I'm sure you realize that God does nothing apart from prayer, don't you? If not, we'll need to discuss it later. Anyway, He sees the desperate needs, finds faithful intercessors to cry out, (actually, He prays through them by His Spirit) and then He answers. Get ready!

Prevailing Prayer

"...blind Bartimaeus, the son of Timaeus, sat by the highway side begging. And when he heard that it was Jesus of Nazareth, he began to cry out, and say, Jesus, thou son of David, have mercy on me." Mark 10:46-47

Bartimeaus simply refused to quit in his appeal for the Lord's mercy. And how wonderful it must have been when his eyes focused for the first time, to look into the face of Jesus! Likewise, the woman with the issue of blood would not be denied (Matt. 9:20). Over and over again throughout the New Testament, Jesus rewards believers who refuse to go away without an answer.

"Ask, and it shall be given you: seek, and ye shall find; knock and it shall be opened unto you." (Matt. 7:7) *"Praying always with all prayer and supplication in the Spirit, and watching there unto with all perseverance and supplication."* (Eph. 6:18) *"The effectual fervent prayer of a righteous man availeth much."* (James 5:16) KJV

It was the same fervency and persistence that God honored through-out the Old Testament. Moses fasted and prayed in behalf of the

Children of Israel for forty days and nights (Deut. 9). Elijah persisted in prayer seven times for rain (1Kings 18). Daniel prayed three weeks for God to reveal the meaning of a vision (Dan. 10). The Bible remains clear: God has been, is and will continue to be looking for believers who will not give up, no matter how long it takes or what it requires to receive an answer. *"Seek the Lord and his strength, seek his face continually."* (1 Chron. 16:11) *"And ye shall seek me, and find me, when ye shall search for me with all your heart."* (Jer. 29:13) KJV

Faith is kept alive through persistent prayer. Without it, faith dies. As we mature in the Lord, we learn to trust Him when He is silent. God's silence is often the sign that we should raise the intensity of our prayers. So if asking doesn't work, knock. Then keep knocking. Why must you keep persistent? Why do you have to ask, seek and knock? Because the longer you seek Him, the less of you remains, and you come to the knowledge of your need for the fullness of the Master in your life. It's a lesson that every believer must learn by "praying without ceasing" (1Thess. 5:17). *"Call to Me, and I will answer you, and show you great and mighty things which you do not know."* (Jer. 33:3)

God stands ready to honor your prevailing prayers with His presence and power. Like Bartimaeus, we cannot give up if we desire to see... to see a glorious Revival! (Excerpts from *The Power of Prevailing Prayer* by Robert)

So what is prevailing prayer, dear Christian? Importunity, persistence, perseverance, tenacity, a pressing in, continual, for extended periods or segmented, with fasting sometimes included... Prevailing prayer is praying until you get an answer!

"God's child can conquer everything through prayer." Andrew Murray

Transform Our City, My God!

"... Why should my face not be sad, when the city, the place of my fathers' tombs, lies waste, and its gates are burned with fire? ....Come and let us build the wall of Jerusalem, that we may no longer be a reproach." Nehemiah 2:3, 17

There has been much said about transformation in recent years, but what actually is it? Well meaning social activists and politicians have tried numerous experiments in city revitalization. Plans and programs and government funds have been poured into such projects. But if we are to be truly honest, they have had very little effect. The inner city of most metropolitan areas are in deplorable condition. Poor housing, low wages, high crime rates, etc. Do you really think that another project or program will do the job? Should we continue to try? Of course! But there is a better way!

The best efforts of men will not get this done. How we need our cities transformed by the power of God... then the revitalization will occur from the inside out. Lives will be changed by the power of the Holy Spirit and these "changed ones" will change the city. This has happened many times in our history and some of the fruit still remains. Schools, orpanages and hospitals have all been established as the result of a fervent love for God and a love for others. Works of mercy begin to flow as compassion for the weak and the poor increases. Righteous government is also established at all levels. Christian love permeates the region as yeast does dough. The thoughts of men start to rise from the base and temporal to the things that are eternal.

Jonathan Edwards wrote in 1746 "bring the God of love down from heaven to earth." He adamently believed that a true Revival will involve a loving concern for the individual as well as for the society as a whole. "Religious meetings with prayer and singing will not promote or sustain a Revival in the absence of works of love and mercy." It will be very important for us to remember these things when the soon coming revival finally arrives at our doorstep. We must step beyond the church and minister to the needs. Filled with His love and with His guidance, we can do no less than roll up our sleeves and participate in the work of transforming our city, rebuilding her walls as it were... by the power of the Holy Spirit. Yes, this includes inovative works of mercy, but also taking positions on the school board and city council and other governmental and political roles... either up front or behind the scenes.

Fervent, effectual, prevailing prayer WILL bring a supernatural transformation! Our God hears and answers prayer! In fact, He is the One stirring us to ask Him for these very things. Remain faithful; press in; don't give up. Pray for a true Revival with regional transformation. This is not optional, beloved. Our sons and daughters are dying in the streets!

The Revealing

"Arise, shine; for your light has come! And the glory of the Lord is risen upon you. For behold, the darkness shall cover the earth, and deep darkness the people; but the Lord will arise over you, and His glory will be seen upon you." Isaiah 60:1-2

I am absolutely convinced that we are now being prepared, individually and corporately, for a great and glorious end: God is about to reveal His sons and daughters! (Isaiah 60:1-2 burns within me.) Yes, there is gross darkness in the earth and no doubt it will increase, but the Lord is about to show Himself strong. We will be His vessels of honor, filled with His glory and moving in His power and authority. This will be a time like none other in history.

His preparatory work is quite challenging and occasionally very painful; do you agree? But don't turn back; don't settle for lesser things. Your loving Father disciplines, even scourges His sons... those whom He favors. Nonetheless, in the midst of it all you are being conformed to His image. Be wise and vigilant, dear saint; unity must be maintained. Repentance and the forgiving of others has to abound if we are to enter into our destiny. Be grateful and don't complain; sufficient grace is available. You must overcome! The whole earth is waiting and groaning for the revealing of the sons of God!

Many are called to this awesome privilege, but few are chosen - why? Because precious few are willing to pay the price of total abandonment of self. Are you willing? Remember, it is lower, not higher, beloved, lower and lower still... true servanthood with lowliness of heart. The weak and foolish, the humble and the broken... these are the ones who will carry His glory. Your loving God is doing a deep work. Have you noticed the dissatisfaction within, the ravenous hunger for something more… and the nagging desire to see His purposes accomplished in the earth? Soon He will call your name and you will arise and shine with great glory… and many will be blessed!

What Are You Preaching?

"And He opened their understanding, that they might comprehend the Scriptures. Then He said to them, 'Thus it is written, and thus it was necessary for the Christ to suffer and to rise from the dead the third day, and that repentance and remission of sins should be preached in His name to all nations, beginning at Jerusalem.'" Luke 24:45-47

Dear minister, what is Jesus saying; isn't this verse clear? *"… repentance and remission of sins should be preached in His name to all nations..."* He, Himself preached the message of repentance: *"Now after John was put in prison, Jesus came to Galilee, preaching the gospel of the kingdom of God, and saying, 'The time is fulfilled, and the kingdom of God is at hand. Repent, and believe in the gospel.'"* Mark 1:14 –15

The Apostles most assuredly preached this message: *"So they went out and preached that people should repent. And they cast out many demons, and anointed with oil many who were sick, and healed them."* Mark 6:12 *"Truly, these times of ignorance God overlooked, but now commands all men everywhere to repent, because He has appointed a day on which He will judge the world in righteousness..."* Acts 17:30

Shouldn't you also be preaching this message? Be filled with love; don't be harsh; testify of God's goodness, mercy and grace. But dear servant, if you do not call sinners to repentance, to change their mind and their direction, you are not fulfilling the command of Jesus. You will be accountable for preaching a candy-coated gospel!

"So I said, `Who are You, Lord?' And He said, `I am Jesus, whom you are persecuting. But rise and stand on your feet; for I have appeared to you for this purpose, to make you a minister and a witness both of the things which you have seen and of the things

which I will yet reveal to you… to open their eyes, in order to turn them from darkness to light, and from the power of Satan to God, that they may receive forgiveness of sins and an inheritance among those who are sanctified by faith in Me.' Therefore, King Agrippa, I was not disobedient to the heavenly vision, but declared first to those in Damascus and in Jerusalem, and throughout all the region of Judea, and then to the Gentiles, that they should repent, turn to God, and do works befitting repentance." Acts 26:15-20

The Burden of the Lord

"I now rejoice in my sufferings for you, and fill up in my flesh what is lacking in the afflictions of Christ, for the sake of His body, which is the church, of which I became a minister according to the stewardship from God which was given to me for you, to fulfill the word of God," Colossians 1:24-25

Are you still playing with the things of God… doing some spiritual things, having nice meetings, and trying to keep everyone happy? Beloved, you will never break through to the next dimension of God's purposes if you remain in this comfort zone. How often you petition God for your own needs and desires. "Give me a bigger house, give me a bigger church, etc." There is nothing wrong with this, *"Ask and it shall be given to you."* But have you cried out to God for *His* purposes to be fulfilled in your life and through your ministry … not for your sake but *"for the sake of His body, which is the church?"* God is looking for those who will ask Him for His burden, His desire for this generation. The Almighty is seeking those who will hold nothing back, those who are willing to pay any price to see His will established in the Church… in their region and throughout the world. Are you one of these?

Giving birth to the things of God is painful, even excruciating at times. You will suffer, cry, and sometimes have to die. (Consider the precious saints who have gone before you!) Are you willing to travail for the burden of the Lord to be established in the earth? There is much joy and fulfillment in store for those who will see this through to completion. By God's grace, you can do this. Press on!

But Satan Hindered Us

"Therefore we wanted to come to you--even I, Paul, time and again -- but Satan hindered us." 1Thessalonians 2:18

What an astounding statement! The great man of God was admitting he wanted to visit this particular church, *time and again,* but was prevented from doing so... by Satan. It seems that the archangel Gabriel also had a problem delivering a message from God to Daniel. The Prince of Persia blocked his advance for 21 days. (Gabriel needed the assistance of Michael to break through.) There is another mention in scripture of stubborn demonic resistance; the disciples were having a problem casting out a demon. In response to their dilemma, Jesus retorted, *"... this kind does not go out except by prayer and fasting"* (Matt. 17:21). What does all of this mean, beloved? You had better pay attention!

The sovereign, Omnipotent gives His faithful servants formidable tasks to perform. He supplies the grace, the anointing, and the necessary guidance. Of course, you must pray, and listen, and move forward. Nevertheless, even if you do, is there an ironclad guarantee of success? Some have foolishly thought so. Dear warrior, we are at war - the battle rages! The enemy does not sit idly by as you advance upon his territory. He is a masterful strategist, a cunning adversary. One can only imagine how many works of God have been thwarted by demonic forces. Are you prepared to wage war?

Let's say that you are called to minister to the drug addicts and prostitutes of the inner city, or you are sent to preach, or to plant a church where few churches have succeeded. What should you do? Remember, Satan hindered Paul; don't you think that he will attempt to do the same to you? How much energy has been wasted on the finely tuned plans of men... how much money? After endless meetings and meticulous preparation they decide, "Let's rent this facility and hire that music group; let's invite _____ to preach." But what amount of time was spent consulting God? How many days were given to fasting and prayer? Who has broken the strongholds and bound the strongman so that you could plunder his holdings, namely, the hearts and souls of men? Usually no one - and another attempt is made, and another failure ensues. Throughout Church history this fruitless scenario has been repeated ad nauseam.

Perhaps you think that your plan is better than the last group that attempted it; maybe you're a better preacher or have a better doctrine. Dear foolish one, haven't you yet learned that it is not about your preaching or your whatever? It is about war, spiritual warfare, taking back the ground that the enemy has stolen. The adversary seeks to hinder you from presenting your message, and the hearer from receiving it. You must (through prayer, and fasting, and whatever else the Holy Spirit directs) hold the demons at bay so that the captives can receive the transforming Word of the Lord! If you will do this the manifest presence of God will flood the region and He will facilitate more than you could ever hope for or imagine.

Unfortunately, there are so few Christians who actually have a vision from God, much less a battle plan or strategy. Who among you seeks to topple the demonic strongholds over your region? Who does more than talk about winning souls? Where are the mighty men and women of God? Yes, you may be hindered, wounded, and even foiled at times, but press on, dear saint. There is One who stands strong; He is ready to crush Satan under your feet! *"And the God of peace will crush Satan under your feet shortly. The grace of our Lord Jesus Christ be with you. Amen"* (Rom. 16:20).

Your Works Are Not Perfect

"Be watchful, and strengthen the things which remain, that are ready to die, for I have not found your works perfect before God. Remember therefore how you have received and heard; hold fast and repent. Therefore if you will not watch, I will come upon you as a thief, and you will not know what hour I will come upon you."
Revelation 3:2-3

The Church is awash with corruption; and yet, grace is espoused to a fault, and sinners are made to feel at ease in their sin. Dear preacher, who will proclaim the fear of the Lord? In days gone by, powerful messages of repentance were delivered, piercing hearts and causing the listener to weep and tremble for fear of God's judgment. It seems as though, in our day, the pendulum has swung to the opposite extreme. We hear of God's love over and over again, but who warns of hell? Who speaks of the terrible consequences of sin?

Dear reader, please consider Jesus' exhortation to the churches in the Book of Revelation: Although He speaks words of encouragement to all who obey, He rebukes sternly, using warnings and threats, reminding those who have become sluggish to return to the works that they first did, to their first love. In no uncertain terms, He exhorts them to get it right and to do it better. What if Jesus were to talk to you like this? Would you whine and make excuses, blame others, or perhaps even quit?

How we need men and women of God, emboldened by the Holy Spirit and filled with His love, to warn about the ugliness of sin, about *"righteousness, self-control and the judgment to come"* (Acts 24:24,25). We need to be strongly exhorted to enter by the narrow gate and become all that God intends for us to be. Will you be such a messenger? If Jesus should return today, He would find many of His servants compromised and asleep. Will you awaken and warn them?

Hungry For His Presence

"...Have you seen the One I love?" Song of Solomon 3:3

All over the world; millions of men, women, and children have been gloriously filled with God's Spirit. Many have been healed and delivered. Still others, seeing a demonstration of God's power, have freely received salvation, the most precious miracle of all. Perhaps you have had the opportunity to participate in some of these wondrous things.

Because of experiences like this, it is extremely difficult to be satisfied with mere religion and religious services. It would only be natural to hunger and thirst for more of the presence of God. Do you understand? Once you have seen God dramatically transform the lives of others, or you have *kissed* the cheek of God during powerful Spirit-led worship; how can you be satisfied with just another thirty-minute sermon and a chorus of *Amazing Grace*? Dear Christian, have you been pacifying your spiritual hunger with good preaching, good music, and good works? There is so much more: **God's presence, God Himself.**

Much of the church doesn't realize that they are "poor, wretched, and blind" and nearly void of His presence. They are satisfied with their own ceremonies, plans, and programs. They are simply not interested in God's *presence*. In fact, they do not know that this is actually possible. Wouldn't you love to see God sweep through your church causing profound repentance with weeping and wailing? Or experience the Lord in such a powerful way as to cause intense intercession, glorious intimate worship and powerful physical manifestations, not to mention the spontaneous release of the gifts of the Holy Spirit? Dear saint, don't we need the God of Pentecost to show Himself strong in our day?

God is looking for a place where He can come and abide; a people that are hungry for His presence. He is about to manifest Himself sometime soon. And when He does, thousands of lives will be transformed, perhaps entire cities. Would you like to be a part of this impending glory? Ask Him to make you hungry!

Do You Want God to Visit Your Church?

"...the house was filled with a cloud, even the house of the LORD; so that the priests could not stand to minister by reason of the cloud: for the glory of the LORD had filled the house of God." 2Chr 5:13-14

Do you really want God to show up at your church? He may change everything about the way you do church; and that could make you very uncomfortable. Do you like the expression of emotions in church? Make no mistake about it; when God is in the house, people become very emotional. True conviction of sin will turn the place upside-down. Your dignity, pride, and format may have to go. And your favorite part of the service may be preempted. Are you willing to allow God to interrupt your Order of Service?

It is quite possible that God is tired of our sectarian, self-centered and self-contained services, no matter how nice the pews are padded, how beautiful the songs are sung, or how good the sermon is delivered. There is so much more, and we are settling for only a small portion. It's time to earnestly desire His *manifest presence*.

Disciple of Jesus, will you begin to seek God's face, to seek the One who blesses, not only the blessings? He will come to those who really want Him and who seek Him with complete abandonment... individually and corporately. The Lover of Souls is looking for a people who will love Him with all of their heart. He wants you to want Him! You can have as much of God as you desire, but most Christians seldom take more than a taste.

How would you seek God's presence? First, repent of all sin, including empty religious practices and lip service, and ask God to create a hunger for more of Him. Ask Him to help you to die to self; lowliness is absolutely essential. He will be faithful to refine you. Wait on the Lord; allow Him to have His way. Don't permit your agenda to quench the Holy Spirit. It is important to remind yourself that there is no need to strive; He longs to be with you. Simply surrender.

God desires to profoundly manifest His presence in your life and in your congregation. He would love to show Himself strong in your midst. Will you invite Him to have His way? Don't be satisfied with anything less.

"Behold, I stand at the door and knock. If anyone hears My voice and opens the door, I will come in to him and dine with him, and he with Me" (Rev 3:20). Beloved, this text is often used for evangelism, but in context it is Jesus speaking to His church. Let Him in!

The Presence of the Lord

"And He said, 'My Presence will go with you, and I will give you rest.' Then he said to Him, 'If Your Presence does not go with us, do not bring us up from here...'" Exodus 33: 14-16

Do you remember these examples of God's manifest presence, His obvious nearness: the pillar of fire in the desert, the Glory Cloud at the dedication of Solomon's Temple, the mighty rushing wind and tongues of fire on the day of Pentecost?

How the Church needs God's mighty presence today, just as Moses needed Him, perhaps even more so. Every type of sin and selfishness abounds; the love of many has grown cold. Poverty holds large segments of the population in bondage; and AIDS threatens to eliminate entire nations. This litany of woe could be recited ad nauseam. The church has been sinfully impotent. We must seek His powerful transforming presence once again.

Jesus said: *"Behold, I stand at the door and knock. If anyone hears My voice and opens the door, I will come in to him and dine with him, and he with Me"* (Rev. 3:20). Dear servant of God, this scripture is often used as an evangelistic tool. In context, however, it is actually Jesus speaking to His Church. Will you open the door and allow Him into His Church? He will draw you to new depths of intimacy and show you mighty things that you do not know. It is from this place of divine fellowship that the *rivers of living water* flow and the presence of God will once again be made manifest to this troubled world. *Lord, we choose to open our door to You. Please come in and dine with us.*

The Spirit of Independence

"Behold, how good and how pleasant it is for brethren to dwell together in unity!" Psalm 133:1

Unity is suffering dear servant of God. The spirit of independence prevails and very little is accomplished in the Kingdom. Oh, of course you want unity. But don't deceive yourself; that is only up to a point. A smile and a pat on the back is not what the Lord has in mind. The Church has been divided for far too long and we use every type of excuse to remain separate. Doctrine is usually the safest and most religious reason for division, but there are much deeper reasons: Suspicion, jealousy, insecurity, pride, racism, and personal offense. Be honest!

Can you see the results of independence? The public certainly can. We have been the brunt of their jokes for years. Because of disharmony, the Church of Jesus has had little influence in the community. The world literally goes to hell while we remain divided. God forgive us. The time is coming when our independence will be broken. Perhaps then we will have the time. After a season of shaking, we may emerge realizing that we really do need our brothers and sisters, even those whom we have held at arms length.

It is very interesting to note that missionaries from various denominations, serving in countries where the Church is oppressed, seem to overcome doctrinal barriers rather easily. The need for fellowship and mutual support seems to enhance unity. God forbid that it would take a wave of persecution for the western Church to comprehend that we need each other.

Yes, you are busy doing what you believe to be God's will. Who isn't? There is enough work and plenty of trouble to keep you occupied for the rest of your life. But what of Jesus' prayer, *"that they all may be one, as You, Father, are in Me, and I in You; that they also may be one in Us, that the world may believe that You sent Me"* (John 17:21)?

Dear minister, Christians of every persuasion truly can work together for prayer, praise, and community outreach including evangelism, youth ministry, and feeding programs. Your people will not become contaminated by associating with those of differing doctrines. What were you thinking? We can stand shoulder-to-shoulder defending the rights of the poor and the oppressed. We can speak boldly against unrighteousness and injustice. This is unity. This is normal. Dear Church, let me introduce you to the brother of independence. His name is pride.

Unity In The Spirit

"I, therefore, the prisoner of the Lord, beseech you to walk worthy of the calling with which you were called, with all lowliness and gentleness, with longsuffering, bearing with one another in love, endeavoring to keep the unity of the Spirit in the bond of peace." Ephesians 4:1-3

Paul reveals so much truth to the Ephesians that it seems to ooze from each page. For your sake, it is well worth reviewing these first verses of chapter four: *with all lowliness and gentleness, with long-suffering, bearing with one another in love...* These words are loaded, dear saint! It may take you an entire lifetime to fully implement just this verse alone.

How often do you find yourself in abrasive situations? A difficult brother or sister makes it uncomfortable or even unbearable to continue in a working relationship. Look again at verse two, *lowliness, gentleness, longsuffering*. By God's grace, lover of God, you can only do this by His grace. He has allowed this problem to continue. In fact, you have already grown a great deal because of it. Your independence is evaporating. You are becoming more dependent upon God and your sense of powerlessness is bringing you a step closer to complete surrender.

But dear saint, unity goes far beyond tolerance. God would never ask you to do the impossible; this is possible! God is telling you to do everything within your means to *keep the unity of the Spirit, in the bond of peace*. He knows that you don't like this person. Nevertheless, His truth remains. Trust God. He will help. Unity requires humility, servanthood, surrender, and gentleness and as already mentioned, longsuffering. You have been progressing nicely. Do not allow pride or a bad attitude to defeat you now. Humble yourself, forgive or ask for forgiveness, and maintain unity. This is the will of the Lord!

The Simplicity of Prayer

"If you abide in Me, and My words abide in you, you will ask what you desire, and it shall be done for you." John 15:7

So many books have been written to help reveal the intricacies of talking with God! Much revelation has come to the Bride through the pen of E.M. Bounds, Andrew Murray, Watchman Nee, and Jeanne Guyon. Unfortunately, legalism and intellectualism have also expressed their logic and methods leaving much to be desired. A manual about how to pray cannot teach you to pray any more than a driving manual can teach you to drive. Yes, you can ingest the basics but you can really only learn by doing. How much time do you spend practicing your prayer life?

There is no need to understand how prayer works. This may only muddy the water. There is no formula. Why do men always want everything neatly wrapped? Your finite mind will never grasp infinite wisdom, but prayer can be as simple as this: You pray, God answers! Learn His will in the matter, believe His promise and ASK.

There is nothing mystical about child-like faith, Christian. A four-year-old jumping from the kitchen chair expects her father to catch her. You too can ask and expect God to answer. He has promised to do so. Just believe.

Long, flowery prayers are OK, and written prayers serve a purpose, but what could be better than speaking to God from your heart? Express your feelings. Praise and thank Him. Repent, cry, question, trust, ask and ask again. This is simple prayer. Anyone can do it. Why not now? *"Ask, and it will be given to you; seek, and you will find; knock, and it will be opened to you. For everyone who asks receives, and he who seeks finds, and to him who knocks it will be opened"* (Matt. 7:7-8).

Pray and Fight

"Finally, my brethren, be strong in the Lord and in the power of His might. Put on the whole armor of God, that you may be able to stand against the wiles of the devil." Ephesians 6:10

Have you noticed the moral decline in our society? Of course you have. Do you think that this has occurred because of the poor decisions made by politicians... or perhaps the failure of Church leaders to speak out against sin? Both answers are valid, but something far more sinister is at work.

Dear servant of God, we are at war. Our enemy the devil is a malevolent strategist. He is intelligent, powerful and cunning and has been plotting the demise of mankind for thousands of years. It only takes a glance at world history to be reminded of his successes. If he cannot overcome using all-out violence and destruction, he corrupts the heart of man, preying upon his weaknesses. And to make it even worse, he clothes himself as an angel of light and seeks to trample spiritual life through dogmatic deception and religious legalism. God help us!

During the 20th century, the wicked one began to take control of the media. Quite a good plan for this *information age*, don't you think?

From the inception of our nation and throughout the 19th century, nearly all of the newspapers were owned by Christians. Sunday sermons were printed in the Monday edition and the editorials earnestly promoted righteousness. Now, newspapers, magazines, TV, and radio have become the unwitting pawns of demonic design. Many columnists are openly anti-Christian. On television, even the children's programs (*especially* the children's programs) are loaded with occult, violent and sensual themes, thus sowing the seeds of disrespect and rebellion. Witchcraft is blatantly promoted!

Motion pictures portray the ministers of God as buffoons. Adultery and divorce are considered normal and homosexuality is depicted as an acceptable alternate lifestyle. Daytime television feeds the viewer with stories ad nauseam that encourage lying, stealing, cheating, and revenge. And many of the news programs are tainted by *agenda*. The apostle, Paul tells us to think on what is true, noble, just, pure, etc. (Phil. 4:8), and yet, living amidst such a sin sick culture, it becomes increasingly difficult to avoid ingesting its sewage.

On another front, prayer has been banned from the classroom, abortion made legal, and the Ten Commandments have been removed from public display. Children are receiving contraceptives in school and if they have an abortion or contract a sexual disease, the law mandates that the parents not be told. What?!! We are in serious trouble, beloved. How has it gotten so out of hand? The wicked one has lulled us into complacency and would soon render the Church irrelevant and powerless, if it is not so already.

How we need the strong arm of God. How we need fervent prayer... and willing disciples to stand against the works of darkness. If not, judgment will come; our nation will decline, and another will take our place. Open your history book once more. Count the many great nations that have fallen from power. Only a fool would think that it could not happen again... to us! Revive us, Lord!

Dispelling the Darkness

"When the Philistines took the ark of God, they brought it into the temple of Dagon and set it by Dagon. And when the people of Ashdod arose early in the morning, there was Dagon, fallen on its face

to the earth before the ark of the Lord. So they took Dagon and set it in its place again. And when they arose early the next morning, there was Dagon, fallen on its face to the ground before the ark of the Lord. The head of Dagon and both the palms of its hands were broken off on the threshold; only Dagon's torso was left of it." 1Samuel 5:2-4

How we need the presence of God in our lives and in our cities! We can clearly see from the text that the presence of God, represented by the Ark of the Covenant, caused Dagon to topple. How much more will the manifest presence of the Holy Spirit dispel the darkness and shatter strongholds in our land.

Are you diligently seeking God for an increase of His manifest presence? There is such a thing, you know. Throughout the Old and New Testaments, you can see stunning examples of miraculous intervention: God "showing up" to bring victory, healing, restoration, etc… God simply being God in the midst of a desperate situation!

We speak of Revival and recognize it by the manifestations that often accompany an outpouring of His Spirit: repentance, healing, deliverance, and salvation. This is all true …and so desired. But isn't revival simply this: the manifest presence of God coming into a region for a period of time, dispelling the darkness and flooding the area with light? His presence causes the wicked one to flee. His presence brings conviction of sin; He permeates even the hardest of hearts… healing flows like a river; His blessings abound. *"The ark of the Lord remained in the house of Obed-Edom the Gittite three months. And the Lord blessed Obed-Edom and all his household"* (2Samuel 6:11). Let it be so, Lord…in our city, in our lives, in our generation.

Declare The Glory of God

"Oh, the depth of the riches both of the wisdom and knowledge of God! How unsearchable are His judgments and His ways past finding out! For who has known the mind of the Lord? Or who has become His counselor? Or who has first given to Him and it shall be repaid to him? For of Him and through Him and to Him are all things, to whom be glory forever. Amen." Rom. 11:33-36

Please receive these excerpts from a message by John Piper. Have you read a better description of God's glory? Let it transform your "small" thinking and teach this to others. Surely THIS God can revive His fumbling, failing Church!

"In the church, the view of God is so small instead of huge and so marginal instead of central, and so vague instead of clear, and so impotent instead of all-determining, and so uninspiring instead of ravishing." "Our pulpits are not as filled with God and the particularities of His glory, but far too many generalities so that our heads don't get filled with the glory of *His eternality*, that makes the mind want to explode with the thought that He never had a beginning; or the glory of *His knowledge* that makes the Library of Congress look like a little matchbox and makes quantum physics seem like a first-grade reader; or the glory of *His wisdom* that has never been or ever can be counseled by any man or any group of men; or the glory of *His authority* over heaven and earth and hell without which no man and no demon moves one inch; or the glory of *His providence* without which not one bird falls to the ground in any forest in the world or without which any hair on any head turns gray; or the glory of *His Word,* which upholds the universe and all the atoms and all the galaxies in it; or the glory of *His power* to walk on water and cleanse lepers and heal the lame and open the eyes of the blind and cause the deaf to hear and storms to be stilled and the dead to rise; or the glory of *His purity* never to sin or never to have one, two-second bad attitude or one evil thought; or the glory of *His trustworthiness* never to break His Word or to let one, single promise fall to the ground; or the glory of *His justice* to render all moral accounts in the universe settled either on the cross or in hell, there would be no outstanding injustices when all is said and done. People clearly to be redeemed or they will burn forever in hell, and there will be no injustice in the universe that has not been settled because of the glorious justice of God; or the glory of *His patience* to endure decade after decade after decade of our slow sanctification or the glory of *His sovereign, servant-like, slave-like obedience* to embrace the most excruciating pain that has ever been designed by humankind; or the glory of *His grace,* which justifies the ungodly or the glory of *His love* that does for us while we are yet sinners."

"Until we preach the particularities of His glory and put contours on our God instead of using broad, sweeping generalizations about His attributes, but make Him look irresistibly, magnificently more attractive than anything in the world, nobody is going to live for the glory of God in our church because they won't know Him."

Prerequisites for Answered Prayer

"And whatever we ask we receive from Him, because we keep His commandments and do those things that are pleasing in His sight. And this is His commandment: that we should believe on the name of His Son Jesus Christ and love one another, as He gave us commandment. Now he who keeps His commandments abides in Him, and He in him. And by this we know that He abides in us, by the Spirit whom He has given us." 1John 3:22-24

This is such an important topic; please pay close attention. There are so many things that you would like to become in Christ. But dear disciple, how effective you would be if only you could learn to have your prayers answered. Volumes have been written about effective prayer and we have heard much about *specific asking, miracle-working faith*, and about *abiding in Christ*. Now consider these words from 1John: *"And whatever we ask we receive from Him, because we keep His commandments and do those things that are pleasing in His sight."* It is quite apparent that if we are to have our prayers answered we must keep His commandments and do what is pleasing in His sight.

There are a myriad of things that please God. (Do a study on this topic.) But let it suffice to say that pleasing God does not come by your striving, but by complete abandonment to His will. And what does John mean when he writes *"keep His commandments?"* He goes on to explain: *"And this is His commandment: that we should believe on the name of His Son Jesus Christ and love one another."* So there you have it again, we are to believe. But that's not all; look carefully. John adds another condition: *love one another.* Have you considered this necessary ingredient for answered prayer? Peter confirms this in his first epistle (1Peter 3:7-12). If you do what is pleasing in His sight and love one another, you will have confidence... and confidence supports faith... and faith receives answers. Do you understand, beloved. We are talking about loving *in deed and truth*, not words alone.

So what are the key elements to answered prayer? Do what is pleasing to God, love one another, ask, believe, and abide in Him. If you do these things your spirit-led prayers will flow unhindered to the throne of grace... and abundant blessing will flow to you, and through you, to a needy generation.

"But whoever has this world's goods, and sees his brother in need, and shuts up his heart from him, how does the love of God abide in him? My little children, let us not love in word or in tongue, but in deed and in truth. And by this we know that we are of the truth, and shall assure our hearts before Him. For if our heart condemns us, God is greater than our heart, and knows all things. Beloved, if our heart does not condemn us, we have confidence toward God. And whatever we ask we receive from Him, because we keep His commandments and do those things that are pleasing in His sight." 1John 3:18-22

The Prayer Meeting

"I desire therefore that the men pray everywhere, lifting up holy hands, without wrath and doubting." 1Tim. 2:8 *"So, when he had considered this, he came to the house of Mary... where many were gathered together praying."* Acts 12:12

Prayer has been on the increase in many parts of the world... and that is a very good sign. Prayer meetings are springing up everywhere. Even the clergy are crossing denominational boundaries to meet together for intercession! As you know, throughout Church history, God has stirred sufficient prayer before He did something of significance. Be attentive, dear saint, God is about to do something.

Because we want to flow with God's Spirit as He leads us into prayer, it would seem wise to maximize the effectiveness of our corporate efforts (Prayer leader please take note). Let us consider some of the common errors that frequently occur during a prayer gathering, whether it be large or small:

1) *The one who is praying dominates the time with longwinded prayers.* Prayers must be Spirit-led; and of course, you are to flow with the Spirit for as long (or as short) as He gives utterance. But do not drone on in the power of the flesh.

2) *Announcements are made within the prayer.* Let's say that Joe broke his arm. The prayer will usually go something like this: "Dear Lord, you know that Brother Joe broke his arm this past Tuesday and was taken to Mercy Hospital etc. etc." It would be better to stop the prayer, address the congregation, explain the situation, and then pray. Surely God knows all of the details; you do not need to remind Him. Also, be sure that your prayer is not gossip!

3) *Horizontal, instead of vertical "prayers"* How many times have you heard a short sermon included in the prayer? In fact, it is seldom directed toward the throne of grace, but rather to the attendees, to teach or exhort. Don't fool yourself, beloved; this is not prayer.

4) *There is a lack of focus upon the One who hears our prayers.* When you pray aloud are you wondering how others perceive your petition? (Is it doctrinally correct, does it sound spiritual enough?) Or, are you fixed upon the Lord...thinking of Him and speaking directly to Him?

5) *The flow of the Spirit is cut short* by a well-meaning pray-er who changes the subject of prayer before the entire objective has been met. For instance: the current topic is spiritual revival in your city. A few people have already prayed for certain aspects of this multifaceted issue, and the Holy Spirit intends for there to be several more prayers offered regarding this subject...but then, someone begins to pray for those suffering with AIDS. Surely this is a noble prayer, and it may indeed be Spirit-led, but the timing is off. Allow there to be a "dead spot" of at least a minute before changing topics, so the fullness of God's purposes can be accomplished.

Ride the wave of the Holy Spirit for as long as He leads. You may enjoy intensive prayer for a half-hour, sometimes for several hours. You will know when the session is over...the steady stream of intercession simply dries up. Here is a rule of thumb: If you have to think about what to pray for next, it is usually time to take a break, or to end the meeting. *Dear disciple, don't become legalistic about these things, but lovingly instruct the people.*

True Repentance

"Then the Lord spoke to Moses, saying, 'Speak to the children of Israel: When a man or woman commits any sin that men commit in unfaithfulness against the Lord, and that person is guilty, then he shall confess the sin which he has committed. He shall make restitution for his trespass in full, plus one-fifth of it, and give it to the one he has wronged.'" Numbers 5:5-7

Do you realize that there are two elements of true repentance: confession and restitution. As you may know, the word *repentance* is from the Greek cognate noun *metanoia*, meaning: to change direction, turn around, change your mind. Yes, you already know this. But, dear Christian, are you DOING it? It is not enough to simply say, "I'm sorry, God," with some half-hearted prayer of contrition.

First, you agree with God that what you did, or said, or didn't do was against His expressed will; this is called confession. But then there must be action taken to turn away from the sin, and all of its trappings. Never forget, God is very serious about your sin.

What about the other aspect of repentance? Restitution is seldom mentioned. If you have lied, the truth should be made known. If you have stolen something, give it back. If you have injured someone, in any way, you must ask for forgiveness. Do you get it, dear saint? There is a bit more to it than merely offering a few mumbled words in semi-sincerity. Have you truly repented? *(In some instances, restitution may be impossible: the offended party is dead, or the whereabouts is unknown. Nevertheless, the blood of Jesus is sufficient.)*

Prophetic Insight

"He answered and said to them, 'When it is evening you say, `It will be fair weather, for the sky is red'; and in the morning, `It will be foul weather today, for the sky is red and threatening.' Hypocrites! You know how to discern the face of the sky, but you cannot discern the signs of the times." Matthew 16:2-3

As we seek direction for this next season, it seems as though God

As we seek direction for this next season, it seems as though God has begun to reveal His plans. Can you see the signs of the times, beloved; have you heard His prophetic word? Make note of these insights and see if they come to pass:

1) A restoration and fresh revelation of *Holy Communion,* is now in progress. The doctrine of Holy Communion has been debated for centuries. Theologians of all persuasions have tried to encapsulate incomprehensible mystical truth into a mere definition. Soon the Lord will make known to those who seek Him the *mysterious* wonders of the partaking of His body and blood, eating and drinking His precious life. (Interestingly, daily communion has preceded other Revivals. Read the journals of the great revivalists.)

2) Extensive preparation has been occurring throughout this generation, with much refining and pruning taking place. Humility and brokenness are being established in the heart and life of the true disciple. Complete dependence upon God, through prayer and deep trust, is emerging.

3) There will be a revealing of the sons of God, a period like none other in history. The glory of the Lord will be revealed through His chosen ones. Apostolic authority and extraordinary power will be made manifest through the weak and foolish. The world will be amazed... and the apostate Church will persecute.

4) This day of glory (Isaiah 60:1-2) will be revealed in the midst of great darkness, great trouble. The darkness increases as sin increases

5) Although we have been enjoying an extended season of mercy, the judgment of God will come... through natural disasters and nuclear terror. Cities and nations will be shaken around the globe.

6) The fear of the Lord will be restored at this time. It will be imperative for the servants of Jesus to be courageous, being a light in the darkness; leading the fearful to a saving knowledge of Christ.

7) The world-wide revival that has been anticipated for nearly a century has begun. Jesus is coming soon!

Your Prayer Life

"... pray without ceasing..." 1Thessalonians 5:17

This is where things get quiet, when guilt rises... or worse yet, self-justification and excuses: How much time do you spend in prayer,

We could write volumes about the value of prayer and the command to pray... or give examples of the Apostles' praying, but you have heard it all before; haven't you? And I'm sure you realize that prayer, in various forms, is mentioned in the Word hundreds of times. (It seems rather interesting that our text, with only 3 little words, merits being a verse by itself. I wonder why?) Not to mention that you are well aware of the fact that God does nothing in the earth except through prayer - correct? Nevertheless, much of the Church remains prayerless, impotent and fruitless... and appears to be on the verge of irrelevance. When will we learn?

If you are truly desirous of becoming a significant player, I mean one who is running the race to win, a true disciple of Jesus Christ, then you must hear this: Search the New Testament and the extended collection of biographical journals (past and present), and you will be hard-pressed to find any servant of the Most High, who accomplished their God-given assignment, consistently bearing fruit, without having an EXTRAORDINARY PRAYER LIFE. Come now; God Incarnate needed to pray - at times He prayed all night. Do you think that you can somehow bear eternal fruit while sidestepping this necessary ingredient? You have been deceived! Endurance, diligence, humility, faith — all of these are essential, but there is no substitute for fervent prayer.

Some would say, "You pray, I'll work." I'm sorry, dear child, if you really want to become like Jesus, you will both pray and work just as He did! Use the following as a guideline, not a law: All Christians should pray at least 1 hour per day. If you are a leader, 2 hours should be the minimum. (Some pray 4 or 5 hours.) Remember this: The more work you do and the more responsibility you have, the more you must pray. There are many who look good and sound good and act like they have spiritual power, but they do not.

Make no mistake, there are times and seasons of prayer just like any other spiritual activity... including seasons of lesser or greater intensity. There are also times of deep brokenness when you simply can't pray very much. (It seems religious to even suggest it.) If you are there now, please don't be discouraged by this teaching. At the proper time, the Lord will revitalize your prayer life... ask Him.

You can gradually build your prayer time, you know. What prevents you from adding 5 or 10 minutes to your daily routine? Maintain this additional prayer until it becomes a part of your life... and then increase it again. Pray in the spirit throughout the day. In this manner, you will begin to live in the Spirit, rather than merely paying an occasional visit. Without a doubt, believe this promise: ".... He is a rewarder of those who diligently seek Him" (Heb. 11:6).

Visit Us

Have you been asking God to visit your church, your region? I mean, are you praying for revival? Many churches have caught this vision over these past several years. Wonderful! - How we need it! Prayer has increased in many places; a diligent seeking of God has begun. He will answer, beloved; keep praying. Nevertheless, let's consider a few other factors:

Despite what others may have said about the absolute need for unity as a prerequisite for revival, history proves this to be incorrect. Many local, regional and national awakenings were easily accomplished by God without requiring the Church to first enter into unity. Having said that, let's earnestly encourage unity; this is God's will. However, what makes you think that heart-felt unity is now attainable when it has eluded our best efforts for nearly two millennium? In fact, the opposite seems to be true; unity is a byproduct of Revival. During the outpourings of the past century, believers who may have never given each other the time of day were seen embracing in genuine brotherly love as the Holy Spirit filled their hearts. Doctrinal differences seem to evaporate in the presence of the Holy One. During the Azusa Street Revival, in an era when African-Americans were forced to use separate drinking fountains, they worshipped and danced together with "whites," even lying side by side on the meeting room floor as they were overcome by the power of God's Spirit. Seek unity, beloved, but there is something that should be of greater concern.

There is yet one remaining blockage, perhaps the primary hindrance to a glorious awakening... and that is pride. Pride will deter a visitation from God because *"God resists the proud."* Examine your heart personally and your church corporately; pride takes many forms. Most assuredly, God would never leave our refinement to our own inept methods. He already has the matter well in hand. Do you now see why the Lord has been allowing so many upsets, reversals and embarrassments? He is dealing with your pride; He is breaking you. The Lover loves you so much that He will bring you to nothingness, so that He can become everything... in and through you.

Do you truly want a personal and regional revival? Allow the Vinedresser to prune you, also humble yourself and seek the lowest place; become a servant. You have sought revival for many years now, haven't you? Still no results? Try humbling yourself... and then pray. *"...if My people who are called by My name will humble themselves, and pray and seek My face, and turn from their wicked ways, then I will hear from heaven, and will forgive their sin and heal their land"* (2 Chr. 7:14). By the way, humility is the foundation of true unity.

The Judgment of God

"For the wrath of God is revealed from heaven against all ungodliness and unrighteousness of men, who suppress the truth in unrighteousness" Romans 1:18

In this hour when an entire generation has grown complacent about the things of God, a revelation of the fear of God will be given. Open your eyes; this is now in progress. Shakings, disciplines and judgments are coming upon the earth. See what God is doing:

Although a child enjoys his Father's love, he may sometimes take it for granted, testing the boundaries, pushing his forbearance to the limit. Surely you have seen this in your own family. Then comes a warning, and another a bit more stern, and perhaps yet another... this father is slow to anger. But then if the child's behavior is still not corrected this loving father must administer some form of discipline... reluctantly, but firmly. And what if the child becomes rebellious, breaking rules and breaking laws? He will probably be apprehended by the police and warned at a more serious level. The discipline will also increase. God forbid, prison and even the death sentence has been issued to the most rebellious.

Do you understand, beloved? Glean some wisdom and know the ways of the Almighty. Our God is loving, merciful and kind. He is slow to anger and abounding in mercy. His grace is abundant, Jesus' blood sufficient to cover all sin. Nevertheless, He is also holy, righteous and just. God will not be mocked.

How foolish to think that God does not bring judgments. The Word of God is full of His warnings and judgments... sometimes intensely severe. Does this mean that He is not LOVE? Of course not! A loving father disciplines, even scourges his favored sons. God's discipline is usually painful, but it is also love, pure love. The intention is always and only to correct and to set one's feet on the right path... that we may know and love the Lord and fulfill our destiny.

OK, but what about the wrath of God, His fierce anger and righteous punishment? It is coming, dear saint. It has come and will come again. Take note of our New Testament text *"For the wrath of God is revealed from heaven."* His wrath IS revealed, a present activity. Not merely delegated to the Old Testament or to the end of the age. The destruction of Jerusalem in 70AD was prophesied by Jesus Himself.

A quick review of world history reveals God's mercy and long-suffering toward the nations. However, eventually judgment comes to those who refuse to repent: calamity, decline, destruction, or sometimes obliteration. This has occurred many times. In fact, more than twenty great civilizations have declined or have been completely destroyed during the course of human events. Do you not think that the 20th Century decimation of Germany, the bombardments and fire bombings and the killing of so many was not the judgment of God unfurled against a nation who started two world wars and murdered six million of His chosen people? Yes, this judgment was delivered through the allied forces. God's judgment often-times came to Israel via an advancing army.

And then there are personal judgments noted in the New Testament: The judgment of weakness, sickness, even death for receiving Holy Communion in an unworthy manner: *"For he who eats and drinks in an unworthy manner eats and drinks judgment to himself"* 1Cor 11:29 There is also a judgment for not forgiving someone who has offended you: *"And his master was angry, and delivered him to the torturers until he should pay all that was due to him. So My heavenly Father also will do to you if each of you, from his heart, does not forgive his brother his trespasses."* Matt 18:34-35 Our Father is very serious about these matters.

You must fear God, beloved, and obey Him. Our nation must fear God. What judgment is stored up for a nation that has killed over forty million babies for the sake of convenience?

"Who shall not fear You, O Lord, and glorify Your name? For You alone are holy. For all nations shall come and worship before You, for Your judgments have been manifested." Revelations 15:4

Judgment or Testing?

"I form the light and create darkness, I make peace and create calamity; I, the Lord, do all these things. Rain down, you heavens, from above, and let the skies pour down righteousness; let the earth open, let them bring forth salvation, and let righteousness spring up together. I, the Lord, have created it. Woe to him who strives with his Maker!" Isaiah 45:7-9

As judgment begins to befall a nation (or an individual) many will ask the question: "Is this truly the judgment of God or is it merely a test, like so many other difficult times in the past?" In fact, there is a large segment of Christianity that has a big problem seeing God as a disciplinary Judge. They prefer to focus on His mercy, grace and kindness. Actually, they are correct, we should focus on these loving attributes; God is love. Nevertheless, let us not loose sight of His holiness and justice, etc... this is also love.

Anyway, how do you tell the difference between testing and judgment (discipline, chastisement)? Beloved, it is quite simple: If you have been walking righteously before God you can assume that any given adversity is a test (either allowed by Him... or directly from His hand) rather than judgment. Surely it would be unjust for our Father to discipline you if you were obeying Him. This would be like a parent slapping their child for no reason. You know the Lord is not like that.

On the other hand, if you are not walking in holiness and have justified your sins, even modified your doctrine to accommodate your sinful lifestyle, you should expect God's discipline/ judgment/ chastisement at any moment. God loves you so much that He will not spare the rod, but will seek to correct your waywardness. This is true love. Nonetheless, it is important to make a distinction between those who love God and hate sin but occasionally stumble because they are weak… and those who excuse themselves.

Here is another interesting point: Judgment and testing often occurs simultaneously. Consider the devastating natural disasters now ravaging our country and other parts of the world. Wherever these calamities strike, the unrighteous are judged and the righteous are tested. And both will grow closer to the Lord if they respond correctly. The Holy One is in the midst of it all helping, encouraging, comforting... and correcting. What an awesome God we serve!

If you are having difficulty with the word *judgment* perhaps you have received some incorrect teaching. Check your lexicon. You will see there are several meanings. Some judgments are meant to correct, while the most severe have no redemptive value; they are final.

During a recent catastrophic hurricane, a city known for its sinfulness was seriously flooded with several feet of water and buried under tons of sludge, chemicals and human waste. This city was completely evacuated and rendered uninhabitable for many weeks. However, the most overtly wicked part of the city remained virtually untouched by the flooding. Could it be the Sovereign Judge left this section unscathed because He had given them over to their own devices, even to a reprobate mind? If so, this is the most grievous of judgments.

Dear servant of Jesus, weep for this city and pray for her. The mayor has publicly declared that they plan to continue in their sinful ways… just as soon as possible.

Complacency

"For consider Him who endured such hostility from sinners against Himself, lest you become weary and discouraged in your souls. You have not yet resisted to bloodshed, striving against sin. And you have forgotten the exhortation which speaks to you as to sons: 'My son, do not despise the chastening of the Lord, nor be discouraged when you are rebuked by Him; for whom the Lord loves He chastens, and scourges every son whom He receives.' If you endure chastening, God deals with you as with sons; for what son is there whom a father does not chasten?" Hebrews 12:3-7

Do you find yourself enjoying the sermons and books that speak of God's grace and mercy, those that tell you you're OK? Do you catch yourself saying, "Yes, I have my faults, but I do the best that I can. That's just the way I am." Dear Christian, if you respond in this manner, you are in for a rude awakening. You may not be OK! You have become complacent with your sinfulness.

Granted, there are those who struggle with sin, they literally fight the good fight of faith. They seek the Lord, and sweat and cry while resisting temptation. They also ask for prayer and become account-able to another, confessing their sins. And yet occasionally, even frequently, they fail. These brothers and sisters need reassurance that they are acceptable to God, that God's mercy and grace are sufficient... *"if we confess our sins, He is faithful and just to forgive us our sins and cleanse us from all unrighteousness."* But much of the Church does not wrestle; they don't put up a fight. They easily submit to temptation and then run to the spout of grace. This cheapens the blood of Jesus and is not pleasing to God.

Throughout Church history the pendulum has swung from one extreme to another, from harsh preaching about hellfire and brimstone to candy coated messages of love, love, love... And either extreme can be detrimental because it is not the complete truth. God is gracious and merciful; He is also holy and just. The Lord heals, comforts and encourages; He also disciplines and punishes His children. It should be well know that a church only hearing messages about the love of God, can fall asleep... lulled into complacency. For at least the past three decades we have heard much about the love of

God... and how necessary this has been. Some have received these teachings and have drawn closer to the Lover of their soul, becoming intimate. Many others have taken this Great Love for granted, believing that a loving God would never punish them. Look around you, beloved; read the headlines; see the fruit of our complacency.

Surely you must warn your own children once in a while: "If you don't clean your room, there will be consequences." "If you don't stop doing that, you will be punished." Of course, the repercussions should be in accordance with the offense. Nonetheless, the threat of consequences usually helps the child to obey, especially if you have lovingly followed through with disciplinary action in the past. Certainly you should obey God simply because you love Him and want to please Him, but let's get real... our flesh is weak and we also need to be admonished. Consider the fact that Jesus sternly warned five of the seven churches in the Book of Revelations.

Sin abounds throughout the land and the *hour of warning* may soon be upon us. Make no mistake about it, your heavenly Father, as a loving parent, will warn His children. (Learn another definition of *grace*.) He will remind you about the consequences of sin... allowing you to experience some of the pain of discipline. The Fear of God, an all but forgotten doctrine, will be restored to His Church for our own good... bringing us to genuine repentance! You need to be challenged, complacent one. Someone needs to say, *"Sin no more, lest a worse thing come upon you* (John 5:14)! The Lord will shake everything that can be shaken. This is true love ...and normal Christianity.

There is another type of complacency, beloved: lack of enthusiasm for the things of God. Where is your zeal for prayer and good works: giving to the poor, ministering to the sick and the imprisoned? "And let us consider one another in order to stir up love and good works, not forsaking the assembling of ourselves together, as is the manner of some, but exhorting one another, and so much the more as you see the Day approaching." Hebrews 10:24-25

The Rise and Fall of Nations

"And I will say to my soul, 'Soul, you have many goods laid up for many years; take your ease; eat, drink, and be merry.'" Luke 12:19

Consider this well, dear saint; let history be your teacher. Nations rise and nations fall... and among many factors, there is usually one common denominator in the equation of their demise. Ancient Egypt, the Medes and Persians, Greece, Rome, in fact, more than twenty great civilizations came to ruination due to the lack of personal discipline and an increase in self-indulgence!

Each nation rose to prominence as the result of sacrifice, hard work, and perseverance. The people were disciplined and unified. But as they became wealthy and materialistic they became lax and complacent. The pursuit of pleasure took preeminence; their sexual appetite was indulged, including homosexuality. As self-control gave way to permissiveness, the once invincible society became weak, and then declined; most of them were eventually conquered.

Dear philosopher and statesman, anyone who touts a liberal agenda beware! You have disregarded the truth of God's Word and replaced it with emptiness. You will be held accountable for your foolish "wisdom." You are leading many astray, even a nation to its grave.

Maintain Unity

"We then who are strong ought to bear with the scruples of the weak, and not to please ourselves. Let each of us please his neighbor for his good, leading to edification. Now may the God of patience and comfort grant you to be like-minded toward one another, according to Christ Jesus, that you may with one mind and one mouth glorify the God and Father of our Lord Jesus Christ. Therefore receive (accept) one another, just as Christ also received (accepted) us, to the glory of God." Romans 15:1-2,5-7

Do you realize how many churches have divided as the result of differing views of doctrine and practice? The numbers are staggering! You would think that the church could see this massive hole in the road and avoid it, but we do not. This is simply stupid!

Dear disciple, the Master has given us a commission: preach the gospel to every creature, cleanse the leper, heal the sick, raise the dead, restore sight to the blind, set the captives free. Does this sound familiar? Oh yes, He also told us to make disciples and baptize in the name of the Father, Son, and Holy Spirit. Nevertheless, we have gotten so caught up in the debate of *when* we should baptize and *the method* thereof, that we have lost sight of the mission. We fight with each other, the world goes to hell, and the devil laughs.

Doctrine is important, beloved, but not as important as unity; please remember that. Your faith should be built upon a relationship with Jesus Christ, not upon doctrine. (This enables you to examine differing views without feeling threatened.) Of course, the core doctrine of salvation and the biblical mandates of morality must never be compromised, but are you ready to divide over eschatology?

Are you willing to die to your pet doctrines? Even your beliefs must go to the cross, dear saint. Or, will pride rise up and squelch any opposition to what you "know" to be absolute truth? Are you positive there will be a 1,000-year reign of Christ on earth? Are you certain that there will not be? There are millions of Christians on both sides of this debate. Only a proud fool would divide over such an issue. And what of Holy Communion, and Holy Spirit Baptism, and eternal security, do you demand allegiance to your interpretation of these issues?

Dear Christian, please surrender your right to be right and live above your differences. You can humble yourself for the sake of unity, can't you? If not, you will probably follow in the footsteps of the many who have gone before you, insisting that they were correct, only to plunge headlong toward disunity, division, and a weakened Church with diminished resources... and the world looks on and laughs. *If you were busy doing the work of the kingdom you probably wouldn't have the time to be agitated about such things. "Look up, for the fields are white!"*

The Writing Is On The Wall

"They drank wine, and praised the gods of gold and silver, bronze and iron, wood and stone. In the same hour the fingers of a man's hand appeared and wrote opposite the lamp stand on the plaster of the wall of the king's palace..." Daniel 5:4-5

Can you read the signs of the times; the writing is on the wall! You are in grave danger, beloved nation. Your foundation has been laid upon God's Word; your system of justice was inspired by the Law of Moses. You have been mightily blessed... perhaps more than any other. There was a time when you sought the Lord and there was great freedom to worship. In fact, the government nurtured the free expression of faith. The family was considered sacred; children were shielded from evil; public service and self-sacrifice were the norm.

How things have changed! Over the years, the love of money and the pursuit of pleasure have blinded your eyes. Prayer has been removed from the public schools and situational ethics have been taught... replacing moral absolutes. Public displays of religious symbols have been outlawed; pornography and sexual promiscuity have been endorsed. Abortion has also been legalized. (Over 40 million babies have been discarded!) You have turned away from your Divine Protector and have embraced far lesser things.

Woe to you, judges, politicians, teachers, and liberal church leaders who have promoted immorality and governmental policies that led to the erosion of your foundation. You have set yourself above God, refusing to obey His ways; you have ridiculed and maligned those who adhere to Biblical principles. You have chosen your own path, the way of foolishness. You have set your own house on fire.

Open your eyes! The increased divorce rate has taken a great toll on your society, psychologically and economically. Children have been seriously affected; rebellion and delinquency are on the rise. Kids are shooting other kids in your streets, and in your schools. (You have removed the Ten Commandments and replaced them with metal detectors!) Drug addiction and alcoholism are pandemic. Tens of thousands are dying from sexually transmitted diseases. Depression and fear have gripped the hearts of millions. Can't you see that these social ills are the direct result of abandoning your Judeo-Christian values?

Return to your roots before it's too late. Why can't you see that? God is merciful; He would much rather show mercy than judgment. He has temporarily held back His hand of judgment in response to the cries of His people, and has given you a leader who seeks the guidance of the Holy Spirit. He speaks righteousness into the land.

Nonetheless, many of your people hate him and desire his removal. Don't refuse to listen; turn from your rebellious ways. Our enemies have increased; they are even now within our borders, planning our demise. Which will we choose? Will we accept the great sacrifice for sin that Jesus' made on Calvary, and choose to walk in obedience, or will we consider Jesus' love misdirected and insignificant?

The Lord will not strive with us forever. Unrighteousness has increased, not decreased. Child molestation is among the rising statistics! If we continue to ignore the laws of God and push Him away, we will be left without His protection. Our enemies will be allowed to have their way... death and destruction will follow.

We must stop the hatred, violence, injustice, and prejudices. Turn away from divorce, adultery, and promiscuity. Stop abortion; stop promoting homosexuality. It is time to turn back to the Lord. *"Seek the Lord while He may be found, call upon Him while He is near. Let the wicked forsake his way, and the unrighteous man his thoughts; let him return to the Lord, and He will have mercy on him; and to our God, for He will abundantly pardon"* {Isaiah 55: 6-7}.

The Battle Rages

"For we do not wrestle against flesh and blood, but against principalities, against powers, against the rulers of the darkness of this age, against spiritual hosts of wickedness in the heavenly places. Therefore take up the whole armor of God, that you may be able to withstand in the evil day, and having done all, to stand... praying always with all prayer and supplication in the Spirit, being watchful to this end with all perseverance and supplication for all the saints." Ephesians 6:12-13, 18

The enemy is at the gate; you can hear the gunfire in the streets. Your nation and your city are under attack; your family and property are in danger. All that you have worked for is about to be destroyed. Will you stand up and fight?

Throughout the ages countless numbers have had to face the challenge of defending their homeland. Mighty men and women of valor have fought to the death, protecting their children. They are to be remembered and honored. Only a coward would run and hide at a time such as this. Only a fool would carry on with business as usual.

Dear disciple of Jesus Christ, at this present hour a battle rages for the souls of men. Can't you see the spiritual warfare that besieges your own country? The wicked one has pulled out all restraints; his attacks are relentless. The children have been overtaken by his wiles; marriages are in shambles; addictions and sexually transmitted disease have run rampant; babies are being discarded. We have been severely ravaged and the worst is yet to come. When will you stand up and fight? Will you defend your family, your city, and nation through radical prayer and fasting? Will you? The enemy is at the gate! Where are the mighty men and women of valor? They have been lulled into complacency, business as usual, watching TV.

How do you rally the troops, beloved? How can we stir them without heaping guilt and condemnation? Ask God for laborers, warriors, intercessors. Ask; He will answer. Revive us, Lord; revive us!

Doing What the Father Does

"Then Jesus answered and said to them, 'Most assuredly, I say to you, the Son can do nothing of Himself, but what He sees the Father do; for whatever He does, the Son also does in like manner. For the Father loves the Son, and shows Him all things that He Himself does; and He will show Him greater works than these, that you may marvel. I can of Myself do nothing. As I hear, I judge; and My judgment is righteous, because I do not seek My own will but the will of the Father who sent Me.'" John 5:19-20, 30

These words of Jesus give us tremendous insight. Would you review them again? Jesus, the Word made flesh, is clearly revealing how He ministered while here on earth. Do you think that it might also give us a clue as to how we, His servants, should do our ministry? *'Most assuredly, I say to you, the Son can do nothing of Himself, but what He sees the Father do; for whatever He does, the Son also does in like manner.*

Dear minister, do you see what your Father is doing? He wants to show you. *"No longer do I call you servants, for a servant does not know what his master is doing; but I have called you friends, for all things that I heard from My Father I have made known to you"* (John 15:15). How we struggle and strive. Is this the way of God? No, I dare say it is not. Seek the Lord; surrender your will in the matter, listen intently, walk slowly, be mindful of your inner peace and the still small voice within. Observe the circumstances, and the words and actions of others. Through all of these, the Holy Spirit will reveal and/ or confirm the will of God.

See what the Father is doing in an individual life or in a village or region. The Lord may be sowing seeds in a particular area, in which case, you sow seeds. He may be harvesting in another place; make your plans to harvest. It is foolish to spend time and money trying to harvest when it is time to cultivate. His harvest fields do not all ripen at the same time! Is the Lord's attention turned toward the youth of a particular neighborhood? Your paramount concern should then be how to reach out to them. One group made three attempts to plant a church, applying the usual methods, but without success. Finally, after seeking the Lord, they realized that He was working among the 8-12 year olds of that area. They, likewise, planted a church for this age group and soon reaped a wonderful harvest of souls. The youth later won their parents to Christ.

God is a God of the now. He must be followed in the now, not by formula and yesterday's programs. If the Church could only learn to hear God's voice and obey, how abundant our fruit would be.

What is God doing in your life? Perhaps this is the most pertinent question of the day. What season are you in? What has He been showing you? Is it the time to go or to wait, to learn, teach, serve, lead, etc? If you can see what the Father is doing, it will be a bit easier for you to trust Him to accomplish His purpose in you and through you. Next question: What is the Father doing in your family, neighborhood, city or nation? Do you want your prayers answered? Pray back to God those things that He has shown to you, the things that He is about to do… and that which He has already begun to do! What then is the way to fruitful ministry? 1) See what God is doing. 2) Pray what He is doing and 3) Do what He is doing! *Lord, please help me to minister as Jesus did, hearing what the Father is saying and then speak it, seeing what the Father is doing and then do it.*

This is normal Christianity.

Some things that our Father has been doing today around the world: He has been refining and purifying His Bride, bringing her to deeper levels of humility, calling His church to radical intercession, developing unity within His body and preparing His people to withstand persecution and carry His glory in a soon to unfold, global Revival. Even now, we are in the midst of the greatest harvest of souls that the world has ever known. (Just because it is not happening in your denomination or region doesn't mean that it is not occurring. Look to the nations and see multiple millions of Chinese, Africans and Asians accepting the Savior.) He has also been at work in Israel setting the stage for the fulfillment of end-time prophecy. Be ready! The best is yet to come; Jesus will soon return!

Personal Awakening

Abiding in Christ, Living in the Spirit
Walking in Humility, Loving God
The Depths of Jesus

In Christ

*" For since by man came death, by Man also came the resurrection of the dead. For as in Adam all die, even so **in Christ** all shall be made alive. But each one in his own order: Christ the first fruits, afterward those who are Christ's at His coming. Then comes the end, when He delivers the kingdom to God the Father, when He puts an end to all rule and all authority and power. For He must reign till He has put all enemies under His feet...Now when all things are made subject to Him, then the Son Himself will also be subject to Him who put all things under Him, that God may be all in all."* 1Cor 15:21-25, 28

Is there still a tinge of pride that remains? If so, it will be difficult to fully appreciate your position before the Father. As long as you enjoy taking credit for your own achievements and feel that you deserve all that you possess, how can you understand you are but dust and that every blessing comes down from the Father of Lights? How can you possibly abide in the presence of a holy God when you think that somehow, by your own efforts, you have earned the right to be there? Selah... before you conclude this is not you, know that self-righteousness is insidious, lurking in the recesses of your heart.

Please understand, dear foolish one. You have only one position before the Almighty, and that is: *in Christ!* (This phrase is mentioned 85 times in the NT!) The Perfect Sacrifice suffered and died for you and He alone is acceptable to our perfect God! What chance does imperfection have to stand before Him? You are hidden *in Christ*; He covers you. Ask God for revelation in this matter. When you received Jesus, His redemptive work on Calvary, you died with Him... and you now live *in Christ*, you pray *in Christ* and you serve *in Christ*. Your joy and fulfillment are *in Christ* and so are your rewards. And when all is said and done and you behold Him in His heavenly glory, you will easily cast your crowns at His feet saying, "You alone are worthy."

The Vinedresser may permit you to suffer a failure, loss, or some type of reversal to help you come to understand this truth... allow Him to have His way. Realizing your position in Christ is the threshold of Kingdom living.

Appreciate the Blood

"Therefore, since we are receiving a kingdom which cannot be shaken, let us have grace, by which we may serve God acceptably with reverence and godly fear. For our God is a consuming fire." Hebrews 12:28-29

When you look into the night sky, or at a calico sunrise, or feel the power of an explosive thunderstorm... when you study the intricacies of anatomy and physiology, or consider physics, chemistry and calculus... not to mention the gentle touch of a baby's hand, do you fall upon your knees in utter amazement and worship the Creator of all things? Who is this Great God, holding the entire universe in the palm of His hand; can you even begin to comprehend His magnificence? *10,000 times 10,000 and thousands of thousands* of angels surround His heavenly throne declaring His majesty and might. (That's more than 100 million angels!)

Dear human, have you taken the time to consider His power and perfection, His absolute brilliance and holiness. Who can compare? This present generation has minimized His attributes... desiring to conform God to our image. You can see God the Father depicted on the ceiling of the Sistine Chapel as a bearded old man extending His finger. Nonetheless, as beautiful as this masterpiece is, it can by no means express the creative dunamis of the King of Glory!

Do you understand? *"Our God is a consuming fire... who alone has immortality, dwelling in unapproachable light, whom no man has seen or can see..."* How foolish to think that mere humans can sashay their way into the presence of One such as this, somehow under the delusion that they have a right to be there, even demanding that the Omnipotent do their bidding. Can you not see? Do you not know that our God is GOD! The earth trembles as He draws near, the mountains melt like wax. The ancients understood; they would not dare to speak or even write His full name. The High Priest entered the Holy of Holies with bells and a rope around his ankle in case he was to drop dead while ministering before the Ark.

The very nature of God, His perfect holiness, is described as a consuming fire, a furnace so hot that none could approach without bursting into flames - Fire and flesh are not compatible! How can you come close to Someone like this? And beloved, the Lord fervently desires that you would come to Him. You know that.

In very imperfect terms, imagine the blood of Jesus as a suit of asbestos, a covering that permits you to enter into His presence. Not only to enter with reverence for worship and petition, but to be lovingly welcomed into His arms, to be intimate with Him. And then to stand beside Him as a joint-heir with Jesus Christ, as a son given authority and responsibility to rule and reign! This is your destiny, blood-covered child of God. The Holy One has made a way for you to enter in.

You will never fully appreciate the blood of Jesus until you understand the absolute need for it.

The Depths of Jesus

"God desires to give Himself to the soul that really loves Him and to the soul that earnestly seeks Him." Jean Guyon, 1685

The invitation to draw near to God is for everyone, educated or not, poor or rich, man, woman or child. The Lover of Souls desires that each of His children would come closer. Your first reply to this loving invitation might be, "That's very nice but I just don't have the time and I don't want to fast and pray or do anything more." This response is quite typical. Many think that they must somehow strive to get close to God. But this is not the case; it is actually very simple. This does not require the bondage of works nor does it entail the *dos* and *don'ts* of religion. It is simply the yielding of your heart to Jesus and the free expression of your love for Him. You can do this, beloved!

Here are a few insights from Madam Jean Guyon, a 17th century lover of God:

Set time aside to be with the Lord. (Try 10-15 minutes to start.) Find a place that is void of distractions. Turn your heart to His presence by faith. Begin to read scripture and pray the scripture slowly, setting your mind on the Spirit. It is not how much you read that matters. You are not here to study, only to quiet your spirit and enter inward. Wait on the Lord; enjoy His presence. Your mind will wander; bring it back again. It is very important to remember that God dwells within you "...Or do you not know that your body is the temple of the Holy Spirit, Who is in you?" (1Cor. 6:19). Look for God within you, not somewhere outside. Retreat into the depths of your being and when distracted try not to think of something different. (This engages the mind.) Withdraw, turning within to the Lord's presence. This process of disciplining the mind will take time but it gets easier. His touch is so enjoyable that you are drawn inwardly to Him. He makes this experience enjoyable so that you will come to Him more often. How He loves to be with you.

As You Come to Him

"...It is the voice of my Beloved! He knocks, saying, 'Open for Me, My sister, My love, My dove, My perfect one;'" Song of Solomon 5:2

Some very simple steps to enter into a quiet, intimate time with your Lord as gleaned from Jeanne Guyon:
- Remember to seek Him within you.
- Close your eyes and open the inward eyes of your soul.
- Come to Him gently.
- Come with a deep sense of love and worship. Offer simple words of love and praise.
- Acknowledge that He is everything. You are nothing.
- Come as a child: weak, bruised, soiled. Offer words of love and repentance.
- Give yourself completely to Him so that He can do in you what you have been unable to do.
- Acknowledge to Him His right to rule over you.
- Once you are in His presence, be still and quiet.
- Do not let your mind wander.
- Begin the Lord's Prayer, slowly, one phrase at a time, with meditation.
- Wait, listen ... Utter words of love.
- Continue in the Lord's Prayer.
- Remain before Him as long as you sense His presence.

Oh the sweetness, the beauty, the stillness, the depth. God is extending His loving invitation to you. What prevents you from drawing near to Him now? Don't be afraid; take just a few minutes now. Close your eyes. Tell Jesus that you love Him, adore Him and worship Him. *I need You, Lord. I love You. Please bring me deeper.*

Humility... Maturing to Childhood

"Assuredly, I say to you, unless you are converted and become as little children, you will by no means enter the kingdom of heaven. Therefore whoever humbles himself as this little child is the greatest in the kingdom of heaven." Matthew 18:1-4

Dear Christian, in addition to wanting our family to love and serve God, most of us have the need to do something of significance. The search for significance seems to be inherent and causes mankind to accomplish and achieve. This is necessary for the development of a society, but usually unbeknownst to us, some aspects of its forward thrust actually hinder the development of the Kingdom of God. As you can see from the teachings of Jesus, God's ways are quite contrary to the natural ways of the world. Ambition and the drive to be successful are not welcome in the Kingdom. Humility, submission, and death to self are. Jesus said *"He who is greatest among you must be your servant."* (Matt.23:11). Even the greatest must become the least to truly be great!

Do you aspire to greatness? Do you hope to bless mankind in some meaningful way? Then you must become like a child. Aspire to become like a humble child: unassuming, unnoticed, and unadmired. A child's words and deeds are usually not considered to be very significant at all. In fact, really great men and women are seldom recognized by their contemporaries, Jesus being the foremost. Would you hope to be like Him? He was spurned and crucified by the same people that He came to give life. Or perhaps you would like to be a John the Baptist. Jesus said that there was no greater man born of woman. Or maybe you want to be like Paul, Luther, Teresa, Guyon, or Wesley. All of these were rejected by those to whom they were sent.

St. Augustine wrote, "For those who would learn God's ways,

St. Augustine wrote, "For those who would learn God's ways, humility is the first thing, humility is the second, humility is the third." But the very mention of humility grates against your soul, doesn't it? In fact, when you began to read this you may have detected a wee bit of resistance. It is a process, my friend, and a long slow death. The fact that you recognize the pride within is a very good sign. This proves that you are advancing. You are maturing to childhood, ascending to obscurity, descending to greatness. You are dying to truly live. This is *normal* Christianity.

The Downward Spiral of Unforgiveness

"If you do not forgive men their trespasses, neither will your Father forgive your trespasses." Matthew 6:15

Unforgiveness is a very serious matter, dear believer, and perhaps secondary in importance only to the doctrine of Salvation. There is no option; all Christians must forgive. In fact, the servant of Jesus must become an expert at forgiving. If you wield the axe of forgiveness effectively, bitterness will be destroyed at the root. If not, misery will follow.

Some offenses are major: the results of violence, rape or murder, or perhaps some great loss. Others are less grievous such as being slighted, or embarrassed by another, unmet expectations, etc. In serious cases of unforgiveness, there is usually a progressive downward spiral: You may toss and turn in bed thinking about it. At first, you begin to experience self-pity, followed by critical and judgmental thoughts. Anger and frustration begin to increase tempting even mature Christians to gossip about the offender. At this point, neutral statements made by the offender may be perceived as attacks and your offense increases. If the offense took place in church, you begin to withdraw from church activities. Eventually you leave and begin to talk about the pastor, people, or policies of the place that you once loved.

Regardless of the cause, bitterness, resentment and even hatred can build, making you an open door for demonic activity (the tormentors that Jesus spoke of in Matthew 18). Do you realize that many addictions have their root in unforgiveness?

All of this has drawn you away from God and perhaps; your very soul is now at stake. Unforgiveness is an extremely serious matter. What will you do about it?

The Truth About Forgiveness

Perhaps the next statement will be a revelation to you; it is to many: Forgiveness is not a feeling; it is an act of your will. So often, after being hurt, you may become angry, upset, out of sorts. You could easily equate these feelings with your ability to forgive. But forgiveness is an act of obedience to God. It is not dependent on how you feel. It is a decision that anyone can make, even when angry. Yes, a difficult choice for some, but a choice nonetheless; and this decision makes the difference between your sins being forgiven or not. That is certainly worth considering. *"If you do not forgive men their trespasses, neither will your Father forgive your trespasses"* (Matt. 6:15).

This is stated with the utmost love and compassion toward those who have been wounded. God loves you so much. He was probably weeping when you were being violated. He did not want this for you. But, you must go on from here, for your sake, and for the sake of those who love you. God speaks so strongly about unforgiveness because He knows the consequences all too well. Every day He sees hearts fill with bitterness, hatred and revenge. Destruction usually follows.

God loves you; He does not want you to spend your life filled with internal strife. Some think that they will forget, in time, and be healed. But this belies the facts. Unforgiveness remains deep within and may cause emotional and/or physical illness. It has been proven that strong unresolved emotional feelings can cause a malfunction of the self-immune system, digestive problems, bowel problems, bone and joint problems, and even cancer. You can make the right choice today. With God's grace available to you at this moment, you can choose to forgive. Please do it now.

Lord, I want to obey You. Please help me. By Your grace, I choose to forgive_____ and _____ and... Please work deep within, causing me to forgive from my heart. Heal me completely. I ask this in the name of Jesus, the One Who has forgiven me. Amen!

The Steps to Freedom

It is now time to walk through the entire process of forgiveness; ask for the Holy Spirit to reveal truth and give you help and encouragement. This is very important: *These steps should be followed whether the offender asks for your forgiveness or not.* In less serious cases, when possible, it is good to go to the one who has hurt you with a humble posture and seek reconciliation. Some offenses can easily be resolved with a simple conversation, without involving others. Of course, humility by both parties would make it so much easier, but even if you alone humble yourself and seek reconciliation, God will be pleased.

When it is impossible or unwise to approach the offender, the following steps should be taken:

1. Make the choice to forgive. Get alone with God, ask for His help, and declare out loud, "I choose to forgive ____for doing or saying ____to me." Do this with each name that comes to mind. (Perhaps you have already completed this step. It certainly doesn't hurt to do it again. There may be additional names revealed.)

2. This next step may give you a bit of a pride attack, but it is vital. Be sure to do it: Ask God to forgive you for the critical and judgmental thoughts and words, and perhaps actions, that you have had toward the one who has hurt you. Gossip and criticism is never justified. Although God understands your woundedness, He cannot excuse your sin; He will however, lovingly forgive.

3. Release these people before God. In other words, don't hold them in bondage as though they have a debt to pay you. Don't say, "I'll forgive them but they owe me." God forgives us completely. He expects us to do the same.

4. Begin the process of forgetting the offense by asking God to remind you each time you indulge in thoughts about your wounding. When you realize that you are thinking about this again, invite the Lord into the middle of it and surrender these thoughts to Him. Remember don't stuff the thoughts and feelings down into you. Lift them up to God. Ask Him to take these thoughts. It may require time but the more you do this, the less you will remember.

5. Pray for those who have offended you and do good to them. Yes, do good to them! Ask God to show you practical ways for you to bless them with good things, help, money, etc. This is one of the best weapons in the whole arsenal to help facilitate your healing and freedom (Matt. 5:44).

6. Ask God to give you new eyes and a new heart toward this person. Do not freeze them in time. God is at work in their life too.

Please remember; this is a process and it will take time. But the end result will be peace within and a deeper relationship with God. Dear friend, God loves you so much. He will help you.

Asking For Forgiveness

"Therefore if you bring your gift to the altar, and there remember that your brother has something against you, leave your gift there before the altar, and go your way. First be reconciled to your brother, and then come and offer your gift." Matthew 5:23-24

What if YOU are the one who has done the wounding? You must humble yourself, beloved, go to the person you have offended, and say six simple words: "Please forgive me for hurting you." It does not matter if you were right or wrong. If you were wrong, admit it. "I was wrong. Please forgive me." If you don't have the courage to speak with them face to face, then at least write them a note. You are not too proud to do this, are you? It is apparent from this scripture that the Lord is not interested in receiving your offering until after you seek reconciliation. This should be a very sobering thought: your songs, your prayers, and your money are unacceptable to God.

The Wrong Way To Do Things

Some "offenders" say nothing and just go about their business thinking that time will heal. Others believe that if they are nice to the person, or tell a joke, that it is the same as asking for forgiveness. Not so. This relieves the tension and permits the relationship to continue; nevertheless, the offense remains and will flare up again. In Jesus' name, humble yourself, go to the person you have wounded and say, "Please forgive me for hurting you." This is well pleasing to our loving and forgiving God. (Note: Don't say, "*If* I have hurt you" as this dilutes the apology. Freely acknowledge that you *have* hurt them.)

Pursue Holiness

"Pursue peace with all people, and holiness, without which no one will see the Lord..." Hebrews 12:14

Holiness is such a touchy subject these days - I wonder why? You can see that the Lord would have us pursue (quest for, follow after, diligently seek) holiness. God clearly requires us to be obedient, to be set apart from worldly lusts and worldly standards. Don't you agree? Then why such a fuss about someone preaching these things; does it make you uncomfortable - Why? This perhaps, is the more appropriate question.

Let's go back to the basics: You are deeply loved and accepted by God. Nothing you do will change that. It was the blood of Jesus that placed you in such a position of grace and favor, not your own efforts. Whew! You can rest here and always return to this comfortable reference point when you fumble and fail. The Lord will always love you. He is love! If this is not established within your heart you can't go much farther. Please believe this truth and walk in it.

As you proceed in your life of faith, the Master leads you by His Spirit, teaching you many things from His Word. A diligent son or daughter begins to put these principles into practice.... giving, serving, forgiving others, and asking for forgiveness when we are the offender. We learn to pray and stand against the wiles of the enemy. We learn to love God and love one another with self-sacrificing love. We shun legalism and embrace the cross, the way of grace, and the path of holiness.

But what is the response to a message about holiness from those who do not obey, the ones who choose not to diligently practice the ways of God? "Don't judge me! I love God too, you know!" "Your speaking of holiness is self-righteous and judgmental. You are a legalist." "Don't you know that we are covered by grace... where is your love?" It is necessary to differentiate between those who attempt to obey and fail and those who want to remain in their sin - There is a BIG difference! Sometimes God will permit a weakness to linger for a season to serve a greater purpose... perhaps to work a deeper humility. But be careful, beloved, therein lies an opportunity for self-deception. You can love and hate your sin at the same time. In your very deepest parts you truly want to keep this sin... and that may be why it lingers. Be honest with yourself.

This brings us to another issue: someone who feels badly about themselves may have the tendency to perceive all corrective teaching, and the call to holy living as critical and judgmental. In a world where many suffer from low self-esteem, how does one present a message of holiness without raising these defenses? Nevertheless, it would seem logical that low self-esteem is not a new phenomenon; Jesus frequently ministered to the downtrodden... but He never shied away from speaking the truth in love. The crux of the matter may not rest upon how one feels about themselves, but simply their level of pride - or humility. Consider this: someone with low self-esteem can be very proud... defending themselves rather than repenting. The humble easily agree with God (and with anyone else) that they have missed the mark, as do we all. There is no guilt and condemnation here. Exhortations, warnings, and the fear of being disciplined by a loving Father are very welcome and deemed necessary.

Preaching Holiness

"Then they said to him, 'Who are you, that we may give an answer to those who sent us? What do you say about yourself?' He said: 'I am the voice of one crying in the wilderness: 'Make straight the way of the Lord,' as the prophet Isaiah said.'" John 1:22,23 *"He who has the bride is the bridegroom; but the friend of the bridegroom, who stands and hears him, rejoices greatly because of the bridegroom's voice. Therefore this joy of mine is fulfilled.* John 3:29

Examine yourself, preacher; this is absolutely necessary. If you are to challenge the saints of God to walk in holiness you must look long and hard at your motives. I will not insult you by reminding you to walk righteously yourself; you are already aware of that. And surely you know that self-righteousness and judgmentalism are a very shaky platform on which to preach holiness. It won't be long before your soapbox collapses and you hurt yourself. *"Pride goes before destruction, and a haughty spirit before a fall."* Pro. 16:18

Nevertheless, let's look a little deeper. Does preaching holiness, in any way make you feel superior? Pray about this before you answer. Dear servant of the Most High, holiness and righteousness must be preached from a heart of genuine humility and love, nothing less will do. Your motives are being purified in this hour of refinement, beloved. You will emerge as a true friend of the Bridegroom... your only desire: to present a beautiful bride to the Worthy One.

Stand For Righteousness

The Scriptures are full of moral imperatives. I mean, they leap from nearly every page of your grace-filled New Testament: We are challenged by Jesus and every Holy Spirit inspired writer to forsake sin, the world and the devil... and to follow the Master wherever He would lead us. Is this not true? Of course it is.

Our society has embraced the self-defeating philosophy of situational ethics; we provide no moral absolutes. The Ten Commandments have been removed from public buildings and schools. Self-gratification and outright hedonism are on the rise. We want everyone to feel included, no one to feel uncomfortable. *Acceptance* is the new politically correct word (replacing *tolerance*). The things that God hates are now accepted, even approved of. If you dare to speak up about any of this you are labeled as narrow-minded, a self-righteous bigot, a right-wing religious kook. Has this mindset also permeated the Church?

We have lost our moorings, beloved; our moral compass has gone haywire. (Not unlike other great societies before they declined.) As a result of our reluctance to raise a standard, many within the churches are uncertain about the moral / social issues of the day, especially the younger generation. Is abortion OK in some instances? If they truly love each other, why shouldn't gays marry? If someone is really unhappy in their marriage, they should have the right to divorce and remarry, shouldn't they? These questions and others like them need to be answered. Who will address these issues?

Will you preach the way of holiness, with grace and love and mercy? (You do know the difference between true holiness and legalism?) Will you declare the truth of God's Word among those who are confused and to those who will reject the truth when told them? Will you continue to love and serve them even after they have rejected your message and call you self-righteous?

There are many who call us self-righteous and judgmental but for the most part, at least amongst the Christians I know, they are truly not this way. There is great love, servanthood and forbearance. They really do speak the truth "in love". Keep loving, dear Christian, continue to serve and give and pray. Let grace and mercy be your calling card. But don't be afraid to stand for righteousness. If not the Christian, who will?

Living in the Spirit

"Come now, you who say, 'Today or tomorrow we will go to such and such a city, spend a year there, buy and sell, and make a profit'; whereas you do not know what will happen tomorrow. For what is your life? It is even a vapor that appears for a little time and then vanishes away. Instead you ought to say, 'If the Lord wills, we shall live and do this or that.' But now you boast in your arrogance. All such boasting is evil." James 4:13-16

When you awoke this morning did your thoughts turn toward the Lord? I mean, did you say "Good morning" or acknowledge His lordship in anyway? Did you ask Him what He would have you do today? If you set your alarm for the very last minute, you probably didn't do any of the above. You rushed ahead in your own strength, seeking to do your own thing. Of course, your willingness to go to work and provide for your family when you would rather roll over is commendable... but not exactly all there is to Spirit-led living. What if the Master would rather you stayed home today; how would you know? This leads to the larger question: Should we assume that maintaining ones usual routine is sufficient for receiving guidance?

Abiding in Christ

"I am the vine, you are the branches. He who abides in Me, and I in him, bears much fruit; for without Me you can do nothing. If anyone does not abide in Me, he is cast out as a branch and is withered; and they gather them and throw them into the fire, and they are burned. If you abide in Me, and My words abide in you, you will ask what you desire, and it shall be done for you. By this My Father is glorified, that you bear much fruit; so you will be My disciples. As the Father loved Me, I also have loved you; abide in My love. If you keep My commandments, you will abide in My love, just as I have kept My Father's commandments and abide in His love." John 15:5-10

Such powerful truth! I'm sure you have read this passage perhaps more than a few times. If you are a true disciple of Jesus, beloved, pay attention; this is the "mother load." John 15 is filled with foundational discipleship secrets.

With little more than a glance you can see the word *abide* written several times - 12 to be exact. (The words *continue* and *remain* are also from the same Greek verb *Meno*). With so much depending on your abiding, it would seem wise to fully investigate its meaning. What does it mean to abide? As previously mentioned, it means to remain. In reference to place it means to sojourn, tarry, not to depart, to continue to be present, to be held, kept, continually. In reference to time: to continue to be, not to perish, to last, endure. In reference to state or condition: to remain as one, not to become another or different, to wait for. (Greek lexicon based on Thayer's and Smith's Bible Dictionary)

Unfortunately, it seems that the Church has the tendency to lower the bar, to "dumb down" as it were. In this manner everyone can feel comfortable and continue as they are. Some would say if you have been baptized, you are now abiding in Christ. Dear naive one, you must not foolishly assume just because you are "saved" that you are abiding. Surely the servants of God would bear much more fruit if they were truly fulfilling the criterion. And make no mistake about it; Jesus is clearly revealing what is necessary. He exhorts and warns us to remain in Him. We must remain connected to bear fruit. In fact, the disconnected branches will wither and be burned. He goes on to promise: *"If you abide in Me, and My words abide in you, you will ask what you desire, and it shall be done for you."* If you abide in Him and His words (note He did not say Word) abide in you, you will have your prayers answered. How awesome! Not a hit and miss type of prayer life that most Christians experience, but the promise of answered prayer. After Salvation, this is arguably the most significant promise in scripture! So, what is required? To abide, and to have His words within you... the ongoing rhema guidance of the indwelling Holy Spirit! His Father is glorified in our fruit bearing. In so doing we prove to be His disciples.

Jesus continues: *As the Father loved Me, I also have loved you; abide in My love. If you keep My commandments, you will abide in My love, just as I have kept My Father's commandments and abide in His love.* Do you see what He is telling you? Remain in His love! But how are you to do this? *"If you keep My commandments, you will abide in My love..."* OK, let's review: 1) You must abide in Christ to bear fruit. 2) You must abide in Christ and His words (rhema) must abide in you for you to ask whatever you (He) desire and have it done for you. 3) You must abide in His love... and to do that, 4) You must keep His commandments; just as Jesus kept His Father's commandments and abided in His love. (In this age of disobedience, *obedience* has become such a despised word. Can it even be mentioned without someone accusing you of being legalistic and self-righteous?)

Take a look at your fruitfulness, dear saint. Are you bearing abundant fruit that remains... or is it less than you would like to see? What is missing? Are you truly abiding in Christ?

Andrew Murray suggested that we actually abide at different levels. A new Christian abides by simply trying to be less sinful, attending church regularly, doing a few kind deeds, placing a few dollars in the offering, and praying for 5 or 10 minutes each day. In such a state of abiding, they can come with boldness to the Throne of Grace and have their prayers answered. Nevertheless, as you go a bit farther in your walk of faith, more is required. Fasting and other personal disciplines become a part of the believer's lifestyle... including extended times of daily prayer. You begin to seek ways of becoming less, lower. Eventually it will cost you everything to abide in Christ; radical obedience will be the expected norm. You willingly and joyfully abandon yourself to His purposes... giving, going, waiting, as He leads. Of course, spiritual power and authority will be granted to those who abide at this level. The reward will be sweet and intimacy with God so precious. Dear friend, this is exactly what Jesus is offering to each of His disciples in this section of scripture... but you must learn to abide. You can do this, beloved. By His grace and in His timing you can do this. How the Father waits for the revealing of His sons.

Lord, I want to learn to abide in Christ. Please teach me and grant all necessary grace. Father, be glorified in my life. "By this My Father is glorified, that you bear much fruit; so you will be My disciples."

Accomplishing the Purposes of God

"and the pleasure of the Lord shall prosper in His hand." Isa. 53:10

As you may know, this verse is speaking of Messiah. Isaiah prophesied these words, incredibly accurate, eight centuries before His coming. He foretold of Jesus' purposes and His suffering and death. Isaiah 53 is an awesome passage. Please take the time to read it.

Dear saint, what is the purpose of your life? Is it to pursue happiness and enjoy the fruit of your labor? I suppose that these are good and valid; God does bless us abundantly. But there is so much more to life, more than just being a nice person, trying not to sin, doing some good deeds and enjoying your blessings. Through this simple scripture, we are challenged to go higher and deeper. Would you like *the pleasure of the Lord to prosper* in your hand? Do you want His desires to be fulfilled through you?

God has a plan for your life, just as He had a plan and purpose for Jesus. You have a mission, something to accomplish. *"I know the plans that I have for you says the Lord..."* (Jer. 29:11). *"We are his workmanship, created in Christ Jesus for good works, which God prepared beforehand that we should walk in them"* (Eph. 2:10).

These verses are not meant for clergy only; the Master truly does have a specific work for all of us. But so many people live frustrated, unfruitful lives because they do not know God's will; or refuse to surrender to it. Submit to Him now and ask for His will to be done in your life. He has been waiting for you to ask.

Knowing the Will of God

"My sheep hear My voice, and I know them, and they follow Me."
John 10:27

Knowing God's will is indeed a vast subject. Volumes have been written. However, God never intended it to be so complicated. Jesus profoundly and succinctly stated, *"My sheep hear My voice."* The confusion and consternation associated with knowing God's will usually begins when your desires run contrary to His. (This is often the case until you are more fully crucified.) An example: two jobs are laid before you. One pays little but offers great opportunities to help others. The alternative offers great pay and some status but keeps you behind a desk.

You seek God: "What job should I take?" Deep within, a quiet voice tells you that you should take the lower paying job. But you are in need of money and the temptation for status speaks very loudly. You become increasingly troubled as you listen to the reasoning that justifies taking the higher paying job. The opinions of friends and relatives only compound the problem. Double mindedness reigns supreme. Unfortunately, many people make the mistake of 'reasoning' rather than 'listening' and they wrestle needlessly with uncertainty and doubt.

If you make the wrong choice, sooner or later you will become dissatisfied, and experience some discomfort. But God, in His goodness, will give you another opportunity. Unfortunately, many continue to justify their wrong choices and live an unfulfilled life, telling themselves, "but the money is good."

Yes, dear servant, knowing the will of God is simple; nonetheless, due to your humanity you make mistakes. You must be willing to risk making a mistake when you are learning to walk with the Lord. Like a child, you should follow after Him with a total sense of abandonment and uncertainty. Don't hesitate, God knows that you love Him and desire to please Him. This is to His delight, you can be sure of that. He will show you the way. Even now you can see a ray of light. *"Your word is a lamp to my feet and a light to my path"* (Psalm 119:105).

Use What You Have

"Therefore take the talent from him, and give it to him who has ten talents. For to everyone who has, more will be given, and he will have abundance; but from him who does not have, even what he has will be taken away. And cast the unprofitable servant into the outer darkness. There will be weeping and gnashing of teeth..." Matthew 25:28-30

Much has been taught about these verses throughout the centuries. It is worth examining again, just in case you haven't understood. This scripture tells of a man who distributes resources to three of his servants. Two servants invested wisely, one did not. The two were rewarded and praised for their diligence. The third seemed to be treated unfairly. Was he really?

Jesus was revealing another nugget of truth: If you use what is given to you, more will be given. If you fail to use it, you'll lose it. Possibly the best example would be your muscles. If you exercise your muscles, they will become larger and you will get stronger. If you do not use them, let's say you lay in bed for a few weeks, you will become weaker and your muscles may even begin to atrophy.

In regard to your natural talents: whether physical skills, intellectual, financial or relational dealings, whatever is given you, however small it is, use it. Use it diligently and use it in an ever-increasing scale. Ask God for Spirit-led goals to increase whatever you do. The same is true regarding the use of spiritual gifts as found in 1Corinthians 12. Exercise their use. Do not let them grow dormant. God gave you these for a purpose. How dare you place them on a shelf? The world and the church need what you have been given. Dear servant, the following words are quite pointed. God forbid that they ever apply to you. *"Every branch in Me that does not bear fruit He takes away..."* (John 15:2).

Can you play an instrument or sing? Can you pray? Are you proficient with accounting skills? Are you good with children or an efficient organizer? Can you fix cars, build, or repair? Do you love to teach and speak about Jesus? BUT, you say, *"I'm uncomfortable in front of others... I don't have the time... I don't know how... I'm not ready to commit... I'm afraid... I've tried that but I've been burned..."* No more excuses, saint; it's time to report for duty. You can do this thing. Use your gifts and talents. *"So the Lord said to him (Moses), 'What is that in your hand?'"* (Exodus 4:2).

Faith That Changes Things

"And these signs will follow those who believe ...they will lay hands on the sick, and they will recover." Mark 16:17,18

Why don't we see more healings? There is no question that Mark 16 is true, but it is not yet happening to any great extent. There are many believers and few healings. Why? Since Jesus chided His disciples for their unbelief, you would assume that faith, or lack there of, would be a primary reason. Unfortunately, the faith of western civilization has been emasculated by reasoning and logic; science speaks louder than faith. It seems as though Jesus foresaw our current condition and asked, *"Nevertheless, when the Son of Man comes, will He really find faith on the earth?"* (Matt. 18:8).

Disciple of Jesus, do you have faith? Of course, everyone has a measure of faith. You sit on a chair without inspecting its legs and bolts, don't you? However, do you have miracle working faith, faith that changes things? This type resonates within your spirit. Do you understand? Paul, the apostle tells the Romans: *"...faith comes by hearing, and hearing by the word (rhema) of God"* (Rom. 10:17). A current, living word from God (rhema) spoken to your heart ignites true faith. When you hear the word of the Lord, and act according to His plan, nothing is impossible!

Unfortunately many prayers are prayed without faith, the mere words of men recited to a brass heaven. But Spirit-led prayers are actually the revealed will of God being spoken back to God. Be assured that these prayers will be answered; sooner or later, they will be answered.

85

Those seeking to minister healing have suffered many disappointments over the years. Have you prayed earnestly for the sick only to see them worsen, and even die? Because of this some have ceased praying altogether. Dear disciple, your Master has instructed you to heal the sick, cast out demons, restore sight to the blind, and raise the dead. By faith, you can do this! You must not give up. Jesus said, *"If you abide in Me, and My words abide in you, you will ask what you desire, and it shall be done for you"* (John 15:7).

Your spiritual bankruptcy has qualified you for a greater measure of faith. Ask and it shall be given, seek and you shall find. Persistently knock and the door to signs and wonders will be opened. Where is the man or woman of God who will do exploits? You used to believe God for mighty things. Believe again. Answered prayer is very *normal* Christianity.

Lord of the harvest, revive my faith and discernment. Help me to hear Your voice and obey... for Your glory and for the healing of the nations.

Amazing Grace & Personal Responsibility

"Then he said to the keeper of his vineyard, `Look, for three years I have come seeking fruit on this fig tree and find none. Cut it down; why does it use up the ground?' But he answered and said to him, `Sir, let it alone this year also, until I dig around it and fertilize it. And if it bears fruit, well. But if not, after that you can cut it down.'"
Luke 13:7-9

Let's take a careful look at this passage: The owner of the vineyard (God the Father) comes to the keeper of his vineyard (Jesus) and tells him that he is dissatisfied with a certain fig tree. He wants the keeper to cut it down... to make room for another. Thus, the keeper demonstrates the mercy of Jesus... His intercession, as it were. "Let me work with the tree one more year. I'll fertilize and dig around it. If it still remains fruitless, cut it down." What does all of this mean?

Israel, the fig tree, produced no fruit. God had been patient with them since the time of the patriarchs (over two millennium). He was about to uproot their religion and plant a new system, a new wineskin. Jesus was asking the Father for just a little more time to preach and minister to them; perhaps then, they would believe and bear the fruit of righteousness.

Dear disciple, can we apply this passage to our own lives as well? John 15:2 states, *"Every branch in Me that does not bear fruit He takes away; and every branch that bears fruit He prunes, that it may bear more fruit.* Note that Jesus, speaking to His disciples, has just said, *"I am the vine, you are the branches."* Every branch *in Me* that does not bear fruit, He takes away. (The NIV says *cuts off.*) He is speaking to believers! Are you bearing fruit, beloved... the fruit of the Holy Spirit, the fruit of obedience, the fruit of righteousness? The Master is graciously willing to work with you; He loves you. He will fill you with His Spirit, pour out His abundant grace and provide numerous opportunities for your growth and development. His mercies are new every morning! However, the Spirit of God will not strive with man forever. It is not so much your weakness of the flesh that will cause the axe to strike its blow...but a lukewarm, unwilling, unbelieving heart.

Bodybuilding

"...let us lay aside every weight, and the sin which so easily ensnares us, and let us run with endurance the race that is set before us..." Hebrews 12:1

I'm sure that you have done exercises at some point in your life. It seems like fun at first but it doesn't take long to realize that a measure of endurance is required. Exercise doesn't become effective until you breathe a little harder, increase your heart rate, and your muscles begin to ache. This process consists of tearing down muscle tissue and building them up again. Thus, they become a little larger and a little stronger. Painful, yes, but obviously beneficial. Everyone would like the benefits but few want to endure the discomfort. And, of course, this is not a one-time activity. It requires diligent persistence if you would desire to reap the maximum rewards.

What a good analogy of your Christian walk, or should I say run! Paul tells you to run the race with endurance. Are you running today or sitting in front of the TV? The God ordained spiritual growth process removes impurities, builds endurance, reduces unwanted weight, and strengthens you. This is the beautifying, refining work of the Holy Spirit.

Have you been through a difficult struggle, I mean, a really difficult time? You were down for the count and couldn't imagine that you would ever get up again. But congratulations, by the grace of God, you did get up. Now, be careful. After such upset it would be easy to stroll; you know, become complacent, like so many others. Don't let the negative experiences of the past bring fear of moving in that area, try again!

Please don't be satisfied with anything less than the fullness of the purpose that God has for your life. How can you stop now after all that you have been through; all that you have invested in this race? The tearing down, the pain, the sweat and the tears have made you stronger. This struggle has made you wiser. And now, there is less of self. You may not have fully realized this yet, but believe God, all of this has been for a very good purpose. You are far more valuable to our Lord now than you were before.

Your Daily Bread

"Taste and see; the Lord is good." Psalm 34:8

Daily bread seems to be an outdated concept. We recite the words *"give us this day our daily bread"* not really understanding the true meaning. In this age of preservatives, we purchase our weekly bread, kept fresh by chemicals and a plastic bag. But daily bread, oh, that sounds so good. The smell, texture, and flavor of fresh bread are very appealing.

Dear servant of God, when you pray you are asking God for fresh, moist, aromatic, flavorful bread... each day. Is that what you are expecting? Or are you satisfied with the stale provision from last week, or last month. Are you seeking the Lord each day for His sweet aroma and His delicious flavor? *"Oh, taste and see that the*

Lord is good; blessed is the man who trusts in Him!"

This word is for pastors and people alike: Don't satisfy your hunger with lesser things: the teachings and philosophies of men, their thoughts and plans. God will give you fresh bread. He desires to give you Himself. Perhaps a scripture will come alive today, a Spirit-led song or a fervent prayer for revival will flow from your heart. Perhaps a fire will be rekindled within you. Eating fresh, daily bread is normal Christianity.

"And Moses said, 'Let no one leave any of it till morning.' Notwithstanding they did not heed Moses. But some of them left part of it until morning, and it bred worms and stank. And Moses was angry with them. So they gathered it every morning, every man according to his need..." Exodus 16:19-21

His Bride... My Purpose

"Let us rejoice and be glad and give him glory! For the wedding of the Lamb has come, and his bride has made herself ready." Revelations 19:7 (NIV)

God has revealed Himself to mankind as the God who loves. In point, the apostle John writes *God is love.* He also desires *to be loved.* The Holy One has shamelessly pursued mankind for six millennium. Have you ever pondered these things? Having done so for the better part of twenty years, I am convinced that the primary reason for God's creation was to produce a bride. Dear friend, the ultimate purpose for your existence is to become the bride of Christ!

The Holy Trinity, knowing intimate fellowship for all eternity, wanted to share Their love with another. *"Let Us make man in Our image,"* They said. Of course, it would be elementary for the Godhead to simply speak humanity into existence. After all, God is God! But to create love, now that could be a challenge. True love, you see, could not be mandated or programmed. It must be freely given. For a created being to sincerely love the Creator, he must have a free will. He must be permitted to choose.

It seems as though the omnipotent Creator can do all things... but one. Perhaps you are aghast at the mere suggestion; nonetheless, it appears to be true. God cannot force you to love Him. Love that is demanded or programmed, like a computer, is not true love and could never be satisfying to the one desiring to be loved. It must be freely given from the heart. This is why your free will is so sacred to God. It is utterly your choice: to love Him or not.

Can you imagine the thought of allowing created beings to have a free will? Consider the Ancient of Days pondering this concept; like a Grandmaster chess player examining the next move. With a smile that lit the heavens, He shouts, "YES! This will work. This plan, despite the pain and suffering, will produce a beautiful, spotless bride for My Jesus."

With free will, enters the possibility of disobedience; sin and every type of inhumanity invade God's pure intention of love. The Omniscient One, knowing everything beforehand, decided to use the devil's prideful rebellion and subsequent plot to cause the fall of mankind, as a testing ground for love. This adversity would become a fertile seedbed where love could be nurtured and grown. Choosing to obey God in the midst of temptation and adversity is synonymous with loving Him.

Free will you say? Yes, a bride with a capacity for loving and a propensity for evil, choosing to freely surrender to Jesus, her husband, the Lover of her soul. What an awesome plan! How will He woo you, beloved, and cause you to love Him? The greatest of love stories is still unfolding. There is a glorious wedding in your future. Shouldn't you be making yourself ready?

How Does God Perceive Sin?

"He has not dealt with us according to our sins, nor punished us according to our iniquities. For as the heavens are high above the earth, so great is His mercy toward those who fear Him; As far as the east is from the west, So far has He removed our transgressions from us. As a father pities his children, so the Lord pities those who fear Him. For He knows our frame; He remembers that we are dust." Psalm 103:10-14

Is He an angry God, insistent on holiness and demanding perfection, offended and indignant because He made a law and you willfully disobeyed? (In essence saying, "How dare you disobey Me!") Is this really who God is? I don't think so. Instead, God views your sin as an obstacle to an intimate relationship. He is more concerned about your relationship with Him than your sin. And because He is concerned about that relationship, He is concerned about your sin. Do you understand? He wants you to be free from bondage so that you can have an unencumbered friendship with Him. He wants you to be free from worry, and fear, and lusts, so that you can grow to love Him and understand His ways. He wants you to become all that you can be.

When someone who loves God is caught in the snare of the enemy, He is not quick to bring judgment and punishment. If that were true, all of us would be destroyed. God looks at the heart. In other words, He looks deeper than the sin to the root problem: your weak humanity. He knows that you are dust and He has pity on you. Does this excuse sin? No, absolutely not. God is perfectly holy and never excuses sin; He forgives sin. You must not sin, but if you do, you have an advocate with the Father... and He forgives. He is merciful and loving and kind.

Make no mistake about it, God does get angry, but He is slow to anger (Read Psalm 103). He much prefers mercy to judgment and will offer mercy anew every morning; even extraordinary mercy and grace to those whom He chooses to bestow it upon. Repent, dear friend, turn away from the things that have ensnared you. Our loving God wants you to come closer.

Mercy, Grace and Healing

"Yes, I have loved you with an everlasting love; therefore with lovingkindness I have drawn you. Again I will build you, and you shall be rebuilt, O virgin of Israel!" Jeremiah 31:2-4

Are you a drug addict or an alcoholic? Are you involved in other habitual weaknesses like overeating, smoking cigarettes, or sexual lust? Do not think that God seeks to condemn you? He desires to heal and deliver you. Do you understand, beloved? God's motivation is always love...always restoration. He sees beyond the sin to the root cause and will speak a loving word to you so that your soul may be healed.

Repentance simply means this: humility and agreement with God's will. It is a turning from your way of doing things, in obedience to God's word. This opens the door for healing and deliverance. You are not repenting because an angry Judge must be appeased, but because a loving Friend wants you to be restored. He is faithful to bring you back into agreement with His way, which is best for you, and for your relationship with Him.

Some have said that we hurt God when we sin. It would seem more accurate to say that the Lord is saddened when you sin because you are needlessly hurting yourself and others. And He misses the intimate fellowship while you are away. This is the heart of a loving Father. There are times, however, when He will warn you of judgment because of your rebellious, self-indulgent actions. There must be boundaries established and warning of consequences for overstepping those boundaries. But you should see these boundaries as guardrails on a narrow road that leads to the center of His loving heart. Do not see them as religious laws that cause bondage to religious ways. Your goal, your destination: friendship with God, a relationship that brings you stability and healing and fruitfulness.

The Author of Perfection is very consistent, dear disciple. He is perfectly consistent and impartial and He has set two standards, one for those who are saved and another for those who are not. You already know of His great mercy and grace toward His children. But the unsaved, (those who have not accepted the sacrifice of Jesus' shed blood) He must judge by the Law. There is no personal relationship, no friendship, and no intimacy, simply law and judgment. God does show great patience and extends mercy; He desires that all would be saved. But finally, judgment must come because God is holy.

Working For Rewards

"And behold, I am coming quickly, and My reward is with Me, to give to every one according to his work." Revelations 22:12

The Master spoke of rewards several times. However, some Christians don't really like to consider this. Perhaps they think it to be too carnal a topic. After all, they would like to think of themselves as serving selflessly without thought of reward. Nonetheless, since Jesus mentioned this, it must be noteworthy. The dictionary definition of reward: A recompense for a worthy act, a payment made in return for service rendered.

There appears to be a reward for your work (Rev. 22:12), for suffering persecution (Luke 6:23), and for ministering to the servants of God (Mark 9:41), etc. You can receive a full or partial reward (2John 1:8), and when you give to the poor, you have treasure laid up in heaven (Matt. 19:21).

Warning! You can also loose your reward; be careful. Wouldn't it be a shame to arrive in heaven only to find very little credited to your account because you had already received the praises of men here on earth? *"Take heed that you do not do your charitable deeds before men, to be seen by them. Otherwise you have no reward from your Father in heaven. But when you do a charitable deed, do not let your left hand know what your right hand is doing, "that your charitable deed may be in secret; and your Father who sees in secret will Himself reward you openly"* (Matt. 6:1,3,4).

You know this is not about earning salvation, don't you? Jesus already paid for that with His blood. However, it is quite scriptural to work for rewards and to lay up treasure in heaven. And don't forget about the crowns (Rev. 3:11)!

What will your reward and treasure be? One can only speculate. Perhaps, there will be a greater awareness of His glory, perhaps greater honor and responsibility in the world to come; God knows. Nevertheless, do remember this: only the works that are Spirit led and Spirit empowered will receive reward, not your own plans and efforts. God's work, done His way, with diligence and perseverance will receive recompense. Don't burn yourself out trying to do something in the 'flesh.' Simply put: listen, obey, and persevere; the Master presents numerous opportunities every week. You will receive a marvelous reward that will last for eternity.

"Eye has not seen, nor ear heard, nor have entered into the heart of man the things which God has prepared for those who love Him" *1Corinthians* 2:9

Minister For Hire

"For a bishop must be blameless, as a steward of God, not self-willed, not quick-tempered, not given to wine, not violent, not greedy for money," Titus 1:7

It didn't begin like this. Your love for God and your willingness to serve far out-weighed any thought of remuneration. You worked long hours for almost nothing and the Lord always provided whatever else you needed. Correct? So what happened? Money means more to you now than it used to. If someone gives you a small honorarium, you grumble to yourself. It never used to matter. Perhaps it has been all of the disappointments and frustrations and offenses. They mount up over the years. No doubt, you have been faithful and have sacrificed a great deal. But, dear minister, this is a reality check. If you are now 'for hire,' your motives are impure. Many servants arrive at this place, thinking that they deserve something for all of their hard work. In the depths of your heart, you know that this is not true because you remember what Jesus said: *"Does he thank that servant because he did the things that were commanded him? I think not. So likewise you, when you have done all those things which you are commanded, say, 'we are unprofitable servants. We have done what was our duty to do'"* (Luke 17:9-10). The Lord will help you get back on course. Ask Him now. He has so many wonderful treasures for you. Don't settle for lesser things.

Master, I admit that I have been seeking temporal recompense. I agree that I deserve nothing. I am simply doing my assigned task. Thank you for your grace and your loving provision. Change my heart and help me return to my First Love. You are sufficient for me.

Loving God

"Hear, O Israel: The Lord our God, the Lord is one! 'You shall love the Lord your God with all your heart, with all your soul, and with all your strength.'" Deuteronomy 6:4-5

The Old Testament scriptures declare the magnificent luster of His multifaceted attributes. He reveals Himself to mankind as: a companion of Adam and Eve who walked with them in the Garden; an awesome judge who condemned the world to destruction by flood; a faithful deliverer rescuing the children of Israel from Pharaoh's iron grip. He is seen as a just lawgiver in the wilderness and is frequently depicted as a provider, protector, and a mighty warrior crushing His enemies in battle. And the titles *Consuming Fire, Ancient of Days,* and *I AM,* should leave you with reverent fear. But there is so much more: God reveals Himself as a Lover.

You can see an occasional glimpse of God's great love for Israel, as He would shamelessly, time and time again, call His backsliding wife to come home. *"And I said, after she had done all these things, 'Return to me.' But she did not return"* (Jer. 3:7). The Old Testament is actually an incredible love story. Have you ever seen God as the wounded husband longing for His wayward wife to return?

We know that God loved the world and He loved Israel, but there is seldom mention of anyone truly loving Him. In this regard, only one Old Testament character stands out. Lest you think that loving God with affection and intensity is distinctly feminine, please consider David. King David was a "man's man," a valiant warrior, a fearless ruler who subdued the land. He was also an anointed musician and songwriter; He danced before the Lord with complete abandonment. And much more than that, David loved God!

Just as God pursued Israel, He pursues you today, dear one. He desires you. Will you love Him as David did, with affection and intensity, with abandonment and zeal? God's expressed desire remains unchanged: *"You shall love the Lord your God with all your heart, with all your soul, and with all your strength."* Will you love Him like that?

How Do You Perceive God?

Did you know that several things affect your perception of God: your parent's view of God, former religious teachings, your culture, your relationship with your father, even your own personality?

Because God has revealed Himself in so many ways, He allows us to understand Him and His nature in a variety of ways. Of course, you are always to honor and fear God and obediently submit to Jesus, as Lord; that's a given. But, you may prefer to draw near to the heavenly Father in a parent-child relationship, seeing God the Father as protector and provider. There is great security in the loving arms of the Father. Nonetheless, if you have had a poor relationship with your earthly father, you may find it difficult to draw near to your Father in heaven.

In which case, you may tend to favor Jesus as brother, teacher, friend, Savior, Lord, Master, seeking to show love through obedience. Likewise, you may choose to draw near to the Holy Spirit. Although He may be the most difficult to relate to because the only visual image we have of the Holy Spirit is as a dove, wind, fire, oil, or rain.

However you relate to the Holy Trinity, there is one sad resounding truth: God deeply loves us, and we consistently fail to love Him as He deserves to be loved. He is calling you to intimacy. Don't offer the Lover of your soul mere religious activities and good works, giving Him a few minutes, or perhaps a few hours. It's time to learn how to love God.

Can you hear Him saying? *"I love you and I want you to love Me. I am filled with mercy and grace. I will forgive and heal and deliver as you turn from sin and return to me. I want to cleanse and refresh you; I desire to revive you. Don't resist My Holy Spirit. Please allow Me to have my way with you. Don't be afraid. I love you."*

This is an extraordinary time, dear saint. Perhaps the greatest revival in history is soon to unfold; and the Lord may soon return! At that day, He will have for Himself a beautiful bride without blemish or wrinkle. He will return for a bride that loves Him. Not a religious bride offering perfunctory service, but one that *"loves the Lord their God with all of their heart, all of their soul, all of their mind, all of their strength."* Let's be honest now; do you love Him like that? Ask Him to draw you close. He has been waiting for you to ask.

More About Forgiveness

"So My heavenly Father also will do to you if each of you, from his heart, does not forgive his brother his trespasses." Matthew 18:35

You may have been taught that forgiveness is a process, a process that begins by making the decision to forgive. For some, this in itself is a very big step. Congratulations! You do realize that the Lord desires to take you through the entire process, don't you? So how do you know if you have forgiven completely "from the heart" as Jesus stated in Matthew 18:35? Here is a simple test:

- When you see the offender, do old memories and unpleasant feelings flood your soul?
- Do you refuse to help the one who has offended you?
- When you hear that something bad has happened to them, are you inwardly happy?

Dear friend, if you answered "yes" to any one of these questions, there is still some forgiveness and healing needed. With God's help, you can clear your heart of this residue. It will take time, sometimes months or years. Bring this to the Lord again today. He will help you continue the healing process. He is pleased with your willingness.

It is important to note that after an offense, in certain instances, trust will need to be rebuilt even when there is forgiveness. Be wise; this also takes time. For example: If your son borrows your car, gets drunk and crashes it, you will forgive him completely, from your heart. But, it will take a while before you give him your car keys again. He will need to prove that he can be responsible. Be careful; don't deceive yourself. There is no need to withhold your love, friendship, or help. True forgiveness will offer all of the above, but can still deny the car keys.

What is Intimacy?

"Let him kiss me with the kisses of his mouth--For your love is better than wine." Song of Songs 1:2

Webster's dictionary defines intimate as: (1) marked by close acquaintance, association or familiarity, an intimate friend. (2) pertaining to ones deepest nature, very personal. (3) essential, innermost. (4) sexual relations.

Intimacy with God is a very deep personal relationship with the One who loves you; marked by frequent conversation, worship, and service. Its foundation is surrender. You submit yourself, your time, fully to Him, and God in turn reveals to you new dimensions of His unfathomable love, His divine nature, and His infinite wisdom. It is pure communion void of idolatry. "Deep to deep. Spirit to spirit."

The following is the writing of a friend who found intimacy with God: *"This morning I saw a beautiful meadow. The Lord had spread out a blanket and I was just sitting with Him, talking and picnicing. He had brought it all, the blanket, the food, the drink. I was even so aware that He had brought the meadow. It's all from Him. When I looked into His eyes, looked at His smile, there was such love. He truly can be trusted with all. It's my human blindness when I forget this. He takes such good care of us even when we don't realize it. He reached out His hand and wanted me to get up and walk with Him. He led me down to a riverbank. I loved standing on the land alone with Him."*

The first step toward intimacy is this simple prayer, "Lord, draw me." You can't come close to God by yourself; it is a work of grace. It does not come by more prayer, or fasting, or good works. You can't even truly love God without His help. When is the last time you prayed something like this: "Lord, I don't love you as I ought. Help me to love you?"

You may not yet be hungry or thirsty for more of God. Will you ask Him to make your heart yearn for more of Him? If you are satisfied with the relationship that you now have with God, you will probably never enter into the beauty and fulfillment of intimacy. Ask Him to make you hungry for more. I promise you, this is God's perfect will.

Consider this: The awesome Creator of the universe wants to talk to YOU. He wants to be alone with YOU. He desires to be YOUR friend. This is too wonderful to comprehend!

The Father's Heart

"Bless the Lord, O my soul, And forget not all His benefits: Who forgives all your iniquities, Who heals all your diseases, Who redeems your life from destruction, Who crowns you with loving-kindness and tender mercies, Who satisfies your mouth with good things, So that your youth is renewed like the eagle's. The Lord executes righteousness and justice for all who are oppressed. He made known His ways to Moses, His acts to the children of Israel. The Lord is merciful and gracious, slow to anger, and abounding in mercy." Psalm 103:2-8

Back to the basics, dear one; Who is God? What is He really like? Have you considered Him to be a hard 'task master?' Sometimes His ways seem difficult, almost too much to bear. Where is the light and easy yoke He spoke of? Even so, you can't help but be dazzled by His glory and enraptured by His loving kindness. Do you remember how He encouraged you, healed you, and helped you? When all seemed lost, He rescued you. Didn't He?

Sometimes you are angry with Him, other times disappointed in Him and you don't want to admit it. "Why wasn't she healed?" "Why did this have to happen?" His infinite wisdom eludes your finite understanding. Notwithstanding, you know that God is love; you learned this years ago. Yet, somehow under pressure you forget things. And then there are your wrong choices and sins, and the consequences thereof.

Surely you don't take pleasure in disciplining your children. Do you think that your heavenly Father does? Know that He grieves when you must be repeatedly disciplined, sometimes with increasingly more painful measures. He is a loving Father who would much rather correct you with His Word and guide you with His eye instead of using a rod. His Word, as revealed by the Holy Spirit, is utterly sufficient to conform you to the image of Jesus. Unfortunately, many of God's children choose to learn the hard way. God loves you, He is good and you belong to Him. Knowing this is enough for today.

Moving Toward Intimacy: a Few Helps

"But it is good for me to draw near to God; I have put my trust in the Lord God, that I may declare all Your works." Psalm 73:28

Today, as you proceed toward the heart of God, share with Him your deepest feelings (hurts, needs, desires). Talk with God as you would a friend; even speak with Him as you read His Word. Frequently practice the presence of God in the car, at work, and at home. Acknowledge His presence and ask questions. Remember that God is within you, not 'out there' somewhere.

It is good to ask God to remind you of His presence within, and to draw you to be alone with Him. And when you are alone, play worship music and be quiet; simply be quiet. Occasionally tell Him that you love Him. You will begin to see things differently. Even resisting temptation can become an act of worship. When you are tempted, turn to the Lord and say, "I love you more than this person, place, or thing. I want you, not what is displeasing to you."

Surely there will be hindrances and distractions. What would you rather do than spend time with God? Of course God wants you to enjoy the things that He has given you. You are free in the Spirit. But you know what keeps you from God. Are these your idols?

Here are a few things that can impede intimacy: a religious concept of God, fear of rejection or punishment, unforgiveness, self-pity, independence, pride, even a negative experience with a parent. Apparent failure to have your prayers answered will also keep you from drawing near to God. Can you relate to any of these? Dear Christian, all of them can be overcome. Perhaps these spiritual exercises may help you:

- Read the Song of Solomon. Carefully note the words of Jesus (the Beloved) and the Shulamite (the church). Ask God to help

you understand His great love for His Bride and His longing to be with her.
- Ask God to arouse a hunger and thirst for more of Him. This should become a daily prayer. He will answer this prayer! He will satisfy your hunger!
- Privately sing a love song to God (Father, Son or Holy Spirit). Pick a familiar melody and sing new words...Ask the Holy Spirit to help you. What prevents you from practicing God's presence now?

The Formula

"For as many as are led by the Spirit of God, these are sons of God." Romans 8:14

Confusion has come because you are looking for a formula, a simple way of doing your ministry. I'm sorry, dear minister; you will find none. The methodical mind rejects this truth. In fact, if "formula" is practiced, legalism and death may soon follow.

For instance, consider this doctrinal question: Should you associate with a sinner or not? The Pharisees chided Jesus for doing so. He was called *a "glutton and a winebibber, a friend of tax collectors and sinners"* (Luke 7:34). Paul, however, tells the Corinthian church: *"But now I have written to you not to keep company with anyone named a brother, who is sexually immoral, or covetous, or an idolater, or a reviler, or a drunkard, or an extortioner--not even to eat with such a person"* (1Cor. 5:11).

Which is it? Are you supposed to keep company with sinners as Jesus did... or not? Is there a difference here between someone of the world and someone in the church? Spiritual discernment is needed, not a formula or a scripture taken out of context. What is the Holy Spirit telling you to do? It seems, in this case, if you are fellowshipping with a Christian who is a known sinner, without confronting their sin, you are guilty of endorsing their sin. Therefore don't do it. But, if you are led by the Spirit to befriend the backslider and later encourage them to repentance, by all means do what the Spirit is telling you. Can you see the need for Spirit-led living?

Without a doubt, you want to understand God's ways and this is often considered to be a monumental task. Nonetheless, all of His ways are accessible to the Spirit-led individual. You will know what to do, when and how to do it. God reveals His ways to His sons and daughters on a "need to know" basis, either to apply to a given circumstance or for the teaching of others. How frequently do you ask Him how, when, or where? How often do you truly listen? Dear servant of God, this is normal Christianity.

What If?

"He who believes in Me, as the Scripture has said, out of his heart will flow rivers of living water." John 7:38

What if the encouraging word that you spoke to the cashier was up-lifting enough to cause her to remain in her job? She went on to purchase the very business where she worked. Over the years, this woman hired several Christians and their giving financed many Kingdom activities.

What if the young man you took the time to lead to the Lord turned from rebellion to become an anointed missionary? What if the Christian tract that you left in the public rest room transformed the life of the reader, and they, in turn, blessed another, and then another? What if your willingness to stay in a difficult marriage inspired others to stay in theirs?

Are you looking for significance in your life? Dear Christian, you are very significant. Your seemingly mundane daily encounters are helping to change the world. Live your life in a way that pleases the Lord and your natural interpersonal contacts will manifest extraordinary results. God lives within you, beloved. His life is spilling out wherever you go. Carry Him unhindered and you will bear more fruit than you could ever imagine.

"He shall be like a tree planted by the rivers of water, that brings forth its fruit in its season, whose leaf also shall not wither; and whatever he does shall prosper" (Psalm 1:3).

There is Nothing I Can Do About It?

"Why are you cast down, O my soul? And why are you disquieted within me? Hope in God, for I shall yet praise Him for the help of His countenance." Psalm 42:5

Servant of the Most High, today you have another opportunity to please God, to listen for His promptings, and to obey. His mercies are new every morning. How wonderful! Today, failure and regrets can be put behind you and you can start afresh. Have you ever looked at life this way, each new day, a blank page that has not been written on? Yes, you will probably awake in that same situation you were in when you retired last night: not enough money, a difficult child or spouse or perhaps a job that you despise. But today is a new day with new insights for old problems, new ways of doing the same old thing. Obviously, some things cannot be changed overnight, but your perspective and attitude can. This will make your difficulties more bearable. You know this to be true. You have experienced it before. Your attitude can make a big difference!

Take a moment to seek the Lord. What can be done to repair your ailing relationship? Have you humbled yourself to ask forgiveness or to extend forgiveness to another? Are you willing to take a job that offers less money in exchange for greater personal fulfillment? What measure can be taken today to reduce your debt and your stress level?

Do not deceive yourself, many choices lie before you. You must not succumb to the lie that there is nothing you can do about your situation. Ask for help. Seek godly counsel. God has the solution. He may require you to wait or He may ask you to take positive action, even now. Why should you wallow in self-pity, or digress to the point of blaming others. You have a choice to make. By God's grace you can rise on eagle's wings far above the circumstances. Your loving Father desires to help you. There is something He can do.

Dear Jesus, I have resigned myself to carry a burden that You never asked me to carry. Please forgive me. Fill me with Your love and grace. Restore my peace. I trust You for the solution. I await Your answer with hopeful expectation.

Appreciate the Beauty

"The heavens declare the glory of God; and the firmament shows His handiwork. Day unto day utters speech, and night unto night reveals knowledge." Psalm 19:1

Does it come naturally or is it something that must be learned? Some can pass by a delicate flower and never notice it's intricate design or the sweetness of its fragrance. Do you notice? Do you recognize and appreciate the beauty of God's creation? He made it all for you.

Your Father, the Creator of heaven and earth, also placed within you the ability to perceive His creative work as "good" and to appreciate it's loveliness. Have you considered God's color schemes, the vast array of blue and purple hues that splash across the horizon? Or the melodic sounds of a babbling brook, the soothing comfort of a dancing flame, or the essence of lilac carried on the cool spring breeze? Our amazing God conceived all of these and then spoke them into existence. Yes, for His pleasure, but mostly for yours.

David looked into the boundless expanse of the heavens and proclaimed the Glory of God. He could not know that the universe was so much more immense than what he saw with his naked eye. When he gazed at the smallest of objects, could he have imagined the existence of sub-atomic particles? He was in awe at what he could see, but even the average school-age child knows more about the universe that David did. Our God is astounding! And what yet remains unknown and unseen? What grand revelation continues to elude the confines of our finite understanding? Praise be to our Maker! He is greatly to be praised for His ingenious, purposeful creativity.

Dear child of God, teach your children to recognize and appreciate the beauty of a sunset, the grandeur of the mountains, or the vastness of the sea. Point it out to them, again and again; and tell them that our God made all of these things... because of His love for them.

An Opportunity Awaits

"Glory in His holy name; let the hearts of those rejoice who seek the Lord! Seek the Lord and His strength; seek His face evermore! Remember His marvelous works which He has done, His wonders, and the judgments of His mouth," 1Chronicles 16:10-12

Would you be enticed by the prospect of an opportunity to spend an hour with Leonardo DiVinci, Albert Einstein, Thomas Edison, or another brilliant, creative man or woman. How fascinating it would be to learn of their insights.

History is filled with stunning examples of human ingenuity. It seems as though God, in His perfect time, reveals nuggets of wisdom and knowledge to mere mortals for the welfare of mankind. How perfect are His ways. How intricate His plans for humanity!

Now consider this, servant of God: Would you be enticed by the prospect of an opportunity to spend an hour with Almighty God, Creator of all things? How fascinating to learn of His insights and, even more so, of His great love for you. What prevents you from spending time with Him today?

Because The Days Are Evil

"Be sober; be vigilant; because your adversary the devil walks about like a roaring lion, seeking whom he may devour. Resist him, steadfast in the faith," 1Peter 5:8

There is a fierce battle raging for the souls of men, for your soul. The purpose: to make you stumble and to pull you away from the One Who loves you. The intensity of the battle is such that every weakness may be tested and exploited, including your physical health and emotional needs. Does the evil one have an open door in any area of your life? Ask God to show you.

Dear island, you do need others. Do not become independent and prideful. Seek help; ask for prayer; become accountable to someone. And of course, be quick to repent. Submit to God and resist the devil. When someone wounds you, forgive them... yes, forgive again. And when you are the one who did the wounding, ask for forgiveness. As the battle intensifies, remember that it is the Lord's battle. Hide in Him; He is your high tower. He goes before you and is your rear guard. He has trained your hands for war. He is your strength. Put on your armor and stand, my friend. And if you should get knocked down, get up. GET UP! You can do it. Don't quit.

This battle has not taken God by surprise. He wouldn't have led you here unless He knew that you were ready for this day. You may not feel prepared, but you know that the Almighty accomplishes His best work in the midst of your weakness. You are in training, valiant warrior; take courage. The day is soon approaching when His life will flow through you unhindered and many will be blessed. *"Lift up your heads, O you gates! And be lifted up, you everlasting doors! And the King of glory shall come in. Who is this King of glory? The Lord strong and mighty, the Lord mighty in battle."* Psalm 24:7-8

Being Transparent

"Therefore most gladly I will rather boast in my infirmities, that the power of Christ may rest upon me." 2Corinthians 12:9

A pointed question: Who are you trying to be? What facade are you presenting to the world, the church, and your family? Many, intentionally or not, portray a certain image: religious, sophisticated, cool, fashionable, casual, sexy, important, intelligent, productive. Most are seeking to conceal who they actually are. Do you do this? Be honest. There are so many people who are insecure, fearful, and lonely. "If they only knew what I'm really like, what I do, what I think about, then they would not like me, hire me or allow me to minister." Going to church is similar to attending a masquerade party. Wounded, sinful people pretend that everything is just fine. Few will let down their guard long enough to receive help... until they are desperate. The chief offenders may be the minister and spouse. They are dying on the inside while trying to present the image of having it all together. After all, the congregation expects them to be perfect.

Why are you doing this? You are fearfully and wonderfully made and precious in God's sight. You are very deeply loved. But, you are also a vulnerable sinner, like the rest of us. Don't you think that you could be healed more fully and better serve others if you would simply be transparent? The crucified life embraces transparency. Flesh is exposed for what it is, nothing but dust. The scriptures have revealed the frailty and sins of several great saints. Haven't you been blessed by reading of their struggles? Won't you testify of your failures, problems and sins? Allow the body of Christ to minister to you… and then give God the glory for healing and delivering you! Others need to hear of your struggles and His grace!

Use a Bushel, Not a Thimble

"...for with the same measure that you use, it will be measured back to you." Luke 6:38

Jesus reveals a multitude of hidden truths. Your ears should always be attentive when He speaks. In this passage, Jesus is teaching you about giving. *"Give and it shall be given to you."* He then inserts a very interesting point: *"...for with the same measure that you use, it will be measured back to you."* What does this mean? Paul restates it like this: *"He who sows sparingly will also reap sparingly, and he who sows bountifully will also reap bountifully"* (2Cor. 9:6).

Nonetheless, it doesn't refer only to the actual amount of your giving. If that were true, the widow who gave two mites would be sorely deficient. Jesus said of her, *"Truly I say to you that this poor widow has put in more than all; for all these out of their abundance have put in offerings for God, but she out of her poverty put in all the livelihood that she had"* (Luke 21:3-4). These verses obviously pertain to the percentage of giving, the amount of sacrifice and trust involved. It is not about the sum that you give, but what it means to you and how much it has cost you! Do you understand? … Now, what about the tithe?

As you may know, *tithe* means ten percent. If you earned $10,000 per year you would give $1,000. If you earned $1,000,000, you would give $100,000. What sacrifice would be involved if the millionaire gave only $1,000? God wants to teach you to place Him first and to trust Him. Some have boldly stated "We are no longer under the law. It is not mandatory to tithe." Of course this is true; but will you continue to use that excuse? Please note: Jesus spoke several times about giving. He is not proclaiming Old Testament law, but a very powerful New Testament principle; and He continues to use this for your training as well as for your blessing.

Dear believer, you will fall behind in your spiritual development if you do not learn to trust God at this level. He desires to bring you far beyond the tithe. There is no way around it. If you are to grow spiritually, you must become a generous giver.

*"'Bring all the tithes into the storehouse, that there may be food in My house, **and try Me now in this,**' says the **Lord of hosts,** 'if I will not open for you the windows of heaven and pour out for you such blessing that there will not be room enough to receive it. And I will rebuke the devourer for your sakes, so that he will not destroy the fruit of your ground, nor shall the vine fail to bear fruit for you in the field,' says the Lord of hosts;"* Malachi 3:10-11

Shining Ever Brighter

"The path of the righteous is like the first gleam of dawn, shining ever brighter till the full light of day." Proverbs 4:18 NIV

Sometimes Christians act as if they already know everything that there is to know about Christianity. They have gone to church for years and have sat in countless Bible studies. They give, do, and pray. What else is there?

Do you realize that the depths of God are unfathomable? His truth blossoms like a delicate rose. The same scripture verse, when read at different seasons of your life, can reveal a much broader truth. Have you experienced this? What you seem so adamant about today will be revealed as only partial truth tomorrow. This is quite normal.

Christianity is a living relationship with Christ. It is not mere religion, the sum total of well organized facts, practices and ceremonies. A studious individual could reach the bottom of religion in a matter of a few years, no matter how complicated, but not so with

Christianity. Spiritual revelation, through a vibrant relationship with the Creator, is ever unfolding. A child will love his father simply because he is their Dad. Children appreciate the gifts, hugs and times spent having fun together. They know very little about who he really is or what he does. As they mature they begin to know him at deeper levels. Dear child of God, do you really know your Father? Do you care to? Have you asked Him to reveal Himself to you? Far too many Christians have memorized scripture verses without wanting to know the Author. They have prayed without an expectation of an answer; and have gone to church because of obligation rather than desire. This leads to boredom and lukewarmness. You know, don't you? There is so much more to God than that.

Even if you have sought the Lord and reached into His depths, there is still more. As you sink to the deeper places, it becomes much simpler, dear friend: Less intellect, more intimacy, less emphasis on *doing,* more on *being*, less self-consciousness, more God-consciousness…and much more inner truth as the *full light of day* reveals your heart.

Are You Losing Interest?

"… for without Me you can do nothing." John 15:5

Dear servant of God, don't be surprised when you begin to lose interest in spiritual things. This is a very normal part of dying to self. In the past, you had purposed in your heart to seek the Lord and had earnestly desired to be conformed to the image of Christ, but now all seems lost. Your wonderful spiritual experiences are but a faint memory. You don't care to pray or go to church. You don't even want to engage in spiritual conversation.

To make it worse, the enemy will take this opportunity to harass you. Your mind may become confused. Anger, frustration, cursing, impure thoughts, criticism of others, all of these things may invade your thinking. You may even begin to judge God or think that He has left you. There doesn't appear to be any good thing remaining within you.

How could this happen? Why does God allow such things? Dear

Christian, it is during this time that you become acutely aware of your own unworthiness. And you can be certain that any attempt to extricate yourself from this wreck will fail. You may think that prayer or some type of religious activity might help, but instead of feeling better you only become more certain of your inability to do anything correctly. Nothing of value seems to flow from you and your prayer life seems fruitless. Your sense of unworthiness grows even deeper.

Even though you refused to admit it to yourself in the past, you really did think that you deserved to be blessed. You had been serving the Lord faithfully for so many years. Secretly, you felt that you should receive some benefit for all of that effort. But now you are beginning to see who you really are; and that is more than a little disconcerting.

Take courage, my friend. This is but for a season. It is a time of cleansing, another level of breaking down and building up. You are becoming more aware of your weaknesses and the things that need to be dealt with. You must trust God more than ever now. Be assured, He has not left you. He is very close and at work in you. Talk to Him even if you can't sense His presence. Bare your soul. He is listening.

Ultimately, you will begin to realize that God is in control of all things. The times and seasons are His and you can do nothing without Him. Until now, you have given only mental assent to this truth. Soon you will *know* it.

The Greater Reality

"If then you were raised with Christ, seek those things which are above, where Christ is, sitting at the right hand of God. Set your mind on things above, not on things on the earth. For you died, and your life is hidden with Christ in God." Colossians 3:1-3

Do you know that you can live in the reality of your choosing? No, I'm not speaking about schizophrenia. Consider this: Today, most of us will believe something that is not true. Some piece of information that you will receive from an outside source is not correct (another person, the newspaper or TV, etc.), yet you will believe it as though it were. Even your perception of any given situation is contaminated as it passes through the filter of your personality, and is compared to prior experiences. Do you know what I mean? How much of what you believe is absolute truth? Interesting concept isn't it? A bit scary too, because opinions are formed and decisions are made based on partial truth and unsubstantiated "facts." Your reality may not be that real.

Having said that, let us also consider those things that are true, for instance the circumstances that you face each day. You may be lonely, impoverished, and surrounded by difficulties. You may be unhappy with your job, or have a failing marriage. This may indeed be truth and *is* your reality. But, dear believer, belief in Christ, I mean true faith has the capability of lifting you beyond your current reality to a greater reality: God is love; He is also faithful. He has chosen you and He is all-powerful. He is your deliverer. He is your healer. He is your Savior. He is….

Please consider the absolute TRUTH of God's Word and choose to live in this *far greater* reality. Peace and hope abound there.

Coming to Yourself

"But when he came to himself, he said, `How many of my father's hired servants have bread enough and to spare, and I perish with hunger!'" Luke 15:17

How precious a moment, what a glorious day, when those who wander away "come to themselves" and begin the journey back home. We are all aware of the story of the prodigal son who took his inheritance and squandered it on sinful living. When he finally reached his lowest point, he came to himself and said, *"…How many of my father's hired servants have bread enough and to spare, and I perish with hunger! I will arise and go to my father, and will say to him, 'Father, I have sinned against heaven and before you'"* (Luke 15:17-18).

Do you remember when you came to yourself? Little is ever mentioned about this point of decision, this place of surrender, the time when you finally decided that you had enough, the moment when you resigned from your struggle of self will. And yet, this may be one of the finest hours of your life. The angels were rejoicing and your heavenly Father was very pleased. He had planned this day before you were born. And prior to this moment? Those were the years of rebellion, anger, and self-pity. Foolishness and unwise decisions were the hallmark of your life. It is amazing that some of these decisions did not cost you your life. Oh, but for His grace and mercy!

Is it logic and reasoning that finally breaks through? Yes, to a certain extent, *"...How many of my father's hired servants have bread enough and to spare, and I perish with hunger,"* but for many, it is much more than that. There are usually a series of negative, and perhaps, very painful occurrences that compound over the course of the preceding days or months, and finally, your will is broken. No doubt, the enemy of your soul has had a part to play; he was trying to destroy you. But make no mistake about it; God was in control. Your proud, self-willed rebellion would not give way to the Truth of God, His love, nor His law. But after your "self" was pressed against the wall, you were ready to listen. Where would you be today if God did not pursue you with this persuasive kind of love?

But coming to yourself does not only pertain to rebellion and submission. It can also mean receiving revelation that you need to change something in your life, or that you need to apologize to someone, or you have been doing something at work or home the wrong way. You finally realize that what you thought was good and pleasing has really been nothing less than selfish and wrong. May God grant you such revelation today, that you would finally come to yourself, repent, and willingly change direction.

Perhaps you are prayerfully waiting for your child, or spouse, or friend to arrive at such a place. Dear saint, be encouraged today. God is reminding you of His faithfulness; He will bring *His* work to completion. Have faith, dear one; He has heard your prayers and has seen your tears. The answer is soon coming!

Remember, you cannot make it happen. The Father of the prodigal didn't run after him, he waited and watched for his return.

Meeting the Needs

"Now if God so clothes the grass of the field, which today is, and tomorrow is thrown into the oven, will He not much more clothe you, O you of little faith? Therefore do not worry, saying, `What shall we eat?' or `What shall we drink?' or `What shall we wear?' For after all these things the Gentiles seek. For your heavenly Father knows that you need all these things."   Matthew 6:30-32

Believer of Truth, are you allowing your needs to define truth or is truth defining your needs? What bondage and unrest there is if you are ruled by your perceived needs. Do you understand? Our Lord has promised to provide all of your needs. If a need arises, He will surely meet it. If this is true, and you know that it is, then the *wanting* of anything more than you already have, would more than likely be considered a *desire* rather than a *need*, correct? Of course, God is also mindful of your desires; He is a good God, but learn the difference between needs and desires.

You desire to be successful, to have more money, a better job or ministry, a bigger house or car. You desire to have a mate, someone to love and show you affection. Dear one, how much of this is truly need and how much is desire? Wouldn't it be better to allow the Word of God to reveal the truth in this matter? You have lived this long without these things, so they certainly could not be considered an immediate need... like food, clothing and shelter. And yet, after you pray a few times, or even for a few years, you become anxious and launch out to meet your own desires, calling them needs. In essence, by doing this, you are saying to God, "Your provision is insufficient!" And you justify your actions with this simple thought: "I need this now; I can wait no longer."

Be careful, saint. You are asking for trouble. When you seek to do it yourself, you are running ahead of God. Abraham did this and Ishmael was born. How many marriages have failed because someone just had to fulfill their need; they married the first one who looked attractive?

The "needs" of others can also become a bondage. Be wise and be led by the Holy Spirit. There are so many needy people. Some will

113

suck the strength out of you. You must love them, but you cannot be God to them. Remember, you are a servant of the Lord; you are not their servant. Yes, serve them; absolutely, yes; this is what a servant of God must do. But know the difference. You come and go as the Lord directs, not as the need demands. If you can learn this, dear minister, you will not burn out so easily the next time.

Convictions and Beliefs

"These likewise are the ones sown on stony ground who, when they hear the word, immediately receive it with gladness; and they have no root in themselves, and so endure only for a time. Afterward, when tribulation or persecution arises for the word's sake, immediately they stumble. Now these are the ones sown among thorns; they are the ones who hear the word, and the cares of this world, the deceitfulness of riches, and the desires for other things entering in choke the word, and it becomes unfruitful. But these are the ones sown on good ground, those who hear the word, accept it, and bear fruit: some thirty fold, some sixty, and some a hundred." Mark 4:16-20

As you may know, there are various levels of believing. The most common and perhaps most superficial would be called an *opinion*. Everyone forms opinions about any number of things. Opinions are based on feelings, insights, experiences, and a compilation of information that may or may not be true. Opinions can change like the direction of a summer breeze. A *belief*, on the other hand, is a bit stronger. It may have been learned during childhood or acquired over the years. These usually have deeper roots and may actually influence your choices. Again, your beliefs, and subsequent philosophies, may or may not be founded upon absolute truth. The third and most enduring belief is called *conviction*. Convictions are very strong beliefs. Some people are even willing to die for their convictions. How sad, when conviction is based upon falsehood. Terrorists have committed mass murder upon the basis of their religious convictions.

Dear Christian, do you know what you believe and why you believe it? Are your values mere opinions or do you hold strong convictions? Here are a few areas where it is absolutely vital to form convictions: Be assured in the very depths of your being that the

Bible is the inerrant Word of God. It is from this foundation that all TRUTH flows. In addition, it is essential to form convictions regarding marriage and family, sexuality, work ethics, your destiny, and perhaps, a variety of social issues, including abortion, race relations, homosexuality, etc. Ask yourself where you stand on each of these issues, then find scripture verses to confirm your beliefs. If your beliefs do not line up with the Word, then ask God to reveal His truth in the matter. He will be very glad to give you wisdom. Remember, convictions should not be formed upon hearsay, or even the convincing testimony of a friend. You should do some research yourself and pray about it. The truth of God's Word has power to mold and shape your convictions. Make a commitment to live according to your convictions and ask the Holy Spirit to empower you to do it.

Many saints who have gone before us have been imprisoned or executed because they were unwilling to deny their convictions. May God grant you the grace to stand firm in the midst of persecution.

Society Abhors Christian Conviction

"For the time will come when they will not endure sound doctrine..." 2Timothy 4:3

It is more than OK to have an opinion. The world loves to listen to the opinions of others. Millions of viewers sit in front of their television watching knowledgeable (and sometimes not so knowledgeable) people discuss anything and everything. It is also considered very good to have beliefs. Western culture can be quite respectful of someone's belief system, bending over backward, not wanting to offend. But having convictions, that's another story. This is when difficulty arises for the Christian. You see, in many western countries, it is perfectly fine for the Muslim to hold strong convictions, and the homosexual, and the pro-abortionist; but let a Christian with conviction share his or her Biblical perspective and they are quickly labeled a fanatic, a fundamentalist, or a religious zealot. Interesting.

Jesus said, "...No one comes to the Father except through Me" (John 14:6). This is, without a doubt, an exclusive statement; and Christians have been bringing God's unique message of salvation to the nations for nearly 2000 years. The world, however, cannot comprehend God's love and has refused to accept His only begotten Son. They brand the true believer as narrow minded, insisting there are many roads to heaven. "How dare you proclaim that Jesus is the only way!" Dear one, the time is coming when Christians who espouse the inerrancy of Scripture and the supremacy of Christ will be seriously persecuted as intolerant bigots. In fact, the persecution has already begun!

Are you ready to take a stand for your utmost conviction: Jesus Christ is the Son of God and there is no other way to heaven except through Him? Will you also take a stand for Biblical righteousness? Stand firm, servant of God. You will be greatly rewarded.

Dear disciple, be careful! You can bring unnecessary persecution upon yourself. Do not be unloving when presenting or defending the truth. Be considerate of those who do not agree with you. Remember, you only have light because God has given it to you. There is no need to be arrogant or defensive. Humbly declare the truth and humbly stand upon it. Allow God to do the rest!

Agape Love

We have heard about love so often that we may have the tendency to quickly overlook another message on this topic. Having said that, please pay close *attention* to the following:

Love is the central theme of the New Testament. We are commanded to *agape* love no less than 55 times. God Himself is *agape* and everything that is commanded of us is predicated upon *agape*!

So what is the definition? Let us simply say this: *Agape* is giving of oneself sacrificially without expecting anything in return. The very essence of Christianity is built upon this foundation. The Church does not function properly, void of blessing and power, because *agape* is lacking. And the messes that we may get ourselves into, at home, at work and at church are often the result of failure to *agape*. It would seem to be an important area of your life to allow God to work on, don't you think?

Consider this: a husband or wife might say, "I do kind things and say kind words; I try to bless my spouse in many ways, but they simply will not respond." I am sorry, dear one. Perhaps some counseling will help, but even if it does not, you must *agape*... with no expectation of a reciprocal response. Do you understand? This is true love.

Do you truly love your spouse ...or your child, co-worker, or pastor? In this day and age when someone no longer meets our needs, or they offend us in some way, we move on. This is obviously not *agape* love and it probably never was. Remember, love is not a feeling. It is an act of your will. Let's close this reading by reviewing God's word. It is He who exhorts you to love:

"Jesus said to him, `You shall love the Lord your God with all your heart, with all your soul, and with all your mind. This is the first and great commandment. And the second is like it: `You shall love your neighbor as yourself.'" Matthew 22:37-39 *"Greater love has no one than this, than to lay down one's life for his friends."* John 15:13 *"These things I command you, that you love one another."* John 15:17 *"And walk in love, as Christ also has loved us and given Himself for us, an offering and a sacrifice to God for a sweet-smelling aroma."* Philippians 1:9 *"And this I pray, that your love may abound still more and more in knowledge and all discernment,"* Ephesians 5:2 *"...love one another fervently with a pure heart,"* 1Peter 1:22 *"And above all things have fervent love for one another, for 'love will cover a multitude of sins.'"* 1Peter 4:8 *For this is the message that you heard from the beginning, that we should love one another,"* 1John 3:11 *""My little children, let us not love in word or in tongue, but in deed and in truth."* 1John 3:18 *"He who does not love does not know God, for God is love. In this the love of God was manifested toward us, that God has sent His only begotten Son into the world, that we might live through Him. In this is love, not that we loved God, but that He loved us and sent His Son to be the propitiation for our sins. Beloved, if God so loved us, we also ought to love one another. No one has seen God at any time. If we love one another, God abides in us, and His love has been perfected in us."* 1John 4:8-12 *"And let us consider one another in order to stir up love and good works,"* Hebrews 10:24

David, the Righteous

"... David did what was right in the eyes of the Lord, and had not turned aside from anything that He commanded him all the days of his life, except in the matter of Uriah the Hittite." 1Kings 15:5

When the Word of God records the life of David, he is called *a man after God's heart*. David's name is mentioned 897 times. (More than any other except God Himself.) His mighty exploits are spoken of in detail. What an awesome man he was... a mighty warrior and a tender-hearted worshipper, a prophetic songwriter and king.

It is quite evident that God sees David as a great man despite the fact that he sinned. Look at this scripture again, *"... David did what was right in the eyes of the Lord, and had not turned aside from anything that He commanded him all the days of his life, except in the matter of Uriah the Hittite"* (1Kings 15:5). What a marvelous epitaph!

Unfortunately, church people too often amplify David's sin and minimize his mighty deeds. How many sermons have you heard recounting the sordid details of David, Bathsheba and Uriah? Yes, sin is sin; it is ugly and painful, and David paid dearly for his failures. But God forgave David and he went on to fulfill his calling... as did Peter, and many other great saints. Know that God sees you as He sees David. He remembers your faithfulness and your good works; He has forgiven and forgotten your sin. Dear disciple, it is time to fulfill your calling. Our God is the God of a second chance.

More About Grace

"I will cry out to God Most High, to God who performs all things for me." Psalm 57:2 *"But you, beloved, building yourselves up on your most holy faith, praying in the Holy Spirit, keep yourselves in the love of God..."* Jude 1:20-21

Have you ever pondered the perplexing interdependence of grace and works... that which God freely gives and that which is required of you? Which is it, *"God who performs all things for me"* or *"keep yourselves in the love of God?"* If you have success, God receives the praise... and rightfully so. But if you fail, it is your own fault. How can this be? Wasn't it *amazing grace "that brought us safe thus far?"* Was it the removal of grace that caused you to fail or were you simply unwilling or unable to receive it?

Consider this: You pray in faith and God answers. Nevertheless, the Lord, knowing that you need something, stirs you to pray so that He can respond. Did you initiate the prayer or did God? Do you understand? I suppose we could debate this, as some theologians have, but one thing is certain: Whether the stirring to pray originated in the heart of God or the heart of man, grace is freely given for you to take the time to make the petition. It is your choice to avail yourself of that marvelous privilege. In fact, grace is freely given to the servant of God for every aspect of the Christian walk. Without God's grace there would be absolutely no hope of accomplishing His will. Your efforts apart from grace are carnal; your wisdom apart from grace is foolishness. It only requires a brief glance at your daily newspaper to prove this point.

So you see, God will surely give grace to do His will. You must simply appropriate it - not really too complicated after all. Verse 5 states it this way: *"Through You... we will."* God gives abundant, amazing grace and you in turn, respond in obedience, waiting, trusting... or doing whatever He tells you. There is no need to strive, no need to worry. No trouble, difficulty or heartache is beyond His grace. And what of His command to care for the poor, the imprisoned or the sick? And what about declaring His great salvation to the lost? Grace, in the form of provision and spiritual power, flows in abundance as you obey the Word (*rhema*) of the Lord.

Dear disciple, as you know, God is in control of all things. He will not allow anything into your life that will not ultimately work for good; He loves you. Life and strength, wisdom and power emanate from His throne... everything that you need. And when He leads you into battle, you will receive the strategy, the armor, and the strength. What fool would proceed on his own when such a Mighty One has promised to go before you?

"For they did not gain possession of the land by their own sword, nor did their own arm save them; but it was Your right hand, Your

119

arm, and the light of Your countenance, because You favored them.
You are my King, O God; command victories for Jacob. Through
You we will push down our enemies; through Your name we will
trample those who rise up against us" Psalm 44:3-5

Satan's Crowning Achievement

"But know this, that in the last days perilous times will come: For
men will be lovers of themselves, lovers of money, boasters, proud,
blasphemers, disobedient to parents, unthankful, unholy, unloving,
unforgiving, slanderers, without self-control, brutal, despisers of
good, traitors, headstrong, haughty, lovers of pleasure rather than
lovers of God, having a form of godliness but denying its power. And
from such people turn away!" 2Timothy 3:1-5

How often it has been said that the homeless addict/alcoholic is
Satan's greatest accomplishment, his masterpiece. Dear disciple, can
this be true? Yes, a destroyed life is frequently the handiwork of the
devil, but certainly not his crowning achievement. After all, a dere-
lict is of no use to him; he lies in the gutter or sits in an institution.

The devil's prize possessions are the nicely dressed, upstanding,
influential citizens who live their life apart from Jesus Christ. Do
you understand? The rich and famous, the intelligent and well
spoken; these are very useful tools! They may be college
professors or movie stars or business executives, etc. They flaunt
their godless lifestyle before the world... enticing others to join
them, "Life is good, live it to the fullest. You don't need God" and
they can present a very plausible argument for there lifestyle. Far too
many embrace their ungodly philosophy of humanism... "Let us
make things better for our fellow man... and let us be kind to
animals..." *"having a form of godliness but denying its power..."*

There are also others, perhaps the least likely of suspects: brilliant
theologians who deny the resurrection of Jesus or clergy who
unashamedly pervert the meaning of scripture to endorse their sin.
These are Satan's crowning achievement.

You must be discerning, servant of God, the battle rages for the
souls of men. Pray, be bold and speak the truth in love.

120

Too Costly A Journey

"Now therefore, the sword shall never depart from your house, because you have despised Me, and have taken the wife of Uriah the Hittite to be your wife. Thus says the Lord: 'Behold, I will raise up adversity against you from your own house; and I will take your wives before your eyes and give them to your neighbor, and he shall lie with your wives in the sight of this sun.'" 2Samuel 12:10-11

Our Father is kind and merciful, but there is little doubt that sin has its consequences. In David's case, these consequences were quite severe. Remember the parable that Nathan delivered to David? David responded with anger and recited the law*: "...and he shall restore fourfold for the lamb, because he did this thing and because he had no pity"* (2Sam. 12:5-6). Unbeknownst to him, David was pronouncing his own judgment; his *fourfold restitution* were the lives of 4 of his children. In addition, his daughter was raped and Absalom tried to take his Kingdom. What grief, what pain!

Yes, beloved, God is merciful and He forgives sin completely, removing all guilt. But most often, He allows the consequences of sin to remain. If someone robs a bank for instance, God will surely forgive them, but they may spend the next 10 years in prison. While in prison, they will have the opportunity to grow nearer to God and to serve Him in meaningful ways, but nonetheless; they will sit in prison, their freedom forfeited because of a foolish sin.

The words you speak to your children and others, your actions, even the sinful thoughts you allow to remain in your mind...all have serious ramifications. Do you speak and act without considering the repercussions? Please remember: what you say and do, will in some way, affect the lives of others.

And then there are the *willful* sins... Before you make a serious mistake, contemplate the aftermath. Please! You are about to embark on a journey that you cannot afford. The price of sin is far too dear. Like a seagoing vessel caught in a tempest, you could suffer great damage and loss. Wake Up! You are about to be shipwrecked! Your short-lived gratification will flee away like the morning dew, but the painful consequences can endure for years to come.

Forsaking All

"If anyone comes to Me and does not hate his father and mother, wife and children, brothers and sisters, yes, and his own life also, he cannot be My disciple. And whoever does not bear his cross and come after Me cannot be My disciple." "So likewise, whoever of you does not forsake all that he has cannot be My disciple." Luke 14:26-27, 33

Dear disciple, this is serious business. Jesus calls his servants to a very radical commitment. Who could misconstrue His statements? The Master is requiring ALL that you are and ALL that you have... or, you cannot be His disciple. Let's stop playing games! Do you desire to follow Jesus or not? There is no time for indecisiveness. Did you say, "Yes, I will follow?" Then why are you walking after Him in such a half-hearted manner, beloved?

Jesus traveled from village to village speaking truth, doing miracles and calling forth workers for the harvest. Some dropped everything and followed; others made excuses. Please be sure to note that Jesus never begged anyone to come after Him. He moved on and sought another. Has the Lord called you? What an awesome privilege! Forsake all now and follow Him.

"Then a certain scribe came and said to Him, 'Teacher, I will follow You wherever You go.' And Jesus said to him, 'Foxes have holes and birds of the air have nests, but the Son of Man has nowhere to lay His head.' Then another of His disciples said to Him, 'Lord, let me first go and bury my father.' But Jesus said to him, 'Follow Me, and let the dead bury their own dead'" (Matt. 8:19-22).

"Assuredly, I say to you, there is no one who has left house or parents or brothers or wife or children, for the sake of the kingdom of God, who shall not receive many times more in this present time, and in the age to come eternal life" (Luke 18:29-30).

And From His Side Came a Glorious Bride

"And the Lord God caused a deep sleep to fall on Adam, and he slept; and He took one of his ribs, and closed up the flesh in its place. Then the rib which the Lord God had taken from man He made into a woman, and He brought her to the man" (Gen. 2:21-22). *"But one of the soldiers pierced His side with a spear, and immediately blood and water came out"* (John 19:33-34). *"And so it is written, 'The first man Adam became a living being.' The last Adam became a life-giving spirit"* (1Cor. 15:45). *"Let us be glad and rejoice and give Him glory, for the marriage of the Lamb has come, and His wife has made herself ready."* (Rev. 19:7).

Dear one, today we will review a great mystery... and will behold the manifest wisdom and providential strategies of our God! As you know, throughout the Old Testament there are prophetic insights (types) of the Almighty's eternal purposes. (i.e., Abraham was asked to sacrifice His *son of promise*, Isaac, but a *lamb* was offered in his stead). Now consider this awesome picture: The first Adam was placed into a deep sleep; his side was opened and a woman was fashioned, his bride, Eve. The last Adam hung upon a tree; His side was also pierced. And from His wound, the Bride of Christ emerged. That life giving flow of blood and water, oh, the thought of it! How marvelous is our God! What a perfect picture!

Before the foundation of the world, the loving Omniscient had a plan... and through the first Adam, God revealed His eternal intention: He would bring forth a glorious Bride for His Son, Jesus... Worship Him, beloved! *"For God so loved the world that He gave His only begotten Son."* Believe Him, you are that precious Bride!

Understanding the Providence of God

"Trust in the Lord with all your heart, and lean not on your own understanding; in all your ways acknowledge Him, and He shall direct your paths. Do not be wise in your own eyes; fear the Lord and depart from evil. It will be health to your flesh, and strength to your bones." Proverbs 3:5-7

123

What a statement, "Understanding the providence of God!" As if a mere mortal could fully grasp the meaning of God's ways! But dear Christian, God does allow you a glimpse once in a while.

You fall from a ladder and painfully injure yourself. During the ride to the hospital, you complain to God, "Why did you let this happen?" While being examined, the doctors find a small tumor that can easily be removed. If it had gone undetected, it would have become life threatening.

You are driving in a rural area and your vehicle breaks down. Your only recourse is to walk the mile or two back to town. As you walk, you complain to God, "Why did You let this happen?" Of course, there have been many other times when you have not understood what God was doing...but, what if: Unbeknownst to you, a tiny blood clot was just about to form somewhere in your body. The increased exercise (which you get far too little of) acts to thwart this from occurring... or, you meet someone along the way that needs your help. Maybe you will have a conversation with God, while walking, that you would not otherwise have taken the time for. Surely you know that this upset will work for good, don't you?

If the inconvenience turns out to your benefit, I suppose you would concede that God's providence knows best. But what if this disquieting does little for you, but is significant to another... Like missing the plane and stressfully waiting for hours. However, on the next flight you find yourself seated near someone who really needs some ministry. Are you still up for it, or are you so filled with self-pity that you refuse the opportunity?

Dear one, God is in control of all things. Please trust Him. If adversity comes from the devil, stand your ground, fight and win. If it flows from another, learn to forgive and persevere. If it comes directly from the hand of God, endure, beloved, and praise Him. Blessings will soon flow, *to* you or *through* you... if you will only learn to trust Him.

Spiritual Maturity

"... that we should no longer be children, tossed to and fro and carried about with every wind of doctrine, by the trickery of men, in the cunning craftiness of deceitful plotting, but, speaking the truth in love, may grow up in all things into Him who is the head— Christ." Ephesians 4:14

Just a few words about spiritual growth: Please understand, there are various levels of maturity and numerous areas of growth and development. For instance: every Christian should be maturing in their depth of relationship with God... through prayer and worship. They should also grow in virtue, faith, obedience, humility, servanthood, etc. Just as a natural child grows to maturity, so it is in the spirit; growth cannot be forced. Although the natural child is most certainly capable of performing adult activities ...and the spiritual child may flow in the gifts of the Holy Spirit (with magnificent results), this, however, does not mean that they are mature. It usually takes years of experience... successes and failures, to fully mature. A teenager thinks himself wise at sixteen. Again at twenty-one and thirty-something, maturity is a perceived certainty. Likewise, some Christians think that they have reached the advanced level while they are yet in the early stages of spiritual growth. Surprise! God has much more for you to learn... not only in your intellect, but also in the very depths of your being!

A child cannot make himself grow up by simply willing it... and neither can you, beloved. God is the Vinedresser. He prepares the soil, fertilizes it, provides the rain and causes the growth. (He will also prune.) This is a lengthy process, dear one. You may excel in one area of your development but fall miserably short in another. Please, don't use either as the standard to judge your level of maturation. Let the Master evaluate your progress and proceed accordingly. This is His work; trust Him. And what is required of you? Love God, and cooperate with His work in your life through simple obedience.

God's Sovereignty vs The Proliferation Of Evil

"Then I saw an angel coming down from heaven, having the key to the bottomless pit and a great chain in his hand. He laid hold of the dragon, that serpent of old, who is the Devil and Satan, and bound him for a thousand years; and he cast him into the bottomless pit, and shut him up, and set a seal on him, so that he should deceive the nations no more till the thousand years were finished. But after these things he must be released for a little while." Revelations 20:1-3

There are several levels of perception regarding this vast subject of God's sovereignty vs. the proliferation of evil. Here are a few, starting with the rudimentary: God is good, the devil is evil, therefore all good comes from God, all bad comes from the devil! Another level of understanding will teach that God is in control, but He gives a free will to men and they must choose between good and evil. The outcome is determined by their choices. Yet another discernment reveals that the devil perpetrates his wickedness upon earth by deceiving our fallen race, using us as his pawns. We must resist the wiles of the enemy and tear down his strongholds.

You may have also learned that by staying close to God and obeying His word, you will be protected from evil. However, if you allow unrepented sin to remain, you will loose this protective covering and open yourself to the attacks of the enemy. The same is spoken about the "covering" of a pastor or a local church: if you step out from under that covering you could become vulnerable prey for the devil.

No doubt, there are myriads of variations for each of these themes and each contain the truth, but dear one, isn't it time to mature to a deeper understanding... grasping the bigger picture? Jesus told Peter, *"Simon, Simon! Indeed, Satan has asked for you, that he may sift you as wheat"* (Luke 22:31). It is quite obvious that God the Father allowed this sifting. Why? Because the All Knowing, All Wise foreknew that it would work for the greater good... for Peter, and ultimately for the many whom he was about to influence. Do you understand? Yes, God is good; the devil is evil. Albeit, our holy God permitted the wicked devil to attack his faithful servant (who was more than likely walking in repentance and covered by Jesus Himself), weakening him to the point of denying Christ. Peter

126

suffered a bitter defeat; his pain was agonizing, he was humbled and broken... but when he returned, he *strengthened his brethren.*

A spiritual child might say: "It is difficult for me to love and serve a God who permits evil." After they grow a bit, they will realize that by this way of thinking, they are actually placing themselves above God...judging God, as it were. Please know this, dear child: God is Love! You may not understand His ways, but nonetheless, He loves you. He would not, no; He could not do evil to you, nor permit evil that wouldn't in some way be beneficial, working for your good.

Most parents love their children; nevertheless, they discipline them. Children are not always given their own way. They must go to school even when they don't want to; they must do chores, or go somewhere with their parents when they would rather stay home and play. A loving parent will also allow their child to face the adversities of this world, knowing that these difficulties will help develop their character. For the same reason, your heavenly Father will allow adversity (whether from the devil or another) into your life, and cause, or even force you to do things that you do not want to do. This is all part of spiritual growth. Will you resist and be rebellious? God desires for you to shine brightly in this hour of darkness. He wants to give you responsibility and authority. Please learn His ways and grow to maturity. Your Father, the Almighty Sustainer of the Universe, *is* in control of ALL things. Please submit to His wisdom and His judgment; trust in His unfailing love!

Understanding Depression

*"So the ransomed of the Lord shall return, and come to Zion with singing, with everlasting joy on their heads. They shall obtain joy and gladness; sorrow and sighing shall flee away. "*Isaiah 51:11

The insidious blight of depression has enveloped much of our world. Millions of men, women and children (including many Christians!) have suffered from some form of depression; have you, beloved? Those who observe this disease from the 'outside' find it difficult to understand. When a family member begins to lose interest, withdraw, or alter their lifestyle through a variety of escape mechanisms, we do not know how to respond.

Foolish statements like, "Cheer up, things will get better" are repeated time and again by well-wishers. However, this does little to aid the victim of depression. Even in Christian circles, loving saints who genuinely desire to help will offer a scripture verse or a hug, but this barely scratches the surface.

The causes of depression are varied and complex, but certainly not beyond God's healing touch. Dear Christian, He loves you and will bring you through this darkness. Yes, you may need counseling or medicine. Thank God for these things, but remember that He is your source and this is only for a season.

Let's paint a picture that may help you understand one type of depression: According to the Scriptures, your body is the temple of the Holy Spirit (1Cor. 6:19). See yourself now as this temple. Of course, your temple is supposed to be a place of worship, a place to meet with the Lord. But, what is this? You are dumping your garbage on the pews (no pun intended).

In fact, you dump the rubbish there every time you are wounded. As a child, and subsequently as an adult, you weren't able to resolve difficult emotional issues. You may have also responded to your pain with unforgiveness and resentment; or you did not respond at all. Depression is often called anger turned inwards. You canned your feelings and toughed it out. Unfortunately, the more wounding, the more garbage is being stuffed deep inside. Your temple, now filled up to the windows, leaves little room for worship and communion with God. You may stand on the periphery and offer a few songs and prayers, but there doesn't seem to be a closeness to God.

The smell from all of this trash begins to be noticed by others, usually by those closest. They are the first recipients of your moodiness, melancholy, outbursts of anger and more. Stress only compounds the problem. Does this sound familiar? So what is the solution? Easier said than done, but the answer is as simplistic as the analogy. It does however, give hope: Empty the garbage and learn how to respond to life so that you do not dump more garbage within. Anyone can learn to do this through prayer and wise counsel. It is well understood that when someone is seriously depressed, they can't seem to find the energy to do much. But you can do this. You really can!

1) Ask God to forgive you for your sins. Repentance is absolutely necessary. This is the first truckload of garbage being removed.

2) Forgiveness is another major tool for removing debris from your life. Forgive all those whom have offended you, great and small. This is absolutely essential for your healing.

3) Receive godly counsel from your pastor, Christian counselor, or trusted friend. Talk about your woundedness and your needs.

4) As you move forward from here, learn how to express your feelings in constructive ways. It is not a sin to be angry; it is healthy. Simply learn to express yourself in a godly way. You may already be pursuing this course of action. Great! Don't become discouraged. Keep working. There is more trash to get rid of. But there is also an end to this work when all of the debris will be removed. You will feel a little better as more is cleared away. God is healing you! *Lord, today please encourage all who are discouraged and depressed.*

Boundaries

"Wisdom and knowledge will be the stability of your times..." Isa. 33:6

Christian psychology, in this present day, has much to say about personal boundaries in relationships... at work and at home. How does this teaching fit in with all that you have been learning about death to self, complete abandonment, and self-sacrificing love? Shouldn't the disciple of Jesus serve without boundaries, giving, and going, and doing without regard for self?

The answer is not complicated, but may seem a bit contradictory. The answer: both yes, and no! Yes, you should give and serve without regard for self. After all, a humble servant does not think, "You are taking advantage of me!" No, he thinks, "What more can I do to serve you?" BUT one must use wisdom and clearly discern the will of God. Is God asking you to do this thing? If He is, you can be sure that He will give you guidance regarding the particulars: when, where, how, how much, how long. Do you understand? If someone asks for your help, the Lord will usually give you a choice whether to respond or not. Feel free to do as your heart directs. If you do choose to sacrifice your time or money, you will receive a heavenly reward (provided you don't boast about it).

Nevertheless, if this person continues to ask for your help and it begins to consume a lot of your resources, you had better be sure that God is in this. You may be distracted from doing the other things that the Lord has asked you to do. If you can't be sure, it would be wise for you to set boundaries. Not because you are concerned with self, but because you want to flow in God's perfect will for your life.

Not only must you occasionally set boundaries regarding the use of time and finances, but you must also show wisdom concerning your emotional and physical health. You certainly don't want to burn yourself out. Be careful with this, however, especially if you have a tendency to baby yourself. You could use this "boundary" to promote your ease. It is OK to stretch yourself... just don't make yourself sick. The Lord will lead you. If you want a model for self-sacrificing servanthood (with boundaries) look no further than to the Master Himself. During His three years of public ministry, He tirelessly poured Himself out... preaching, teaching, and ministering to the needs of others. But Jesus also knew when to rest. He would withdraw from the crowds and spend time with His Father. You must do the same. So you see, boundaries are also necessary for the one who is dying to self. Use wisdom and discernment, dear disciple; these are your safeguards.

What about Abuse?

What if you are being physically abused in a relationship? Dear one, you must know that God loves you and He does not require you to linger under the imminent threat of danger. Yes, the abuser needs help, but not from you. You must remove yourself from this perilous situation. The Lord will show you where to seek refuge. Tell someone about this immediately... and flee. *"When they persecute you in this city, flee to another."* Matthew 10:23

Bad Decisions

"And let the peace of God rule in your hearts..." Colossians 3:15

It is well worth mentioning again that many of the opinions that you have and the decisions that you make are issued from an imperfect perception of reality. Your feelings of inadequacy or superiority, your unhealed wounds, prior experiences, and prejudices, all of these play a role in helping you form an impression of an individual, or of any given occurrence. That is why it is so important, no, absolutely vital, that you allow the Holy Spirit to guide your decision making process. What a mess we, the Church, have made due to carnal determinations.

You may say, I have a bad or good feeling about that person or this situation; but don't assume that God has given you that feeling. As holy as you may be, you are still human, and humans are influenced by a plethora of previous experiences.

Take the time to seek God, wait on the Lord; listen for His voice. Discern if you are sensing a peace within. There is a significant difference between a troubled mind and a troubled spirit. Many feelings such as fear, doubt, and inadequacy have their source in the mind (emotions). A Holy Spirit led decision will give you inner peace even though you might later wrestle with fear and doubt. Do you understand? If not, God is very willing to teach you; ask Him.

On The Verge Of Total Ruin

"And you mourn at last, when your flesh and your body are consumed, and say: 'How I have hated instruction, and my heart despised correction! I have not obeyed the voice of my teachers, nor inclined my ear to those who instructed me! I was on the verge of total ruin, in the midst of the assembly and congregation.' Drink water from your own cistern, and running water from your own well. Let your fountain be blessed, and rejoice with the wife of your youth. For why should you, my son, be enraptured by an immoral woman, and be embraced in the arms of a seductress?" Prov. 5:11-15,18,20

Words cannot describe the pain that is caused by adultery. Its ever-widening ripple effect is eroding the very fabric of society. Marriages and families are destroyed, children are raised in single parent homes, sexually transmitted diseases are running rampant, and the welfare system is strained to the point of rupture. In addition, the financial losses due to divorce are astronomical. (Do you know that recent statistics reveal those cities that have a high rate of divorce also have a higher incidence of suicide?) Who will sound the warning? Where is the pulpiteer who will squarely address this extremely urgent matter? Teachers, please teach us!

Of course adultery is nothing new, you can read about it in the ancient writings, nonetheless this insidious offense is so prevalent these days... and seems to be increasing, brazenly depicted on TV and movie screens as a totally acceptable practice. Please be careful, beloved; don't think that it could never happen to you. The enemy of your soul lurks in the shadows waiting for the opportune moment. Be wise, heed the word of the Lord. There is great destruction awaiting those who indulge in extramarital sexual relations. Do not play the fool; run away from any occasion of sin. Yes, God is merciful but the consequences of this sin are disastrous!

Resisting Sexual Temptation

"If your right eye causes you to sin, pluck it out and cast it from you; for it is more profitable for you that one of your members perish, than for your whole body to be cast into hell." Matthew 5:29

You may ask for prayer, you may even belong to an accountability group. This is all well and good, but why do you still succumb to sexual temptation? Dear Christian, have you plucked out the source of your problem? Is it your computer, or the things that you watch on TV, the books and magazines that you read; what do you allow yourself to see and hear?

It seems that everywhere you turn these days, sex is being promoted; society is increasingly endorsing sexual sin, even perversions... but this does not give you an excuse. Reread what Jesus said: *"If your right eye causes you to sin, pluck it out and cast it from you; for it is more profitable for you that one of your members perish, than for your whole body to be cast into hell"* (Matt 5:29). Incredible! The Lord is very serious about this matter of resisting temptation. He speaks of taking extreme measures... doing whatever is necessary to avoid sin. It would be very wise to heed His word.

If your computer is the source of temptation buy some protective software and have a family member set the password. Otherwise, get rid of your Internet access. If you are tempted to buy sexually explicit material, go to exotic clubs, or patronize prostitutes, you must stay away from these places. Literally walk, run, or drive in a different direction so that you don't have to pass these occasions to sin. Do you understand? Do whatever is necessary!

Here are a few other recommendations to aid in your stance against sexual sin: Don't watch TV programs or read articles that promote sexual themes...even if they are not pornographic. Dress yourself quickly after bathing. Don't go to beaches where you are surrounded by those wearing seductive swimsuits. (Find a spot on the beach where you are able to turn away from lustful gazing.) *"But I say to you that whoever looks at a woman to lust for her has already committed adultery with her in his heart"* (Matt 5:28). Stop wearing sexy clothes. You will attract the kind of attention that may eventually lead you into sin. Avoid sexual conversations and jokes.

Is there a certain someone at work or at church that stirs you to temptation? Dear saint, why would you place yourself in jeopardy by maintaining contact with this individual? Too many sorry fools have said, "I can handle this," just before they fell. Break that relationship now! Stop kidding yourself; there are several things you can do to avoid compromising situations. Jesus is very serious about you gaining victory in this area of your life. How serious are you?

The Power of Example

"For as by one man's disobedience many were made sinners, so also by one Man's obedience many will be made righteous." Rom. 5:19

We all know that this scripture speaks of Adam's sin and Jesus' work of redemption. But it also brings to mind another vital truth: the power of example. You see, one man's disobedience *can* cause many to sin. There are people watching you, dear Christian. Some are waiting for you to fail so that they will have an excuse. They will tell themselves, "If it's OK for them to do, so can I." Let's use divorce as an example... A marriage is in serious trouble, and there does not seem to be much hope of repairing it; you are ready to give up. God is watching, beloved... and so are other couples with similar problems. What will you do? You know that God hates divorce; He is a God of reconciliation. Surely, this is the most agonizing time of your life, but if you choose the easy way out, you will not only miss what the Lord desires to do in you, and in your family, but you may become a stumbling block to others. There is a lot more riding on this decision than you think.

On the other hand, if you choose to seek counseling and do whatever is necessary, as painful as that may be, God will be pleased and will supply the needed grace. And eventually, as you learn self-sacrificing love (agape), your marriage will be healed. Those couples within your sphere of influence, who wrestle with difficulties, may take courage upon hearing of your success, and decide to work on their marriage as well. So, also by your obedience, many will be persuaded toward righteousness.

The Art of Listening

"Listen carefully to my speech, and to my declaration with your ears." Job 13:17

Verbal communication is such an interesting skill. Two distinct personalities with differing thoughts try to express themselves to one another. Of course, using proper vocabulary is an essential part of it all, but have you considered that even when using common language, many people don't fully understand what the other is trying to say? The spoken word is being filtered through the hearer's past experiences and personality (emotional makeup.) For example, if someone has low self-esteem, or has in some way been offended, they may actually perceive a complement to be an insult! It is truly amazing that anyone is able to clearly communicate their thoughts and feelings about any given topic...and have them totally understood in the manner in which they were expressed.

If you are conversing face to face, the added complexity of facial expressions can make it even more confusing, either helping or hindering the receptivity of the message because body language sometimes contradicts the words that are being uttered. So many things have been thoroughly messed up do to misunderstandings and misinterpretations. Dear servant of God, knowing this, strive to understand what others are saying to you, and also strive to make yourself understood. The Holy Spirit will help you.

The best place to start: simply take the time to listen to what the other person is saying. Many people tend to listen only half-heartedly. They are too busy rehearsing silently in their heads what they are going to say next... Or, they override what the other person is saying, reacting to a single comment without waiting for the entire concept to be fully stated. Please learn to wait and take in all that the other person is saying. Repeat back to them what you believe they said, and if you don't grasp it, please ask them to explain themselves; this is merely common sense. One more thing, listen to yourself once in a while. Are you the one doing all of the talking; are you dominating the conversation? Allow the other person equal time. Please be slow to speak and quick to listen.

Kindness

"Let, I pray, Your merciful kindness be for my comfort, according to Your word to Your servant. Let Your tender mercies come to me, that I may live" Psalm 119:76-77 *"And the natives showed us unusual kindness; for they kindled a fire and made us all welcome, because of the rain that was falling and because of the cold."* Acts 28:2 *"What is desired in a man is kindness"* Proverbs 19:22

Dear believer, you can be sure of this: our God is very kind. For certain, you will find no one who is kinder, more merciful, more compassionate, and more loving. This is who God is! There is no doubt that He has shown His kindness to you on numerous occasions whether you have recognized it or not. Beloved, if God has so loved you, shouldn't you demonstrate this kindness to others? Let these few words from Mother Teresa serve as a reminder for you today.

"At all times and within reach of every hand, spread love wherever you go, first of all in your own house. Give love to your children, to your husband or wife, to the next-door neighbor. Let no one ever come to you without leaving happier. Be the living expression of God's kindness, kindness in your face, kindness in your eyes, kindness in your smile, kindness in your warm greeting!"

Humble Yourself

"...Yes, all of you be submissive to one another, and be clothed with humility, for God resists the proud, but gives grace to the humble. Therefore humble yourselves under the mighty hand of God, that He may exalt you in due time." 1Peter 5:5-6

So, you are being asked to take the lower place again; how do you feel about that? No one really likes to become less, especially when the world tells you, 'bigger is better.' Your flesh cries for recognition and appreciation, but God looks for humility and lowliness. Yes, beloved, God is calling you, once again, to get lower; surely you recognize His ways by now. He builds using burnt bricks, gold refined by fire. The lower, the better!

When you have two opportunities set before you, always check your spirit before accepting the one that pays the most and gives you the best exposure. Surely your flesh would love that, but is this God's will? Perhaps, but then again, maybe not. Are you humble enough not to be a hindrance to the release of God's power flowing through you? You're not really "dead" yet, are you? Think about it: do you want to be a big fish in a little pond or are you willing to become a little fish in a big pond... and grow bigger? Maybe you would prefer the former, but you will be settling for much less than your full potential. To achieve your optimum you must humble yourself.

You see, beloved, there are so many who look good, sound good, and act like they have power... but they do not. In God's economy, humility, servanthood, and selflessness are the ways of true effectiveness and power. Your quest: to love God above all things, to love others as yourself, and to be willing to pay any price for the glory and honor of His name to be proclaimed throughout the earth. Will you trust Him once again to perform His word? *"Therefore humble yourselves under the mighty hand of God, that He may exalt you in due time."* There is true greatness in store for you... if you will only trust Him!

The Supremacy Of Love

"And now abide faith, hope, love, these three; but the greatest of these is love." 1Corinthians 13:13

Who doesn't strongly desire to have the faith that could move mountains, do miracles, and bring healing to the sick? How effective you would be in all that you do. Or, perhaps you would desire to have great spiritual revelation and the knowledge of things to come. Your teaching and preaching would be absolutely stunning. Every minister longs for such grace, but please remember this: love is greater!

Take another sober look at this famous passage: *"Though I speak with the tongues of men and of angels, but have not love, I have become sounding brass or a clanging cymbal. And though I have the gift of prophecy, and understand all mysteries and all knowledge, and though I have all faith, so that I could remove mountains, but have not love, I am nothing. And though I bestow all my goods to feed the poor, and though I give my body to be burned, but have not love, it profits me nothing"* (1Cor 13: 1-3). Please God, give your Church... men and women of faith and power; how we need You to do this. Nevertheless, love is greater!

Dear reader, you may never remove a mountain, or have a grand revelation (Here's hoping that you do), but at this very moment you have within your grasp the ability to love. The Spirit of the living God, the all-glorious Lover of the world, dwells within you. Step aside and allow Him to love through you today. Give to the poor; visit the sick and the imprisoned; spend time with someone who is lonely, spend time with your family... not from a sense of duty or any other religious motive, but simply because you love God, and love others as yourself. Love is greater, beloved; pursue love!

I Knew You Before

"Before I formed you in the womb I knew you; before you were born I sanctified you; I ordained you a prophet to the nations." Jer. 1:5

This scripture is very intriguing, isn't it? God is telling the prophet that before he was formed in his mother's womb, *"I knew you."* What does this mean, disciple? Obviously, his body was not yet formed; God must have been speaking of his spirit. God knew Jeremiah's spirit before he was formed, before he was born! And not only did God know him, He had set him apart for a purpose.

Now, imagine this: before *you* were born, in fact before *you* were even formed in the womb, God knew *you*. He may have had a conversation with your spirit in heaven that went something like this: *"I love you and you are Mine. I have set you apart and have a good plan for your life, a mission for you to fulfill. You will be sent to earth and placed in human form. Because you will be born in sin, you will be separated from Me; you will be lost... In fact, you will have no Spirit-life in you. But I will cause you to seek Me, and allow you to find Me; I will fill you with My Holy Spirit and you will love Me and serve Me, according to My purposes. When you return home, I will bless you and honor you and we will remain together for eternity! However, you will not remember any part of this conversation, but you will remember My voice. Trust Me; I will be in touch with you."* (paraphrased T.D. Jakes)

And then... you are formed in your mother's womb, and you are born into this sin-infested world. You are placed into the family that God chose for you, the city, country, and the culture... at the perfect juncture in time. You live in the neighborhoods that God preordained, and go to the schools, and have the jobs that God has ordered. He speaks to you at different times in your life, just enough to keep you on track. (Most of the time you are not sure that it is He, but the voice is vaguely familiar.) He also ordains, or allows the numerous experiences (good and bad) that are necessary to cause you to seek Him, and will help prepare you to fulfill your mission. He sends others into your life to explain the way of salvation and gives you abundant grace, allowing you to submit to His glorious redemption through faith in Jesus Christ... and ultimately, you will begin to love Him above all things. Your salvation and has always been in God's heart, beloved; it was always His plan for you. Happy is the one who does not resist the wooing of the Holy Spirit. If the Almighty One loves you this much and can orchestrate your life to such a degree, don't you think He can adequately bring you to the next phase of your journey... to the fulfillment of your destiny?

Ascending To The Lowest Place

"And this will be the sign to you: You will find a Babe wrapped in swaddling cloths, lying in a manger." Luke 2:12

How you long to see the Glory of God made manifest as in the days of Solomon, when the glory cloud filled the temple. His presence was so intense, so tangible, that the priests could not stand to minister (2Chr. 5:13-14). You have delighted yourself in the Lord and have sought His face in worship conferences and special prayer services. These meetings have been good, but never as glorious as you would have desired; and this begs the question: "How can I see God's glory made manifest in the world today?"

Dear servant of the Most High, understand the lowly state in which Jesus came, *"wrapped in swaddling cloths, lying in a manger."* His glory was made manifest in humility! He ascended to the lowest place and became a servant. Can you imagine the King of Glory washing feet? He suffered and died, crucified as a criminal!

Do you truly want to see His glory? Don't strive for it by reaching to the high and lofty things that are found in places of grandeur. The glory of God will probably not fall upon the comfortable, singing the latest worship chorus. Seek for His glory by descending to the lowest place. This is what Jesus did. Go to the prisons and hospitals and ghettos of this world. Find the darkest of places and see Him shine ever so brightly as you minister to those in desperate need. Go in humility; go in lowliness... wash feet! His power is demonstrated in your weakness and His love in your servanthood. If you cannot get lower than false humility and peripheral religious activity, you will probably miss the awesome display of His manifest presence. Ascend to the lowest place and behold the glory of God!

Glory in This

"Thus says the Lord: 'Let not the wise man glory in his wisdom, let not the mighty man glory in his might, nor let the rich man glory in his riches; but let him who glories glory in this, that he understands and knows Me, that I am the Lord, exercising loving-kindness, judgment, and righteousness in the earth. For in these I delight,' says the Lord." Jeremiah 9:23-24

Dear one, do you think that God is impressed with your gifts and talents? Come now; He was the One who gave them to you! With no effort whatsoever the Almighty can cause a donkey to talk. Why should He think it a great accomplishment that you can preach, prophecy or heal the sick?

Those things that please God are those that issue from your surrendered heart: sacrificial love, sacrificial giving, radical obedience, and true humility. Don't think of yourself more highly than you ought. Do not glory in what you can do, or say, or in your position of status and authority. Glory in this: you are His; and you know Him; and you are beginning to understand His ways!

Is there really a need for constant affirmation, a need to appease your inferiority complex, or your wounds of rejection, by striving for success, seeking attention, or looking for applause? Why do you need to tell yourself, over and over again, that you are "something"... looking at your achievements and comparing yourself with others? You are affirmed in Christ; you are His! Surrender all, beloved, even the very depths of your needy personality; you are now living for the glory and honor of His name!

Conflict Resolution

"I, therefore, the prisoner of the Lord, beseech you to walk worthy of the calling with which you were called, with all lowliness and gentleness, with longsuffering, bearing with one another in love, endeavoring to keep the unity of the Spirit in the bond of peace." Ephesians 4:1-3

Dear saint, this is a very important truth; please take it into serious consideration: Men and women handle conflict differently. One party wants to resolve the issue while the other seems to pull back. Of course, this is not a new revelation, but why does a man shy away from a potentially volatile discussion (argument)? Dear woman, it is usually not because he is afraid of intimacy, as some have suggested. There are many men who are very good at expressing their inner feelings. Men are afraid of conflict because conflict stimulates a reflexive physiological response. Do you understand? Among other things, God has fashioned man to defend and protect. When conflict arises, hormones are secreted that can make a man feel aggressive. If he is confronted by an angry wife, he becomes very uncomfortable and does not know what to do with this surge of adrenaline. He certainly cannot act-out in violent behavior... so he defends himself with a few gruff words, turns, and walks away.

Husband, these feelings are very natural, but certainly no excuse for losing your temper; learn to control yourself. Learn to listen to your wife before she feels the need to confront you. You must take the time to communicate, allowing her to share her heart with you. Wife, please understand how a man functions, and learn a better strategy for discussing your needs. Without a doubt, you must express yourself (Your husband cannot read your mind.), but learn how your spouse can best hear and understand your needs and concerns. God will help!

One of the first steps toward better communication would be to simply ask your partner this question: "What would be the best way for me to express my needs and concerns to you? I love you and don't want to nag. I know that you love me too, and want to hear what I have to say."

The Kingdom of Heaven

"Not everyone who says to Me, `Lord, Lord,' shall enter the kingdom of heaven, but he who does the will of My Father in heaven." Matthew 7:21

So much has been written about the Kingdom of Heaven, the Kingdom of God. What does it all mean; do you know? Let us ponder this mystery. Matthew is the only writer who uses the term *Kingdom of Heaven*; the other gospel writers use *Kingdom of God.* It is safe to conclude that these two terms are most often interchangeable.

The following is a magnificent description of the Kingdom written by Rufus Jones (1863-1948): *"The entire teaching of the Kingdom of God has a mystical aspect. It is a society, or fellowship, both in earth and heaven, both human and Divine. Its capital is not in some foreign land, its King is not a distant Sovereign; any member of the Kingdom at any spot on earth can see Him if his heart is pure. The Kingdom is the life of God exhibited in human fellowship. It is the heavenly life appearing here in the midst of time, the sway of God in human hearts. It is a human society that grows on and flowers out and ripens its fruit, because its unseen roots are in God the Life."*

Throughout the scriptures Jesus divulges the secrets of the Kingdom. He says, "the Kingdom is like a man who sowed good seed, like a mustard seed, like leaven, and a treasure hidden in a field, like a merchant seeking a beautiful pearl, etc." He also states that it will not come as one looks for some type of external manifestation…as with an earthly Kingdom; the Kingdom of God is within you!

Dear disciple, have you entered in? It is a wonderful place of abiding peace, spiritual power, and abundant fruitfulness, a place of obedience and abandonment of self, intimate communion and childlike faith. In fact, you cannot enter without child-like faith. You must be born again! Those who humble themselves and become like a child will be the greatest in this kingdom… and some who are now first, will be last, and the last will be first.

In God's kingdom, you must give to receive, become a servant to be a leader, and submit to authority to be given authority. You must forgive to be forgiven, and you must "die," to truly live. Only those who are willing to deny self and follow Christ to Calvary will fully experience this glorious kingdom. Those who cling to the security and pleasure of this life will barely cross its borders; they will practice religion instead.

It is possible to gain a glimpse of this kingdom by stepping into the vestibule for a brief season. It is also possible to enter deeply and remain forever.

The Gift

"For by grace you have been saved through faith, and that not of yourselves; it is the gift of God, not of works, lest anyone should boast. For we are His workmanship, created in Christ Jesus for good works, which God prepared beforehand that we should walk in them." Ephesians 2:8-10

A close friend has just given you a wonderful gift, something that you really wanted and needed. Nonetheless, you continue to pester them until they divulge how much they paid for it; and then you reach for your checkbook and write them a check for the entire cost of the gift. Beloved, this would be rather insulting, wouldn't it? Even more than an insult, it would be cause for offense. This gift can no longer be considered a *gift* because you purchased it yourself! The love, effort, and sacrifice made to acquire your present has now become cheapened, demeaned.

Unfortunately, so many people (usually because of faulty doctrine) treat the precious gift of salvation in the same manner. Please reread Ephesians 2:8-10; also consider Romans 6:23: *"For the wages of sin is death, but the **gift** of God is eternal life in Christ Jesus our Lord."*

Dear Christian, you are not a Christian because you have earned your salvation, nor are you in the process of earning it. Your salvation has been purchased by Jesus Christ, by His blood, His suffering and brutal death, by His glorious resurrection. The only begotten Son of God loves you and gave Himself for you, paying an indescribable price for your freedom! Do you understand?

You may say, "but *'faith without works is dead'*" (James 2:20), and rightly so. As a Christian, you must do good works. However, please note that you are not saved *by* your good works, but saved *for* good works (Eph. 2:10). There is a glaring difference. God has a purpose for your life; He freely saved you by His great sacrifice, and now expects you to do those things that He has prepared for you to do.

What an insult it must be to the Lord for anyone to think that they should do more than repent and graciously receive God's precious Gift... As it were, for them to take out their checkbook and try to pay, by good works, for the unparalleled gift of eternal life. Be careful, beloved; rest completely upon His merit and not upon your own. *"...not by works of righteousness which we have done, but according to His mercy He saved us..."* (Titus 3:4-5).

Striving About Words

"Remind them of these things, charging them before the Lord not to strive about words to no profit, to the ruin of the hearers. Be diligent to present yourself approved to God, a worker who does not need to be ashamed, rightly dividing the word of truth." 2Timothy 2:14-15

The discussion is getting a little intense, even a bit heated. The "junior Bible scholars" quote the passage, exchange cross-references and with thumbs in their respective lexicons, get ready to define the next Greek cognate noun. However, the point being made will help no one to become more holy, nor will it draw anyone closer to God. This is an intellectual debate, beloved, and a useless vanity. And to make matters worse, there are non-believers or new Christians within earshot. Will they benefit from your discussion? Of course not, they will probably be harmed. The non-believer will see nothing but disunity (again!) and the new believer will become confused.

The doctrinal purist places more emphasis on a single word than is appropriate. And although they don't realize it, give a higher regard to their scriptural interpretation than to Jesus Himself! The intellectual, on the other hand, will delve into the Word to satisfy their inquisitiveness, giving mental ascent to spiritual truth. The proud will adamantly defend their position to a fault. But the humble and the spiritually hungry will receive a morsel from the Lord's table and be fed. Ahhhh, fresh bread!

Dear disciple, did you get the point? There is seldom a need to publicly defend your doctrinal position or to display your intellectual understanding of the Word. This could actually be harmful to the listener. *"We know that we all have knowledge. Knowledge puffs up, but love edifies. And if anyone thinks that he knows anything, he knows nothing yet as he ought to know"* (1Cor. 8:1). Let your heart be filled with love and servanthood and a genuine hunger for the Word of the Lord, a word to your heart... not for your mind alone.

Blessings From Above

"I have shown you in every way, by laboring like this, that you must support the weak. And remember the words of the Lord Jesus, that He said, `It is more blessed to give than to receive.'" Acts 20:35

How we all want the blessings of God, more of His Spirit, more of His love and power. Material blessings would also be nice once in awhile. *The Prayer of Jabez* (1Chr.4:10) has become quite popular over these past years, and what truth has been expressed! This generation needs to revisit the "blessing principle" as set forth by Bruce Wilkinson. "Bless me abundantly, Lord! Fill my *blessing box* to overflowing, enabling me to spill out a river of blessings to others."

Nevertheless, Bruce points out that there are deeper levels of blessing than simply receiving good things from God. The greatest of blessings are obtained through the sacrificial giving of oneself, whether that be finances, your time, the sweat of your brow or your intercessory prayers.

If you should desire for God to bring you to this place of abundant blessing, ask Him. But don't be surprised when you begin to be interrupted by those needing your help... and sometimes asking for more of something than you can afford to give. Will you see these requests as an opportunity to be wonderfully blessed, or will you consider them to be an intrusion into your already busy life? How many rewards have been left unclaimed because you have stepped past these opportunities, considering them to be an annoyance. And instead you complain and take your ease in front of the TV or choose to do something equally unfruitful.

Beloved, the richest blessings are reserved for those who, with complete abandonment to the purposes of God, humble themselves and become a servant. It is far more blessed to give than to receive!

See Jesus

"...Assuredly, I say to you, inasmuch as you did it to one of the least of these My brethren, you did it to Me." Matthew 25:40

This is especially for caregivers, those who minister to the sick, care for children or the elderly, or the handicapped. Dear servant, may God bless you abundantly; for you have chosen to serve in the lowliest of places. Few notice or ever realize the degree of your sacrifice... long hours, little pay, very little gratitude; but the Lord knows and He will reward you accordingly.

The demands are great and discouragement is not uncommon. There are times when you are literally run ragged by the hectic pace. At other times, boredom and the mundane can be overwhelming. And servants are asked to do such humble things; no amount of money would be sufficient. You get tired, sometimes very weary. Be careful, dear servant; so many caregivers overextend themselves and don't receive the necessary rest. After a season, you can become emotionally drained and physically exhausted. Even with the love of Jesus in your heart, you can burn out. Do you feel that way now? When you become like this, it is easy to loose your compassion and loose your temper. The Lord understands, and He will help you.

Mother Teresa, while caring for Calcutta's poor and dying, discovered an invaluable secret, something that gave her strength and joy in the midst of absolute squalor... for many years. You too can practice what she had learned: *She saw Jesus in the faces of those whom she served.* Would you wash the feet of Jesus or clean His soiled garments? What an honor, what a privilege! Would you feed Him? Would you visit Him if He were lonely or incarcerated? Surely you would! Don't you see? The parent that you care for, the child, the one who has soiled themselves or needs to be fed... this *is* Jesus! He has come to you disguised as someone in need. Don't be fooled by their personality, behavior or appearance. See Jesus! Can you recognize Him; will you minister to Him? *"...Assuredly, I say to you, inasmuch as you did it to one of the least of these My brethren, you did it to Me"* (Matt. 25:40).

You have been seeking intimacy with God? What could be more

intimate or more personal than meeting His "needs?" Many Christians stand in church and worship from afar; but when you serve in this manner, your worship actually becomes hands-on. You are being given the opportunity to touch the very face of God!

Take the time to rest, beloved; get away for a vacation. Ask for assistance! If you are caring for a loved one at home, even if you must pay someone to relieve you for a few hours, do it. The Lord has given you the privilege of servanthood, but He also knows your physical and emotional limitations. There is a notable difference between a trudging forward with persevering endurance... and doing this work with a measure of wisdom. Be wise. The Lord will renew your strength and your compassion.

The Bible

"Your word is a lamp to my feet and a light to my path." Ps 119:105

Dear disciple, have you been feeding upon His Word lately? A devotional reading is no substitute for reading the Bible. This is simply a reminder to do so. The following, author unknown, is an extravagant synopsis of all that is included within: "The Bible contains: the mind of God, the state of man, the way of salvation, the doom of sinners, and the happiness of believers. Its doctrines are holy, its precepts are binding, its histories are true, and its decisions are immutable. Read it to be wise, believe it to be safe, and practice it to be holy. It contains light to direct you, food to support you, and comfort to cheer you. It is the traveler's map, the pilgrim's staff, the pilot's compass, the soldier's sword, and the Christian's charter.

It's where paradise is restored, heaven opened, and the gates of hell disclosed. Christ is its grand subject, our good its design, and the glory of God its end. It should fill the memory, rule the heart, and guide the feet. Read it slowly, frequently, and prayerfully. It is a mine of wealth, a paradise of glory, and a river of pleasure. It is given you in life, will be open at judgment, and be remembered forever. It involves the highest responsibility, rewards the greatest labor, and condemns all who trifle with its holy contents." Read it today, beloved.

Jesus, the Prophet

"Therefore the sisters sent to Him, saying, 'Lord, behold, he whom You love is sick.' When Jesus heard that, He said, 'This sickness is not unto death, but for the glory of God, that the Son of God may be glorified through it.' Now Jesus loved Martha and her sister and Lazarus. So, when He heard that he was sick, He stayed two more days in the place where He was." John 11:3-6

What an interesting passage. Lazarus was sick; his sisters sent someone for Jesus to come heal Him and *"when He heard that he was sick, He stayed two more days in the place where He was."* It seemed as though Jesus wasn't really concerned. He nonchalantly replies, *"This sickness is not unto death, but for the glory of God..."* and then goes about His business, delaying for a total of four days before He shows up. He purposely waited for Lazarus to die!

Mary may have been angry with Jesus when she ran to meet Him. *"If You had been here, my brother would not have died."* After all, she had been at his bedside for several days... watching her loved one suffer, struggling to stay alive. Jesus didn't do what she thought He should do, when she thought that He should do it.

There are a few points that we can glean from this passage. First and foremost, this story is really not about Lazarus or Mary; neither is it about suffering and death. Beloved, it is clearly a revealing of the manifest presence of God! It was not recorded for us to learn more about Lazarus, but about our magnificent Jesus. The Holy One is magnified and glorified! God may allow you to go through difficulty so that when He finally does intervene, your family, neighbors and co-workers will witness His marvelous works. Secondly, in these verses, we can see Jesus as prophet. A prophet usually looks beyond the present; He sees the future. His seemingly cold remarks and delayed action showed little concern for Lazarus. But Jesus was not regarding the present situation; He already saw the outcome.

Perhaps you have felt like Mary, (or the disciples in the storm struck boat). You question Jesus' concern for your current problem. Dear one, God sees past your problem. He already knows that everything is going be just fine... even better than you could imagine. Have faith, disciple, trust Him; see as He sees.

How we struggle to stay "alive," no doubt like Lazarus did. Our flesh wants to live. The Master will delay giving comfort, encouragement or deliverance so that your self-life will suffer another fatal blow. Remember, this self that you love so much, often hinderers the work of God. Don't be angry with the Lord if He should seem slow to respond. This is for your good and for God's glory.

Clothed With Humility

" ...Yes, all of you be submissive to one another, and be clothed with humility, for God resists the proud, but gives grace to the humble."
1Peter 5:5

Anyone who has worked on a troubled marriage or resolved a family quarrel has learned a bit about dying to self. Overcoming a doctrinal difference or any other type of church wrangling offers another fine example of death to self. In order to truly resolve matters like these, it takes a bit more than a simple compromise; it takes a piece of your heart. If you are one of these, congratulations! You are learning to forgive and to lay down your life for the sake of another. You are growing to maturity.

However, those who demand their rights, foster a prideful love of self, often disguised as a just cause. They divorce instead of reconcile, trashing the covenant made before God. Or they become estranged from siblings or parents after a serious quarrel. If the upset occurs in church... when disagreeing with a peripheral doctrine, or for that matter, what color the carpet should be, they move out, and move on. Beloved, let's hope that this is not you. You know this to be displeasing to the Lord. He desires for you to be an overcomer, not a quitter. He is looking for a loving, tender heart that will submit to another, not a willful heart that finds no contentment unless things are done my way. Please remember, the Lord has allowed the adversity to help refine you. If you always take the path of least resistance you will lose in the end. Seeking your own personal happiness over the expressed will of God will leave you empty and fruitless. Submit, and grow!

Your Perception of Time

"All flesh is as grass, and all the glory of man as the flower of the grass. The grass withers, and its flower falls away, but the word of the Lord endures forever." 1Pet 1:24-25

Have you ever wondered why time seems to pass so quickly, especially as you grow older? I have spoken with many elderly folks and nearly all of them say the same thing: "Be sure to do the things that you really want to do while you are young and able. Life goes by so fast." It hardly seems that way when you are five years old, waiting for your birthday or Christmas; it takes forever. One would assume that busyness would cause time to pass quickly; and it does. Nonetheless, after your life is saturated with responsibility, you would think that your perception of time would remain constant, but not so. With each passing year the days and months seem to whiz by at an increasingly rapid pace. How can this be? There are still 24 hours per day, 365 days per year.

I pondered this great mystery and mused before the Lord... and then one day, a twelve year old gave me some insight. He said, "When you are seven years old, one year is one-seventh of your life; when you are seventy, one year is one-seventieth of your life." Eureka! It dawned on me that we can only perceive time, its passing, according to the time that we have experienced. I mean, our grasp or under-standing of time is completely dictated by the number of years that we have lived. When you are five years old, one year seems like such a lengthy period because you have only lived for five years. Therefore, one year is a large chunk of your life. When you are fifty, one year is a much smaller portion. That is why it seems to pass more quickly! God is so perfect; perhaps He has planned this perceived speed-up of time especially for the homesick soul who longs to be with Him in heaven.

Dear child, now that we have solved this age-old enigma, is there any practical application? Simply put: "Life goes by so very fast; only what is done for Christ will last." According to the leading of the Holy Spirit... Do it now! Worship Him now! Serve Him now! Love Him with all of your heart, NOW!

On Being A Man

"From the days of John the Baptist until now, the kingdom of heaven has been forcefully advancing, and forceful men lay hold of it." Matthew 11:12 (NIV)

Dear man of God, what does it really mean to be masculine? It seems as though this present generation has become confused, maybe because there are few good examples or role models. The pendulum has swung to opposite extremes, either to some form of machismo, or to a sissified femininity. However, this must change, beloved, if we are to become imitators of Christ... if we are to train-up the next generation of men.

TV and movies, over the past few decades have increasingly portrayed the man of the house as a bumbling, emasculated idiot, and at best, a mild mannered, "nice guy." But is that who he should be? John Eldredge, in his compelling revelatory work, *Wild at Heart,* depicts the true nature of man to be a William Wallace (*Braveheart*) type, born to fight a battle, "with an adventure to live and a beauty to rescue." Not a mealy-mouthed coward, unable or unwilling to fight the good fight.

Consider Jesus, dear man; He is your example of true manhood: tender and loving, yet bold and courageous. He humbly surrendered Himself to the purposes of His Father while resisting the temptations of the devil, wielding the Word of God, His mighty weapon. He boldly spoke the truth, rebuking the Pharisees, even over-turning the tables of the moneychangers. He could also weep unashamedly with those who mourned... but He was never out of control. He wasn't afraid to be different. Jesus was diligent to accomplish His mission; He endured and persevered in the midst of intense opposition. He loved His Father; He loved the people; He gave His all. You are in the process of being conformed to His image, mighty man. Press on!

God-Given Appetite

"The laborer's appetite works for him; his hunger drives him on."
Proverbs 16:26 (NIV)

Hunger for food, sexual desire (libido), the need to be successful, the thirst for adventure, the quest for God: these are all very natural, providentially inspired appetites of the male gender...inherent to his nature. It would be wise to understand this, dear Christian. God has placed these drives within you for a purpose. Consider the sexual urge: This is of God... and what a wonderful gift it is. How foolish to blame the devil for all of the sexual feelings that come your way. Of course, this is not to say that some sexual thoughts are not implanted by demons, but God has given you a sexual appetite, first and foremost, for the purpose of procreation. Food was made to be pleasurable so that we would be sure to eat. In like manner, the Creator intended that much pleasure be derived from sexual relations thus ensuring the continuation of the human race. The Lord also delights in your pleasure. He loves you!

In the normal flow of things, depending upon your libido, sexual thoughts will come, and in some cases, become more frequent the longer you go without sexual relations. (Just because these thoughts and feelings are normal it doesn't mean that you can dwell on them; you must overcome them.) This is why Paul advises the unmarried to marry, rather than *"burn with passion."* He also reminds the married couple not to deprive one another, least they fall prey to the enemy (1Cor.7: 5).

After relations with your spouse, these thoughts / feelings should subside... and will again increase after a few days or weeks depending upon your own body. Unfortunately many Christians consider this recurrence as a demonic temptation instead of a normal body function... and begin the usual wrestling match with self-condemnation... lamenting, "Will I ever get past these thoughts?"

Surely you must exercise self-control with this or any other appetite. Sexual immorality is a sin, just as gluttony and selfish ambition are appetites that have gone awry. Do you understand, dear man? God has placed certain things within you... for your good and for the blessing of others. Recognize their origin, but you must also learn to control yourself. By the power of the Holy Spirit you can do this.

The extra surge of adrenaline that a man experiences when confronted or feels threatened is also natural and God-given. But if it is not controlled, violent words or actions will follow... this too is sin.

Cheap Grace

"What shall we say then? Shall we continue in sin that grace may abound? Certainly not! How shall we who died to sin live any longer in it?" Romans 6:1-2

Dietrich Bonhoffer, a 20th Century German theologian, was perhaps the first to coin the phrase "cheap grace." Have you ever heard this term? Among other things, it means an abuse of the application of the precious blood of Jesus. Rather than fighting the good fight of faith and wrestling with the rulers of wickedness, the abuser of grace simply submits to temptation without much of a struggle and then appropriates "the blood" to cover over their sin. This isn't you, beloved, is it? True repentance requires you to turn from sin with the full intention of never doing it again... (Of course, with God's help.)

You do not need to fight this fight alone. How much better it would be to confess your sin to another who is trustworthy... and ask for their prayers during a time of temptation. If you are serious about overcoming, you must do whatever is necessary. In this day and age, there are support groups for nearly every area of weakness, but be careful, steer clear of groups that merely pat you on the back and in essence say, "you're OK; we all do it." These can actually encourage repeated failure by glossing over sin.

In fact, you should always feel badly after committing a sin; you never want someone to make you feel OK about it. In saying this, let it be clear that feelings of guilt and condemnation that come after true repentance are not of God and are quite counterproductive. If this is your experience, receive some godly counsel. At times, it is very beneficial to hear someone declare to you, "your sins are forgiven."

Many of us are weak, dear saint, fumbling and failing; our flesh is weak. But you must not give in without a fight. *"Put on the full armor of God... and having done ALL, stand."* This is what Paul told the Ephesians. Call on the Lord and hide in Him; He will make a way of escape. Get help; ask a confidant for prayer. You may have to distract yourself; the battleground is usually in your mind. Get up; get moving; do something else. If temptation presents itself right before you, turn away; flee! Remember, when you successfully resist a temptation, it becomes a little easier to resist the next one, but when you give in, it is a little easier to give into the next one. You must take a stand sometime! Draw the battle line NOW! Do not fold at the first sign of temptation. Fight! In the power of the Holy Spirit, submit to God, resist the devil and he will flee!

Some who are addicted wait until their lives are shattered, their families destroyed... until the pain becomes greater than the pleasure. Many fools have said, "I can handle this" and they eventually lost everything. You don't have to let it go this far; ask for help NOW! The Lord has been waiting for your complete surrender. Give Him every aspect of your life. He will help you; trust Him!

Leaving Town?

"Trust in the Lord, and do good; dwell in the land, and feed on His faithfulness. Delight yourself also in the Lord, and He shall give you the desires of your heart. Commit your way to the Lord, trust also in Him, and He shall bring it to pass." Psalm 37:3-5

Did the Lord call you to this region? I mean, you either moved here or were raised here... and at some point you must have heard God tell you that this is where you are to be. He may have said: "Go to that place and start a ministry ... or support one." "This is your new job, this is where you are to raise your family." "Here is the neighborhood that I chose for you to live in, the school to attend, etc." If this is true, why are you thinking about moving again? The call of God has led you to this very place.

Adversity comes and goes, dear one. It is that way everywhere you live... because it is God's training ground. Remember, He is in control of all things and allows obstacles and difficulties for your spiritual growth and development. If you run from this challenge you will just have to face it someplace else. However, if you have been called here for a specific mission, your leaving town will hinder the purposes of God.

Obviously things didn't happen the way you thought they would. You should realize by now that they seldom do. Don't be discouraged; be of good cheer. Trust the Faithful One. You know that He will not abandon you. If He has truly called you here, He will make a way. In the meantime, praise Him and give thanks. Do whatever is necessary to maintain your foothold in the community. Take a lower paying job; make do with what you have; hang in there. The Lord has a good plan... and this time of testing is part of your preparation. At this point, many take the easy way out and end up settling for far less. But you, dear disciple, are running this race to win. Press on! Oh how wonderful it will be to enter into the fullness of your God-given purpose!

Your Favorite Sin

"...let us lay aside every weight, and the sin which so easily ensnares us..." Hebrews 12:1

How often you espouse an undying allegiance to our Lord. "I will do your bidding, Jesus; use me!" Nonetheless, there lingers within you a hindrance... something that stunts your spiritual growth and development, occasionally tarnishing your witness. Is it your pride, or perhaps a particular self-indulgent habit, your anger or critical spirit? What is it that you refuse to completely surrender? It is very unpopular to speak like this when much of the world wants to hear of God's love, mercy and grace. Most certainly, you are not disqualified because of your weakness. But for those desiring to win the prize, those who want to shake free from the mediocrity of this current form of anemic Christianity, it is absolutely essential to be challenged, rebuked and disciplined. Are you willing to receive this?

The Master lovingly affirms you and builds you up. His love is lavished upon you; blessing you far more than you (we) deserve. God is merciful, gracious, and slow to anger, abounding in mercy. He realizes that we are weak and flawed. He lovingly has referred to

155

us as *dust*, even *grass* that withers, but make no mistake: He requires you to get it right; He wants you to stop sinning!

In your struggle with self and sin, remember that the question of obedience is never *"Can I or can't I obey,"* but *"Will I or won't I?"* The scripture declares that you will not be tempted beyond what you can bear - the Lord makes a way of escape. Grace is abundant where sin abounds, but you must avail yourself. What are you actually doing to gain victory?

In the past, your pet sin has given you pleasure... or in some way afforded escape or gratification or comfort. This is why you have continued to do it. You thought that it fulfilled a need. And then God began to gently convict you. If you don't respond, He will probably increase the pressure until you begin to feel the sting, the downside of sin. No doubt, the pressure will increase until you submit to His will. However, things could be worse; God could leave you alone, giving you up to your own devices. (Now that's a scary thought.) Acknowledge your sin, beloved. It does no good to justify yourself or blame another. Surrender this sin to the Lord... and take all necessary measures and precautions to avoid reoccurrence.

Kissing His Wounds

"and they will mock Him, and scourge Him, and spit on Him, and kill Him. And the third day He will rise again." Mark 10:34

Can you imagine what was done for you at Calvary? Who could fathom the depth of God's love, unless it was demonstrated? Even so, full comprehension can hardly seem possible. The day is coming, however, when full understanding will burst into your reality. Jesus Himself will descend from heaven with all glory and splendor. The brightness of His coming will dispel all doubt. Jesus, the Lord of all, is also the Lover of your soul! You will look into His eyes and be overwhelmed by His presence. Some will tremble with fear; others will faint in dreadful remorse. But those who have longed for His appearing, will worship Him with awe and delight; falling at His feet, kissing Him, even kissing His wounds. You will finally comprehend the mystery of His love, and lavish upon Him your unending praise and gratitude. Dear Bride, your wedding is at hand!

Religion

"If anyone among you thinks he is religious, and does not bridle his tongue but deceives his own heart, this one's religion is useless. Pure and undefiled religion before God and the Father is this: to visit orphans and widows in their trouble, and to keep oneself unspotted from the world." James 1:26-27

The challenge does not lie in your ability to perform religious duties: going to church on Sunday, learning the tenants of your particular persuasion, memorizing scripture verses, giving an offering, and saying your prayers every night. Of course these things are worthwhile and they do require disciple and commitment, but is this what Christianity is all about? Some would think so.

The practice of religion has frequently hindered true spiritual life... causing the adherent to be satisfied with the *good* found in their activities rather than advancing to the *best*. All too often we consider ourselves to be good Christians because we attend church on Sunday, while falling far short in the areas that are vitally important: spending quiet-time with the Lord, learning to love the unlovable, forgiving the one who has offended you and asking for forgiveness when you are the offender, giving your money to those in need, comforting the broken-hearted, caring for your aging parents.

Be careful, beloved. Christianity is all about your heart attitude, coupled with a loving response, not dutiful religiosity.... a heart filled with love for God and for your neighbor, trusting, serving, giving and going as the Holy Spirit leads you.

What Should I Do?

"And those who know Your name will put their trust in You; for You, Lord, have not forsaken those who seek You". Psalm 9:10

A few things to consider when engulfed in a difficult situation:

Ask God! Take the time to seek His counsel. Don't react or respond in the flesh. The natural man always wants to take the easiest way out. Be careful; in prolonged conflict it is quite tempting to believe a deception. In fact, you may find yourself looking for someone to agree with your desire to give up: "It's OK to quit; you've endured this for long enough. You have to think about yourself now." Oh how pleasant, these words to the weary soul. But is this God?

What about all that He has spoken to you regarding endurance, perseverance and overcoming? Has that changed; has God changed His mind? Of course, everything within you wants to hear "YES, He is giving me release." But you must be absolutely certain. Even if He permits you to go, is this His perfect will? (Can you be fully satisfied with something less than His perfect will?) Far too many have abandon ship when it could have been brought safely into harbor; and in doing so have suffered untold loss. Ministries have declined and businesses have failed, families divided, and children gone wayward because someone would not stay the course.

Has He not kept you until this very moment? Surely He has been faithful in the midst of every storm. Nonetheless, here is the question of the day: Will you continue to trust Him?

Do you answer "Yes, I trust you, BUT....."? Shouldn't you say instead "Yes Lord, I trust you. Let your perfect will be accomplished in this situation. In the crucible of adversity conform me to Your image"?

Let it be perfectly clear that we are not encouraging you to stay in a physically abusive relationship. Go... get help now!

To Be Significant

Significant: important in effect or meaning, fairly large, substantial.

This is well worth discussing because most of humanity strives for some measure of significance... especially through the use of their gifts and talents. Those with creativity paint, sculpt, write books or play music etc. Some build structures, businesses or countries. Others find fulfillment in serving. The possibilities are endless. With six billion of us now inhabiting planet earth, how rewarding it would be to do something that would make you feel unique. Even some criminals are compelled to be the best at what they do!

We run into a problem though: What is considered significant to man, may not be so in the eyes of God. Men scramble for the world's attention, acquiring money and material possessions. Political and corporate power are coveted. We love titles, positions and platforms that say, "I'm somebody; I have arrived." Be careful, beloved; don't fall into this trap.

It is the small and obscure things that may be the most significant. For instance: when you spend time with your child, teaching, loving, encouraging, and correcting them, you are fashioning an arrow to be launched into the world... straight and true, hitting its mark, a child fulfilling their God-given purpose. Now that is significant! What about the Sunday school teacher who prayed, prepared the lessons and then taught someone like a little Billy Graham or Charles Finney. .. imparting a love for God and a heart for the lost. Would you consider their part-time Sunday school ministry to be significant? Probably not; and more than likely, neither did they at times. And then there is the faithful intercessor who prays in the secret place. No one knows, no one sees. They are overlooked and considered to be less, while the do-er is considered to be more.

Your reward will be sweet, concealed one. Do not grow weary in well doing. Others may consider you to be of little significance, but God has called you to greatness! Be content to receive your commendation from the Lord. Don't seek the temporal recognition that this world offers; it is shallow at best. Seek that which is eternal. There are many who are now first who will be last... and you who are hidden will be revealed with great honor and glory!

To Those Who Correct Others

"When you become outraged over a person's fault, it is generally not "righteous indignation" but your own impatient personality expressing itself. Here is the imperfect pointing a finger at the imperfect. The more you selfishly love yourself, the more critical you will be. Self-love cannot forgive the self-love it discovers in others. Nothing is so offensive to a haughty, conceited heart as the sight of another one." Fenelon circa 1690

Consider this profound truth as revealed through God's servant, Fenelon. Are you critical and judgmental; quick to correct others sometimes with harshness? This is not how the Holy Spirit operates; He is gentle and patient. Knowing we are but dust, He leads us out of darkness a step at a time. God usually gives revelation of our faults one by one, as we are able to bear them. He then gives time for us to work on these areas. Grace is applied, much grace. Yes, pressure too is applied at times, but not fiery criticism. As a representative of Jesus Christ you may be presenting Him as angry and mean. This is not acceptable, dear servant.

Wouldn't it be much better to remain silent and pray. Allow God to go before you and speak to the individual about this area of their life. (This may take months or years according to Divine priority.) Of course, do and say what the Lord tells you, but don't react from your own soulful, impatient flesh; be led by the Spirit.

Lord, please forgive me for my judgmental and critical thoughts and complaints. Help me to be quick to pray and slow to speak.

Only One Explanation

"The Spirit Himself bears witness with our spirit that we are children of God, and if children, then heirs--heirs of God and joint heirs with Christ, if indeed we suffer with Him, that we may also be glorified together. For I consider that the sufferings of this present time are not worthy to be compared with the glory which shall be revealed in us." Romans 8:16-18

Dear one, there is only one logical understanding: All things are within His control, everything! If that were not true, He would not be God. It is quite clear that He can allow or prevent any given situation. Yes, the awesome, loving, merciful Father of lights has permitted this difficult thing to occur. We tip-toe around the issue and subconsciously blame Him but wouldn't it be better to simply discuss it?

Of course, you know that our loving Lord is not the author of evil... pain, suffering, or sin. He is perfectly pure; He is love. Satan is the worker of iniquity. And to be completely honest, we ourselves have brought much pain upon ourselves by disobedience and poor choices. But even then, God could have prevented it, couldn't He?

This is where most people stop and an unspoken hardness of heart commences; we begin to distance ourselves from God. Yes, you might continue to attend church, but something has changed; spontaneity and enthusiasm start to fade. And you become like the millions of others who have lost their zeal to love... and to serve.

Lover of God, please know that there is something happening that is far deeper than the immediate. Can you not see beyond? You have been chosen by God to spend eternity with Him, to know Him intimately, to be by His side and to rule and reign with Him. What type of preparation would be deemed necessary for such a spectacular honor? Think about it!

If you were to become a physician, a professor, or a president intense training would be required, would it not? Twelve years of elementary and high school , four years of college, and another four of post graduate work, then there would be internship with several more years of work and life experience to follow. Great personal sacrifice would be required. All of this for a mere 30 or 40 years of temporal fulfillment and fruitfulness. We are talking about eternity, beloved, being wed to the King of Glory for all of eternity! What preparation would be too great?

Are you willing to patiently endure the trials of this life... with a hopeful expectation of the glory to come? Please trust your God; He loves you and is overseeing your preparatory work. Yes, He has allowed this thing to happen, but only because He loves you and knows that you will come through it... a radiant bride without spot or wrinkle. Soon you will gaze upon His glorious beauty and the former things will be remembered no more. Joy will flood your soul; life with Him forever more!

I have had the wonderful privilege of observing my own daughter prepare for her wedding. Nearly one year of personal beatification, reception plans, gowns, invitations, flowers, music selection, etc., and she was only marrying a wonderful man. You, beloved, are to become the bride of Christ, the bride of the Creator of the Universe!

The Ways of Paul

"For I am the least of the apostles, who am not worthy to be called an apostle, because I persecuted the church of God. But by the grace of God I am what I am, and His grace toward me was not in vain; but I labored more abundantly than they all, yet not I, but the grace of God which was with me." 1Cor 15:9-10

Let's take a closer look at this passage... a 2 verse exegeses, as it were. In verse 9, we can see Paul's humility... he calls himself unworthy. How easily we say, "Paul persecuted the Church." Nevertheless, have you considered the memories that he tried to forget, the scars upon his heart? He and his associates, filled with religious zeal and perhaps self-righteousness, would enter the home of a Christian and seize them by force, causing bodily harm. No doubt there were insults hurled and other cruelties perpetrated as parents were torn away from their screaming, bewildered children. These captives were either tortured, imprisoned or murdered. Could it be possible that during these violent episodes, hatred filled Paul's heart... even demon's? Anyway, Paul knows who he used to be and what he did, and he fully appreciated the wonderful grace of God. He could clearly state, *"But by the grace of God I am what I am..."* sensing absolute unworthiness, and knowing that neither His calling, nor his fruitful apostolic accomplishments were by his righteous self-effort.

However, he goes on to reveal a major key to his effective ministry: *"His grace toward me was not in vain; but I labored more abundantly than they all..."* He knew with every fiber of his being that God had called him and that he was afforded abundant grace to fulfill his mission. His strength and ability was in Christ alone, (*"yet not I, but the grace of God which was with me"*), but he also applied his best effort, straining and pressing toward the goal. Paul was diligent, he worked hard, he was disciplined, committed and he persevered. In fact, he stated that he *"labored more abundantly"* than all of the rest of his peers! He had his eyes set on the goal. *"Do you not know that those who run in a race all run, but one receives the prize? Run in such a way that you may obtain it. And everyone who competes for the prize is temperate in all things. Now they do it to obtain a perishable crown, but we for an imperishable crown. Therefore I run thus: not with uncertainty. Thus I fight: not as one who beats the air. But I discipline my body and bring it into subjection...."* 1Cor 9:24-27

So what did we learn, beloved? Amazing grace, how sweet the sound... His favor, His anointing, His power and strength are all abundantly available to me. I can do all things through Him. Oh yes, one more thing: my surrender and obedience, my labor and commitment, my diligence and perseverance... by His grace.

Eyes to See

Did Paul grow weary, dear one? Was he discouraged; did he ever despair? You can be sure of it! *"For we do not want you to be ignorant, brethren, of our trouble which came to us in Asia: that we were burdened beyond measure, above strength, so that we despaired even of life"* (2Cor. 1:8). Nevertheless, he was able to press on. It seems that the secret was found in his ability to believe God's promises and to look beyond the temporal, in the midst of adversity, to see the joy of eternity, the eternal weight of glory.

In a society that demands instant gratification, patience and deferred gratification are a rarity. But you, dear disciple, must learn to wait... to see the eternal, to look beyond the circumstances. Can you see? Even if the situation never changes and the pressures increase, not diminish... you can see heaven, can't you? Great glory awaits you, honor and reward. And you will finally be with Him! Praise Jesus now! Even if there is no fruit on the vine, praise Him and give Him worship. The Magnificent King has chosen you!

Read this passage and be encouraged, believer, in Jesus name:

"And since we have the same spirit of faith, according to what is written, "I believed and therefore I spoke," we also believe and therefore speak, knowing that He who raised up the Lord Jesus will also raise us up with Jesus, and will present us with you. Therefore we do not lose heart. Even though our outward man is perishing, yet the inward man is being renewed day by day. For our light affliction, which is but for a moment, is working for us a far more exceeding and eternal weight of glory, while we do not look at the things which are seen, but at the things which are not seen. For the things which are seen are temporary, but the things which are not seen are eternal." 2Cor 4:13-14,16-18

Lord, fill me with hope. Let the eyes of my heart truly see eternity... and the joy that awaits me.

Taking Risks

"Then he who had received the one talent came and said, `Lord, I knew you to be a hard man, reaping where you have not sown, and gathering where you have not scattered seed. And I was afraid, and went and hid your talent in the ground... '" Matt 25:24-25

You will not find the words caution or cautious in the Bible... and yet so many of God's people think it to be an attribute; it is not. In fact, the man in our parable was called wicked for his cautiousness. *"But his lord answered and said to him, `You wicked and lazy servant, you knew that I reap where I have not sown, and gather where I have not scattered seed. So you ought to have deposited my money with the bankers, and at my coming I would have received back my own with interest.'*

At the root of caution is fear and doubt. And in this case, laziness was also present "What if I fail in my business ventures; what if I make a poor investment? Even if I put it in the bank something could go wrong; perhaps I should just hold on to it for safe keeping." This servant was clearly fearful. *"Lord, I knew you to be a hard man, reaping where you have not sown, and gathering where you have not scattered seed. And I was afraid..."*

164

Take note of those who have gone before you. There have been many weak and foolish vessels called to do great and mighty things. (We are in good company.) Nevertheless, one obvious characteristic is present in them all: They were men and women of courage! No doubt they were fearful and anxious at times, but ultimately, by faith, they were willing to take the "risk" and step forward. Surely, doubt will attempt to crowd in, saying, "What if you are wrong?" Sometimes (many times) you will not be absolutely sure. This is why faith becomes necessary. In fact, the concept of faith so pleased God that He chose to weave it into the very fabric of creation. I mean, He hides Himself in the spirit realm and asks us to seek Him, believe Him and trust Him.

What prevents you from moving forward, beloved: fear of failure or worry of what others will think? Do you have financial concerns or fear for your personal safety... or that of your family? Don't all of these stem from pride, or a lack of trust in the Lord? Be bold, dear disciple. Of course you must pray and have wisdom and receive godly counsel, but then step forward boldly; God will help you. If you do make a mistake, He will even use failure to help guide you.

An Act of Rebellion

"They did not cry out to Me with their heart when they wailed upon their beds. They assemble together for grain and new wine, they rebel against Me..." Hosea 7:14

How often does woundedness, discouragement or disappointment result in an act of rebellion? It would be wise to recognize this propensity so that you can more easily defend against it. I mean, you normally resist temptation; you are strong in the Lord... and then comes a season of discouragement, or you become offended by another's words or deeds. It's not long before self-pity festers and you begin to use all of this as an excuse to sin, usually a sin of self-indulgence. You buy something you don't need, eat or drink more than you should, allow yourself to see something that you shouldn't, or commit a sexual sin. Does any of this sound familiar?

When you see this pattern reoccurring, take a stand. Say, "no farther" and stand your ground. Jesus will help you. These difficult periods do have a half-life; they'll not last forever. Remember, praise Him and don't complain... and forgive those who have offended you. This is the quickest, most direct route to the other side.

No Partiality

"For there is no partiality with God." Romans 2:11

Have you wondered how God can love you intimately, as a favored son or daughter, and yet remain completely impartial, without favoritism? This is worth looking at!

You would like to think that you could have special treatment. A beloved son should receive a break once in a while, shouldn't he? You work very hard for God. He'll let it go this time, won't He? He doesn't really expect you to give; He knows you can't afford it. Besides, you're too timid to be a witness; He understands. Perhaps inwardly you somehow believe that God should "lower the bar" for you. This is a dangerous place to be, dear child.

You have drawn closer to the Father, even becoming intimate with Him at times. You approach His throne with boldness because of Jesus' shed blood. But what is this? Does your closeness now give you license? You excuse your actions by thinking, "God loves me; He wants me to be happy." "He will surely allow me this." "He wouldn't really make me do that." Don't deceive yourself, beloved; Abba is no respecter of persons. He shows no favoritism; all of His children must live by His standards. His "rules" are absolutely perfect and create the necessary environment for your spiritual development...even the testing of your love for Him. He loves you so much that He may not allow you to get away with anything.

Have you ever attempted to get on the "good side" of your parents or teacher or boss? This won't work with the Almighty. As you grow more intimate with the Father, your familiarity should also stir an awesome reverence, the deepest respect. You seek to obey His every word and meet His every desire. This is the true nature of intimate self-sacrificing love.

Motive: The Third Level

"... Both the inward thought and the heart of man are deep."
Psalm 64:6

So, you have stopped lying and stealing and fornicating; very good! And you have been learning to control your anger and your heart attitudes like jealousy, criticism and judgmentalism etc. You have also been working on your thought-life. Praise the Lord! You are coming along very nicely. However, there is another level to consider, dear child... and that is motive. (Why you do the things you do.) Beware, there are many good things done with the wrong motivation... and this may effect the outcome and will surely determine your reward.

Jesus warned us about giving or praying publicly... so that we will be seen by men and receive their honor or admiration. He said that we should not expect a reward in heaven for doing these things since we would have already received it on earth. You understand, don't you?

Can you see your motives, beloved? Mind you, I'm not speaking of deep-seated psychological factors, but those reasons that lie just beneath the surface, things that can be easily seen... if you will only take the time to look. This is very important. So much of what you do centers around you, what will benefit you or please you.

Nonetheless, don't be discouraged; God is at work. He is in the process of transforming you from being self-centered to becoming Christ-centered. He is teaching you to pour yourself out; not for the praise and approval of men, not even for your own spiritual growth and development, and not for the promised heavenly reward, but for Him alone, for His pleasure and for His glory.

Suffering, My Friend

"Blessed are you when they revile and persecute you, and say all kinds of evil against you falsely for My sake. Rejoice and be exceedingly glad, for great is your reward in heaven,..." Matt 5:11-12

The doctrine of suffering has all but been forgotten over these past four or five decades, especially in the western Church. Blessing and abundant life have been preached instead. Surely these are truths from God's word, but perhaps it's time for the *full gospel* to be preached once again. Of course, suffering is not a new teaching. Through the centuries it has been taught ... and taken to the extreme as are most truths. Nevertheless, the fact remains that God uses human suffering to accomplish His purposes. He even gave His only Son to suffer and die. Remember, this was His perfect will, His divine plan. If you disagree, you may only be seeing a limited view of God.

The following are excerpts from an extraordinary book, *The Heavenly Man* by Brother Yun with Paul Hattaway. Yun suffered incredible hardships, persecutions, torture and imprisonment under the Communist regime in China during the 1980's and 90's. His comments challenge Christians around the globe to embrace suffering and fully abandon themselves to the purposes of God.

"The Lord wants us to embrace suffering as a friend. We need a deep realization that when we're persecuted for Jesus' sake it is an act of God's blessing to us." "We can grow to such a place in Christ where we laugh and rejoice when people slander us because we know that we are not of this world...When people malign you, rejoice and be glad. When they curse you, bless them in return. When you walk through a painful experience embrace it and you will be free! When you learn these lessons, there is nothing left that the world can do to you."

" The first time I went to prison I struggled, wondering why God had allowed it. Slowly I began to understand He had a deeper purpose for me than just working for Him. He wanted to know me and I to know Him, deeply and intimately."

"Whenever I hear of a house church Christian has been imprisoned for Christ in China, I don't advise people to pray for his or her release unless the Lord clearly we should pray this way. Before a chicken is hatched it is vital it is kept in the warm protection of the shell for 21 days. If you take the chick out of that environment one day too early, it will die..."

"There is always a purpose behind why God allows his children to go to prison. Perhaps it is so they can witness to the other prisoners, or perhaps God wants to develop more character in their lives. But if we use our own efforts to get them out of prison earlier than God intended, we can thwart His plans, and the believers may come out not as fully formed as God wanted them to be."

"My brethren, count it all joy when you fall into various trials, knowing that the testing of your faith produces patience. But let patience have its perfect work, that you may be perfect and complete, lacking nothing." James 1:2

Opportunity Abounds

Here are a few interesting statistics: During an average lifespan of 70 years you will have lived approximately 25,550 days. This would be 3,640 weeks or 840 months. Consider the numerous opportunities that are given throughout your lifetime to praise and worship the Master... and to love and serve your family, friends and coworkers.

Each day presents new challenges to forgive someone or to love the unlovable, new occasions to become less so that He can become more... in you and through you. Will you take advantage of these opportunities, beloved? Who you are, and who you will become depends upon the seemingly insignificant choices you make each day. And the magnitude of your reward in heaven may also depend upon how well you respond to each God-given opportunity. Pay attention; the clock is ticking!

Adolescent Christianity

" till we all come to the unity of the faith and of the knowledge of the Son of God, to a perfect man, to the measure of the stature of the fullness of Christ... but, speaking the truth in love, may grow up in all things into Him who is the head--Christ--" Eph. 4:13,15

Do you remember, as a child, when you would stand against your wall and place a pencil mark to measure how tall you were? From time to time you would recheck it to see how much you had grown. Our text speaks of growth, dear saint, and exhorts you to grow *"to the measure of the stature of the fullness of Christ."* In essence, your big brother, Jesus, has made His mark on the wall and challenges you to grow up to the fullness of that mark! Are you making some advances?

Truth is, it seems that very few Christians ever mature beyond adolescence. Most teens get into a phase where its "all about them.," the world revolves around their needs and desires. (I hope that this does not offend you.) There are a lot of Christians who never get past making decisions based upon what is best for them and "theirs." Sacrifice is only made when there will be some residual effect... benefiting the benefactor in some way. In other words, there are very few who will give of themselves in a sacrificial way without wanting to receive something in return.
Here are some sure signs of spiritual maturity:

- Self-sacrificing love (Agape)
- You learn to love the unlovable
- Deeper levels of trust and contentment
- Complete reliance upon God through prayer
- Genuine humility
- You are quick to admit your faults,
  quick to forgive others and to ask for forgiveness
- Christ-awareness that transcends self-awareness

You may excel in one area and lag behind in others, so don't evaluate your maturity based on only these few guidelines... but sacrificial love, in its many forms, is definitely the high-watermark of Christian maturity.

Please realize it is not a single deed or even a series of events that denotes maturity... and not the fact that you can preach or do miracles. But your life poured out for His glory and honor, this is your goal.

Holiness... Your Mindset

"For by one offering He has perfected forever those who are being sanctified." Hebrews 10:14

It has always intrigued me to consider the numerous mind sets held by true Christians regarding the various aspects of spiritual life. Take the process of sanctification for example: Some stand before the Lord saying, "I am who I am; I can't change; grace will cover me." They make little effort to alter anything about their lives... depending upon the Lord to do it all. There are others who adhere to methods and formulas to make themselves holy. Many times these border on outright legalism. Which is it: no effort, great effort, or somewhere in between?

Perhaps a brief overview of the New Testament would be helpful. You will find every gospel and nearly every epistle exhorting the reader to turn from sin and walk in holiness. In fact, Jesus tells His disciples to *"strive to enter by the narrow gate"* (Luke 13:24). Striving means to apply great effort, straining, sweating, etc. Make no mistake about it, the New Testament is filled with imperatives... principles, necessities and commands. But all are to be fulfilled by grace... with God's help, not your effort alone.

You strive and rest all in the same breath, dear worker. This is a great mystery that has eluded theologians for centuries. Work diligently, pursue holiness and godliness... even strive, as it were, while resting in His all encompassing grace and covered by the precious blood of your suffering Servant. He is in you and you are hidden in Him throughout this entire lifelong process. Remember, in God's eyes, because of Jesus' sacrifice, you are already perfected... forever!

Be Hard on Yourself -Easy on Others

"And whatever you do, do it heartily, as to the Lord and not to men"
Colossians 3:23

Have you heard this expression before? Worth considering, isn't it? How often you are just the opposite...excusing yourself while judging others. Let this be a rule of thumb in your interpersonal dealings and your attitude of heart.

Now let's make this very clear: We're not implying that anyone should be harsh with themselves, beating themselves while striving for perfection. This is a sign of emotional sickness. But dear one, shouldn't you be challenging yourself to get it right, to do it better? This is a character quality that is sorely lacking in the body of Christ.

Endeavor to do all things with excellence but offer abundant grace to those who do not. Earnestly desire to walk righteously before the Lord while offering mercy and compassion to those who do not.

Want to be a Martyr?

"... Lord, I am ready to go with You, both to prison and to death."
Luke 22:33

How many dedicated, God-loving Christians have boldly declared, "I will die for you, Lord"? The thought is almost romantic... in a sense. Oh the glory of dying for Jesus. Surely a noble aspiration, absolutely selfless...giving one's life for the Lord. The thought of suffering is a bit less appealing though. "Just let it be a quick death, Lord." The truth is, hundreds of thousands of our brothers and sisters are being martyred - even now, in this generation. Do you ever think of them, or pray for the ones who are being tortured at this very moment? Quite a vast difference between the noble aspiration and the actual reality. Wouldn't you say?

Don't loose heart, dear one. Perhaps you will never have the opportunity to surrender your physical body to suffering and death, but there is something afoot that you can respond to. And this challenge

172

has been heralded throughout Church history: *"If anyone come after me let him deny himself and take up his cross daily and follow me."* It is time to die, beloved… to die to yourself, to die daily! Surely, it would be easier to just die once and then go to heaven.

Dying to self, to all of your selfish ways, your pride, and the lusts of the flesh is a formidable venture. Nevertheless, this is your martyrdom, dear saint. The Lord is searching to and fro for those who will die to themselves, loving Him above all else and loving others. *"Precious in the sight of the Lord is the death of His saints"* (Ps 116:15). And you thought this scripture applied only to physical death?

Take up your cross with joy; there is no place for complaining and self-pity. You have been given a great honor - to die for Christ. Die to the deepest depths of self; surrender your rights, your time, your everything… being led by the Spirit in all of your ways. The Master will help you; He loves you. Trust Him!

The Kingdom of God awaits you… here on earth, as it is in heaven.

A Letter to One Who is Discouraged

"So likewise, whoever of you does not forsake all that he has cannot be My disciple." Luke 14:33

I'm sorry that you are feeling discouraged. I hope that after some rest and prayer you will feel better. I can only encourage you to revisit your call… seeking God, asking for His guidance. It would be a shame to see you turn back if it was His will for you to proceed. I don't know why God has not yet given full provision, but He will. I myself am deeply in debt. I fully believe that what we are asking of God will cost us everything. If we should loose our houses and cars and everything else, we must be willing to move forward. There is so much at stake.

John Lake, when working in Africa, received very little provision for himself and his workers. He called them together, explained the situation and freely released them… knowing that some may actually starve. But no one would go home! As a result, several people did die from disease secondary to inadequate nutrition, including wives and children! Where was God in all of this? But then it came, an outpouring that saved over 100,000 souls and launched John into a healing ministry that is well documented!

It will cost you everything, dear friend. We are at the point where we are moving far beyond mere words and the ethereal concepts of self-sacrifice. I can promise you the Lord will always provide your needs as you seek Him and His kingdom first; this is His Word. I can promise little else. Having said that, know that you are greatly appreciated.

Be sure that you are very honest with yourself though. There are many other factors that come into play: interpersonal relationships, loss of freedom, self-sacrifice and additional work, etc. You must count the cost in these areas too.

I believe that we are about to see a glorious outpouring of God; this is why we live. We have no other ambitions, no other driving goals or desires. We are asking God for a magnificent regional transformation. Not only for a few souls or healings, not even for a fruitful, successful ministry, but for the spiritual revival of an entire region! The cost has been, and will continue to be enormous. Some may even die. I do not mean to sound dramatic, but why should we be asked to pay any less of a price than John Lake or the saints in China or the early Christians? I hope that you will go on with us... but if not, I can truly understand.

The Easier Way

"...choose for yourselves this day whom you will serve, whether the gods which your fathers served that were on the other side of the River, or the gods of the Amorites, in whose land you dwell. But as for me and my house, we will serve the Lord." Joshua 24:15

Be aware, beloved, throughout your entire Christian walk there will be decisions to make, opportunities to choose this way or that. Many Christians seek the path of least resistance… in dealing with interpersonal relationships, or financial matters, and those things which would allow them to exert the least amount of physical energy. Can you relate? Choose your course wisely.

First and foremost, choose according to the known will of God, His written word... and by rhema, the living word that He has spoken to you personally. One will not contradict the other. But you already know this rudimentary truth, don't you?

The challenge lies in those areas where you are not quite sure of God's will in the matter; at least you don't think you are. Or when extreme pressure is applied either externally or from within.... demons, friends or foe. During these times of intense adversity even those who know and love God may disobey His Word and choose the easier way. Let this not be you, dear disciple. Seek the Lord and seek wise council. Don't run away unless you are running from sin. Endurance and perseverance are the key... and there is abundant grace for that.

Please remember this absolute: You have been given the glorious, unspeakably matchless gift of eternal life and you are now being conformed to the image of Christ. You are in the process of becoming a beautiful bride without spot or wrinkle. Surely you don't want to choose lesser things. Choose Jesus, beloved. Difficult or not, always choose His way.

The Fear of Loss

"Are not two sparrows sold for a copper coin? And not one of them falls to the ground apart from your Father's will. But the very hairs of your head are all numbered. Do not fear therefore; you are of more value than many sparrows." Matthew 10:29 –31

How often we speak of complete surrender and total abandonment. Such a lofty goal, isn't it? But there are very practical reasons why this has been mentioned so often throughout the ages. Take note, beloved; this applies to you:

Losing something, anything, can be a painful experience... in varying degrees according to the importance that you have placed upon it My heart goes out to those who have lost children or loved ones - how agonizing. And a fire or violent storm can take every last possession. Will you release these to the Lord, dear one? It is surely time to do this. Nevertheless, allow us to go on to another dimension of this subject: the *fear* of loss.

175

Total surrender and complete abandonment to the purposes of God allows such freedom. You simply give yourself entirely to the Lord. This includes your family, finances, material possessions, health, reputation, job or ministry, etc. If you are afraid of losing any of these things you will be hindered in your Christian walk. In fact, you can not enter into the fullness of freedom or the totality of true discipleship until you do. Do you understand?

If you are afraid of losing your health, you will carefully guard your health. You would have a very difficult time going someplace that would put you at risk... either from disease or violence. Well, I guess that cuts out all missionary work overseas or inner-city. Likewise, if you are afraid of losing your money or property, you will be less generous, even stingy. This prevents you from being generous to the work of God... seriously limiting your fruitfulness and your reward. And your reputation? How could you ever be a witness for Christ if you are afraid of what others will think of you?

Do you see? Complete surrender is the only way to go; it is not an optional nicety. No one can enter into the fullness of Christ while clinging to self and protecting their well-being! Give it all to Jesus, Christian; you can trust Him!

Dear Jesus, I confess that I have not trusted You. I cling to the people, places and things of this world and have made decisions based upon the fear of loss. Please forgive me. I surrender ALL to You, Lord. Help me to trust You with every aspect of my life.

The Race

Can you envision the starting line of the Boston Marathon, or any great footrace for that matter? Thousands of excited participants pack the street awaiting the official signal...and the race begins.

Dear saint, you probably started the Christian race with the same enthusiasm. Needless to say, zeal can dwindle amidst the vicissitudes of life. Not only are you expected to actually run this race, but it seems that the road is filled with potholes and obstacles; and it gets narrower as you proceed. The other runners have the propensity to bump into you and venomous snakes and roaring lions linger in the shadows, awaiting an opportunity! Nevertheless, in the midst of it all, God is at work. You are being transformed by the power of the Holy Spirit; and are called onward to the deepest levels of His love.

Oh, that each year would be the equivalent of one mile; then perhaps, we would be near the finish line. But it feels, at times, as though we have just begun. There have been long stretches when bounding strides have been made with minimal effort. It appeared as though no adversity could affect us; no temptation could trip us up. We would pray, and preach, and serve, and were *faster than a speeding bullet, able to leap tall buildings in a single bound.* Well, not exactly. And then came the times of failure, sin, or discouragement, when the night was so dark that we could not see where to walk ... much less run this "stupid" race. We had no strength, no desire, and no hope; it seemed as though the contest was over. Have you ever been there? Perhaps you're there right now; that's why God has placed this book in your hand. Anyway, somehow, by God's grace, we got up and began running again.

You can do this beloved. By His grace you can win this race. Don't turn back now; you have come so far. Revival is at the door. The wonderful promises that God has made are unfolding as we speak. Your life's purpose is about to be fulfilled!

Judgment

"So we make it our goal to please him, whether we are at home in the body or away from it. For we must all appear before the judgment seat of Christ, that each one may receive what is due him for the things done while in the body, whether good or bad. Since, then, we know what it is to fear the Lord, we try to persuade men." 2Cor 5:9-11 (NIV)

"For we must all appear before the judgment seat of Christ..." what does this mean, redeemed one? The dictionary defines judgment as: the act of judging or assessing a person or situation or event. You are a blood bought, blood washed child of God; your

sins are forgiven. Where does judgment fit here? There is a plethora of teaching regarding the Judgment Seat of Christ... some of it is not entirely biblical. It has frequently been stated that there is no judgment for those who are in Christ, that everything is *under the blood*, and yet Paul is quite obviously reminding the Christians of Corinth that they will be held accountable for their deeds while living on earth....

The apostle clearly says that he makes it his goal to please the Lord because he knows that he too will appear before the judgment seat of Christ. He even goes on to say that because he knows what it is to fear the Lord, he persuades men... presumably to behave in a manner that is pleasing to God. (NKJV uses the phrase *the terror of the Lord.*)

Regardless of what you have been taught or what you think that this means, it is well worth considering this text ... and to live your life in a manner that is pleasing to God. There is no question that you will appear before Him *"that each one may receive what is due him for the things done while in the body, whether good or bad.* This is the Word of the Lord! *"So then, each of us will give an account of himself to God."* Romans 14:12

While it is difficult to be absolutely certain what this judgment will mean for the Christian, apparently there will be rewards, crowns and treasure given for self-sacrificing good works, for enduring temptation and for overcoming, etc... and there will be a loss of reward for that which was not good. "If what he has built survives, he will receive his reward. If it is burned up, he will suffer loss; he himself will be saved, but only as one escaping through the flames." 1Cor 3:14-15 (NIV)

The Simplicity of Truth

"... And I pray that you, being rooted and established in love, may have power, together with all the saints, to grasp how wide and long and high and deep is the love of Christ, and to know this love that surpasses knowledge--that you may be filled to the measure of all the fullness of God." Ephesians 3:17-19 (NIV)

The depths of God? ... far too deep to totally comprehend. I mean, what mortal can truly know Him, His ways. But throughout your lifetime, now and again, you may receive a revelatory glimpse. How great is our God! We will spend eternity fascinated by His beauty, wisdom and power... His perfect love.

Nonetheless, dear explorer, there is simplicity in the midst of the wonderment – elementary enough for a child to understand: God loves me! (Meditate on that for a few decades!) In addition, we are given only two directives: Love God above all things and love your neighbor.

Yes, while we grow in grace, virtue, knowledge etc. we collect much truth and experience. We try to assimilate, evaluate and then reevaluate as we progress to deeper levels. Albeit, having climbed mountains, wept in valleys and wandered in the desert, this simple truth remains: God loves me... and He desires that I love Him!

Don't get to cerebral, dear pilgrim. You may loose sight of the central theme: ♫ *"Jesus loves me this I know..."*

Appropriating Grace

"And the grace of our Lord was exceeding abundant with faith and love which is in Christ Jesus." 1Timothy 1:14 (KJS)

Of course you know that the standard definition for grace is "unmerited favor"... unearned, undeserved loving benevolence toward us! The frequent use of this word assumes that we comprehended its meaning; but do we really? I mean, is it given proportionately, in measure... more or less, now and again? Is it given to all? Does it mean that something *just happens* without effort on your part? Let's take a look at this: Some would like to think something *just happens* without effort on your part, and use it as an excuse for a lack of diligence or commitment. Others apply effort apart from the grace to do God's specified will, and they fail. So it is clear that we are not speaking of self-effort, but an intricate weaving of grace and Spirit-led effort with Spirit empowerment.

When speaking of Salvation, grace means the free gift of God, paid in full by the blood of Jesus, no human effort whatsoever. But if a humble student graduates cum laude, they would tell us it was by the grace of God; and yet great effort was applied. Or, an overweight person, by God's grace, was able to lose those extra pounds. Was effort applied, how foolish; you can be sure it was... and lots of it. But with God's help (grace) it was possible to go to the gym on a regular basis, and stay on the diet.

This leads us to the next question: timing. Was grace always available, or was it given at a specific time... and that's why the favorable results occurred? Interesting thought, isn't it? The answer: both *yes* and *no*. Yes, God's timing surely comes into play; and according to His purposes, additional grace may be given. Nevertheless, man's willingness to respond to grace must be taken into consideration... especially when God's expressed will is violated. Grace is always available to accomplish God's will, but it may not always be appropriated. Paul surely understood this when he wrote, *"... and His grace toward me was not in vain; but I labored more abundantly than they all, yet not I, but the grace of God which was with me"* (1Cor. 15:10).

You see, dear one, grace is abundantly available to everyone (the humble) *"But he gives us more grace. That is why Scripture says: 'God opposes the proud but gives grace to the humble'"* (James 4:6 NIV). You cannot see it, touch or taste it; nonetheless, like gravity, you can recognize and feel its effects. Similar to an antibiotic held in your hand, able to cure your infirmity, grace abounds; it surrounds you and is readily available to you. With it you can receive healing, strength, the fortitude to overcome and the ability to do mighty exploits in the name of the Lord. However, beloved, it must be appropriated and acted upon in faith, by the leading of the Holy Spirit... just like the medicine must be taken as prescribed. If you would simply grasp this truth, you could earnestly say: *"I can do all things through Christ who strengthens me."*

What does all of this mean, dear saint? Listen for the prompting of the Holy Spirit; move forward in faith; utilize the abundant grace provided to you... be diligent and apply your best effort.

The Gospel of Self-Sacrifice

For at least three decades we have heard the message of prosperity and blessings… and surely you will find these truths in the scriptures. Unfortunately when taken out of context they can become a theology in and of itself, leading it's adherents to spiritual ruin.

"Now godliness with contentment is great gain. For we brought nothing into this world, and it is certain we can carry nothing out. And having food and clothing, with these we shall be content. But those who desire to be rich fall into temptation and a snare, and into many foolish and harmful lusts which drown men in destruction and perdition. For the love of money is a root of all kinds of evil, for which some have strayed from the faith in their greediness, and pierced themselves through with many sorrows. But you, O man of God, flee these things and pursue righteousness, godliness, faith, love, patience, gentleness." 1Tim 6:6-12

Dear disciple, it is time to mature. Do you recall the words of President Kennedy "Ask not what your country can do for you, but what you can do for your country?" This principle is sound. Spiritual maturity demands personal sacrifice. You didn't join a "bless me" club when you became a Christian, did you? *"If anyone come after Me, let him deny himself, take up his cross daily and follow Me."* You spend far too much time considering your pleasure, comforts and financial security.

Your Personality

"And the Lord passed before him and proclaimed, 'The Lord, the Lord God, merciful and gracious, longsuffering, and abounding in goodness and truth, keeping mercy for thousands, forgiving iniquity and transgression and sin, by no means clearing the guilty, visiting the iniquity of the fathers upon the children and the children's children to the third and the fourth generation.'" Exodus 34:6-7

Modern psychology would tell us that apart from our God-given traits, the development of our personality is influenced by a variety of factors, among them being our genetic make-up. Personal appearance and stature are simple examples; or if born with a slower metabolism you may respond to life differently than one born with, let's say, Attention Deficit Disorder. Your environment and socio-economic parameters would also be added in. And personal experiences in the formative years... affirmation and encouragement as opposed to neglect and abuse will most assuredly play a major role in personality development. (One who is affirmed faces life with a sense of self-worth and confidence, while the latter may spend a lot of time and energy seeking validation.) It would seem that before we even get started, we are either handicapped or enhanced. Because of this, our "enlightened" society has inferred, "it's not my fault;" I was already predisposed. And we deflect the blame and refuse personal responsibility. Dear saint, this is a major problem.

Let us freely concede that we are predisposed to sin; we have a sin nature, and *"The iniquity of the fathers (are visited) upon the children and the children's children to the third and the fourth generation."* (This is God's reference to the aforementioned developmental factors.) Nonetheless, each individual is given a free will; options are presented, choices to be made. Will we obey God, or will we not? Most certainly, negative influences can cause a propensity to lean in a particular direction, but anything short of the real or perceived threat of physical harm, leaves each individual accountable for his or her own actions. If this were not true, there could be no justice... on earth or in heaven. You are personally responsible for what you say and do. And according to the nature of your actions you will either be rewarded or adjudged.

There is, however, one more thing to consider: the Blood of Jesus Christ. Run to Him now, beloved. His life-giving flow will wash you clean. He makes all things new; you can begin afresh today!

Transformation vs. Modification

"And do not be conformed to this world, but be transformed by the renewing of your mind, that you may prove what is that good and acceptable and perfect will of God." Romans 12:2

I'm sure that you are well aware of the methods used to modify someone's behavior: scolding, discipline (including corporal punishment), imprisonment, etc. Sometimes these are necessary to redirect the wayward. Every society has developed it's own methods, and severity will vary. (The Church too must discipline; although, of course, not in corporal ways.) More than likely, as a child, you have experienced discipline to a lesser or greater degree, depending upon your hardheadedness… and the disposition of your parents. You did what you where told because it proved to be painful if you did not. You learned to do, or not to do certain things; your behavior changed in one way or another. Nonetheless, you probably grumbled and complained under your breath. Your heart and your attitude remained unchanged. Therein lies the challenge.

Dear lover of God, there is a vast difference between behavior modification and true internal transformation. The fear of consequences will surely affect your actions, but the Lord seeks to bring you far beyond these external changes. He wants you heart. He loves you and wants you to find peace and fulfillment in the life He has given to you, to submit willingly, to obey with joy.

How difficult it is to do what should be done only because it should be done. What drudgery to round the gristmill one more time, running the rat race, fulfilling your duty… all the while wishing you were doing something else. "Isn't it better to do my duty rather than not do it?" you ask. Of course! If you do not work, your family will not eat. But there is a better way, beloved! You are to *"be transformed by the renewing of your mind."* There is a place of peace and contentment in the Lord, where you find joy in the ordinary and see glory in the mundane… doing all things as unto Him. Ask the Lord to bring you to such a state. If you tarry here, you will find pure gold!

Feed on the promises of His Word, dear one, worship Him, and rest in His presence. Your value, your self-worth is in Christ, not in what you do or what you have. Look beyond the temporal to the eternal. You are a child of the Most High God, a joint heir with your Brother, Jesus. For all of eternity you will behold His glory and fulfill an eternal purpose. Surely you can rejoice in this! Your life on earth is merely a preparation.

Discipline Your Mind

"Finally, brethren, whatever things are true, whatever things are noble, whatever things are just, whatever things are pure, whatever things are lovely, whatever things are of good report, if there is any virtue and if there is anything praiseworthy--meditate on these things." Philippians 4:8

You have probably read this passage a dozen times and yet you continue to dwell on the negative, fearing the worst. The enemy spews his lies: "You will never succeed; you will never be well; you will never pay all of your bills; your children will come to harm." When something goes wrong, the evil one blames you and you are also quick to blame yourself. Guilt and condemnation flood your soul and discouragement soon follows. Dear child, it is time to take action. Please don't believe these lies. You will be defeated before you even get started.

It is interesting to note that meditation and worry are nearly the same thing. Your mind is beholding something positive and filled with life, or something negative, leading to discouragement and defeat. You are not responsible for the initial thoughts and subsequent feelings that flood your mind; nevertheless, you are responsible for what you continue to dwell upon. Take control of your thoughts!

This will require the grace of God (which is abundantly available to you) and diligent practice. When you find yourself thinking about that same old litany of negativity, realize that this is a pattern, something that you do far too often. Also consider the number of decisions that you have made based upon these inaccurate thoughts, the lies that you believe. Now that's a bit frightening! You don't go somewhere, because you think that you are not welcome (a lie). You won't speak out because you believe that others don't want to hear what you have to say (another lie). You won't try something new because you are afraid that you will fail (yet another lie).

Dear blood purchased, precious possession of God, your loving Father wants you to succeed; He delights in your progress. No matter what you have done, your history is behind you. A glorious future lies ahead. God has good plans for you... and for your family. Meditate on these things!

There are some who may feel barely in control of their mind. You have not lost your mind, beloved! It is stress and warfare that makes you feel this way. You have a sound mind. Feed on the Word of God, perhaps only one paragraph at a time. He sent His Word to heal you and deliver you from destruction.

It will take time and effort to change ingrained patterns of thought, but this is not only necessary, it is absolutely possible. Please be aware of the lies that you believe about yourself and disregard the negative things that others speak against you... and remember the promises of God's Word. You can do this, beloved. The Lord will help you. *"You will keep him in perfect peace, whose mind is stayed on You, because he trusts in You."* Isaiah 26:3

The Personality of Father God

"And because you are sons, God has sent forth the Spirit of His Son into your hearts, crying out, 'Abba, Father!' Therefore you are no longer a slave but a son, and if a son, then an heir of God through Christ." Galatians 4:6

How can it be: kind and severe, merciful and just, benevolent and calamitous? Who is this God... and how should we relate to Him? The Church has waffled between fear and familiarity. Many are afraid to come too close.

It is no accident that God has revealed Himself as Father, dear child. He wants you to know Him and to understand. Let us consider for a moment an earthly father. (Note that I did not say *your* father, unless of course, he was perfect. Far too many people have difficulty relating to Father God because of the sins of their own parent. Let's try to step past that for now.)

There are multiple facets to everyone's personality; don't you agree? A father can play with his children with all gentleness and then strap on a gun and a badge and bring the "bad guys" to justice with domineering authority, using lethal force if necessary. Tender words of love can flow from his lips as well as strong words of rebuke... righteous anger. A loving father knows when to lavish blessing and also when to withhold for a season. He encourages and corrects; his motives are always for our good, always loving. He helps with our character development... even pushing us out of the comfortable nest, having us do things that we would rather not, completing tasks that we would rather neglect. If this can be true of a human father, how much more so for your Father in heaven. Do not cling to an understanding of God that is too narrow, one or two dimensional. He is a loving Father, who can be many things at the same time (yet He never changes). Do you understand? Our God is an Intimate Lover with a strong arm of justice, the Wisdom of the Ages who delights in simplicity, the Ultimate Perfectionist who forbears our imperfections by the blood of Jesus.

Religious men say you must fear God, and you must. They say you must respect Him, correct again... with awesome reverence, for sure. They also infer familiarity denigrates His holiness and breeds disrespect. But is this really true? Consider an earthly dad playing with his kids on the living room floor, tickling and giggling... but then it is time for bed. You know that he means what he says; you have learned to respect his word. (You have foolishly disobeyed in the past, suffering the consequences.) But deep respect, even the fear of adverse consequences should not prevent you from playing with him at the very next opportunity. Intimacy and fear *can* stand side by side, but *perfect love casts out fear!*

Please don't hesitate to come near to Abba. Do you still not feel His love? You will, beloved, trust Him. Come with abandonment, as a

186

child. Run past the torn veil; leap into His outstretched arms; sit upon His lap. He wants you to enjoy being in His presence; you can truly enjoy Him... even telling jokes and laughing together. You can also unload your burdens at His feet and cry rivers upon His shoulder. This is your Father; this is who He is ... and soooo much more!

You Command Me!

" Thus says the Lord, the Holy One of Israel, and his Maker: 'Ask Me of things to come concerning My sons; and concerning the work of My hands, you command Me.'" Isaiah 45:11

What an incredible statement; God is telling us to command Him? If you have a problem with intimacy and familiarity with God, this one will surely take you over the edge.

Can a mere man command God to do anything? What a foolish thought; I mean, God is God! We are His servants; He commands us, right? Absolutely! But that's not the entire story... unless of course you have become fossilized in the crevasse of lifeless ecclesiastical dogma. Is it possible to have such intimacy with the Father that He will actually entertain your commands and do what you ask?

Oh the bliss of child-like faith; I'm sure you are well aware of the need for it. Imagine this scenario (as suggested by Rolland Baker): Your adorable grandchild in whom you delight and consider perfect in your eyes, bursts into the room. He or she is filled with joy, bubbling with enthusiasm. They begin to rouse you, "Papa, take me to the park! Take me for some ice cream!" Will you not do what they say? Yes you will, and even more. *"Ask, and it shall be given you; seek, and ye shall find; knock, and it shall be opened unto you."* Matthew 7:7

Compatibility

"Behold, how good and how pleasant it is for brethren to dwell together in unity! It is like the precious oil upon the head, running down on the beard, the beard of Aaron, running down on the edge of his garments. It is like the dew of Hermon, descending upon the mountains of Zion; for there the Lord commanded the blessing--life forevermore." Psalm 133:1-3

What a blessing to work with people that you can get along with. There seems to be such a sweet flow of unity. You have the same heart. *"Behold, how good and how pleasant it is..."* Why is it then, that the Lord usually places you with those who are irritating in some way? They either seem to know it all, or talk about themselves too much, or have a negative view about almost everything. Or, you may find yourself being jealous of *their* giftings. Do you know what I mean? If unity is so precious why doesn't God always join you together with those of like mind and heart?

Dear student of Love, you must learn this lesson well because therein lies an invaluable secret, something that will release spiritual power into your life and ministry. "What is it?" you ask: Death to self! Yes, again we hear of its value. Humble yourself, *submit to one another in love*, die to your preferences; die to your own agenda. Live in the unity of the Holy Spirit.

The Master has wisely joined you with those who are different from you to bring balance, truth, and new ways of doing things. They can also enhance your spiritual life by giving you ample opportunities to love the unlovable. (You said that you wanted to be like Jesus, didn't you?) Come now; let's move forward; die to yourself; forgive, if necessary, and move forward. Forgive again tomorrow and the next day too... And learn to accept the idiosyncrasies of others. They are learning to accept yours!

When brothers or sisters in the Lord learn to live like this, everyone on the team submits to one another in love. The atmosphere of self-sacrifice (the yielding of self) produces a sweet fragrance unto our God. He will surely draw near and command a blessing!

Exercise Godliness

"For everything God created is good, and nothing is to be rejected if it is received with thanksgiving, because it is consecrated by the word of God and prayer. If you point these things out to the brothers, you will be a good minister of Christ Jesus..." *"For physical training is of some value, but godliness has value for all things, holding promise for both the present life and the life to come."* 1Timothy 4: 4-6, 8 (NIV)

Have you noticed that there is an increase in health consciousness within the Church? This is a good thing; many westerners are overweight, even obese (including children). Some, however, have gone overboard with health foods and dietary supplements, taking 10-15 tablets at a time. Is this wise, beloved? The health gurus will probably take issue with this, but let us defer to the Word of God.

Beware; some Christians would put you in bondage by forbidding certain foods, even telling you to eat no meat whatsoever. Please reread 1Tim.4: 4-6. Not only should you step away from such legalism, but also you will be a good minister if you instruct others to do the same. Of course, all foods are to be taken in moderation; don't use this writing to excuse overeating or unbalanced dietary habits. Nonetheless, know that it is perfectly OK to eat all types of food, even reptiles! *"He saw heaven opened and something like a large sheet being let down to earth by its four corners. It contained all kinds of four-footed animals, as well as reptiles of the earth and birds of the air. Then a voice told him, 'Get up, Peter. Kill and eat.' 'Surely not, Lord!' Peter replied. 'I have never eaten anything impure or unclean.' The voice spoke to him a second time, 'Do not call anything impure that God has made clean'"* Acts 10:11-15 (NIV). Don't be foolish; be free.

Some will pay exorbitant prices for "all natural" foods. They read every package and never drink anything but the purest mountain spring water. God bless you, dear one; what are you doing? Perhaps you think that you are being a good steward of your health, but instead, you may be fully absorbed in self, self-preservation. Wouldn't your time and resources be better spent caring for others? You may be in bondage and don't realize it.

Also know that physical exercise is good and it is necessary for health, but don't become addicted to physical fitness. This can be very stimulating to self-life. You are either dissatisfied with what you see in the mirror... or you admire it. Exercise yourself in godliness; practice it like you would practice any skill. Adjust or modify your responses to unkind words, to unpleasant situations, to adversity. Learn to love the unlovable and forgive completely. Learn to be truthful at all times. If you exercise like this, you will surely shed a lot of excess weight.

Denying Yourself

"Then He said to them all, 'If anyone desires to come after Me, let him deny himself, and take up his cross daily, and follow Me.'"
Luke 9:23

How often you have heard this scripture and nodded your head in agreement. Do you really know what it means to deny yourself? Wouldn't it be wise to consider the practical application of all scripture? Especially, as in this case, when the ramifications are so profound. I mean this is bedrock, a foundation of discipleship and a prerequisite for following Jesus Christ. It may be quite interesting to find out what this particular verse means to you.

Some may think it refers to denying themselves an extra desert or putting a few dollars in the offering plate; but I can assure you it goes much deeper than that. The rich man was asked to sell all he had and give to the poor, the one who felt obligated to his family responsibilities was told to *"let the dead bury the dead."* Jesus informed the willing disciple who promised to follow Him anywhere, that He didn't have a home or even a bed... an unspoken rhetorical question left hanging, "Can you live like this?" Dear disciple, count the cost. It will cost you everything!

Here are only a few examples of self-denial:
- Turning off the TV to read the Word or to pray
- Giving up your leisure time to help another
- Giving to the poor instead of spending on yourself
- Giving up your reputation to be a witness for Christ

- Giving up your probable earning potential to serve in menial ways for minimal wages
- Giving up the deepest desires of your heart to fulfill the call of God
- Forgiving another completely when you would rather harbor ill feelings

Before you take a morbid, martyristic view of discipleship also consider the joy: the fulfillment and the intimacy with God. What price is too great to become a friend of God and to experience the wonders of His love as He pours through you?

How we strive for carnal achievements. Vast amounts of money, long hours and intense study are invested in the pursuit of success... to become a physician or an attorney, or many other careers for that matter. Self-denial is a necessary companion on the way to the top. Why can't you deny yourself in the pursuit of God and for the fulfillment of His purposes?

Reformation

*A fresh look at our doctrines
and the ways of doing church*

I am Of Christ

"Now I say this, that each of you says, 'I am of Paul,' or 'I am of Apollos,' or 'I am of Cephas,' or 'I am of Christ.' For when one says, 'I am of Paul,' and another, 'I am of Apollos,' are you not carnal? Who then is Paul, and who is Apollos, but ministers through whom you believed, as the Lord gave to each one?" 1Cor. 1:12, 3:4

Luther and Wesley were great men of God; they brought much spiritual insight and reform. Nevertheless, they probably wouldn't be pleased to know that entire denominations bore their name. Thank God that the world is not blessed with Zinsendorfians and Watchman Neeites, too. (Just a bit of humor.)

Each of these "prophets" were given spiritual truth that has been of great benefit to the Church. Martin Luther for instance, uncovered a long forgotten foundation of our faith: *We are saved by grace through faith, not by works. We are justified by faith!* Thank you Martin Luther! And John Wesley, with his brother, Charles, carried Revival to many, transforming a nation. Holiness was restored to the Body of Christ. But do *all* of the spiritual insights and practices of these men or any man, as good as they may be, deserve undying allegiance? Remember beloved, no servant of God is perfect, nor do they perfectly interpret the scripture.

It seems that God will bring illumination to an individual or a group... and the organized church quickly rejects it. They are then persecuted for their beliefs / practices by the powers that be, and are forced to break away. Unfortunately this group does not possess the entire truth either and within a few generations they become legalistic or liberal, ecclesiastical and ceremonial and God must raise up another to enlighten the former light bearers. The foundation of Christian doctrine, *the Apostle's Creed*, cannot be denied, but our understanding of peripheral doctrines and practices should remain fluid. Let us be open to the present day workings of the Holy Spirit.

Within the past 40 years, the Spirit of God has uncovered so many buried truths and practices: prayer and fasting, Spirit-led worship, spiritual warfare and deliverance, the Baptism in the Holy Spirit, divine healing and the other spiritual gifts, sacrificial giving, intimacy with God and truths regarding the Bride of Christ. There have also been fresh insights into the role of women in ministry, the priesthood of believers in general, and a renewed emphasis on personal holiness. In addition, the Holy Spirit has been stirring some serious intercession for Revival. Those who have missed or rejected these ongoing "illuminations" have really missed a lot.

It is more comfortable, and gives a greater sense of security to cling tightly to the former ways... and some traditions are good; Jesus has initiated them Himself. Nevertheless, if we blindly adhere to the fossilized practices of the past, we may overlook what God is currently doing; and worse yet, persecute those who are flowing in His latest work. Throughout Church history, that error has been repeated time and again. Will we continue to be so foolish? The Church is desperately in need of another Reformation! Who will post *The Ninety-Five Thesis* in our generation?

The Perception of Truth

"For now we see in a mirror, dimly, but then face to face. Now I know in part, but then I shall know just as I also am known."
1Corinthians 13:12

What you believe to be definitely true may not be the truth! After all, you only *"know in part."* Do you understand that your perception of truth is influenced by several factors? Hopefully, the Holy Spirit is gaining the most sway, but there are also personal experiences, prior teachings, parents, culture, even your personality. All of these factors clearly shape who you are and what you believe, both in the natural and in the spiritual. It is absolutely essential that you realize this: Only a percentage of what you believe to be true is really TRUTH.

Dear believer, there is a period of time during your spiritual development when you are vulnerable to assimilating non-truth. You believe your parents, pastor, and teachers without question, even if the doctrine being taught has been faulty for hundreds of years, handed down from one generation to another, wrong each time.

Indeed, the Bible is the standard of truth; nonetheless, there are few who wholeheartedly agree with each other's interpretation. Leaders of various Christian backgrounds, all born of the Spirit, all knowing Hebrew and Greek will arrive at a variety of conclusions when researching the same verses. How can this be? Someone must be incorrect.

Make no mistake about it, doctrine is very important. You need to know what to believe for salvation, holiness, and victorious living, etc. Even so, are you able to hold peripheral doctrines in an open hand, enabling you to receive something more? There is no compromise suggested here: *Jesus Christ crucified and risen for the forgiveness of sin* is absolute Truth. But will you continue to fight and divide over eschatology, baptisms or eternal security? It is time to grow-up, saint; learn from Jesus.

Has this reading disturbed you? Perhaps your faith is built upon doctrine. This is not good. Like a house of cards, remove a doctrine and the whole house collapses. If your faith leans too heavily upon doctrine, you may be threatened by change or may become dogmatic and legalistic. A doctrinal purist may even isolate from others for fear of contamination. This is actually very weak faith.

Jesus is truth, dear friend. Your faith must be built upon a personal relationship with Jesus Christ. His Holy Spirit will lead you into all truth. Come to Him once again as a child, with child-like faith, and relearn His truth.

Doing Things Differently

"Call to Me, and I will answer you, and show you great and mighty things, which you do not know." Jeremiah 33:3

Let's get right to the point. Is it working: the way you do church? You continue to do the same things the same way and expect different results. Without wanting to be offensive, dear friend, this is the definition of a moron! Finally, someone comes along and says, "This is not working; we need to do things differently." Eureka! The genesis of a New Beginning, a paradigm shift, a Revival!

It doesn't take much discernment to see that the church, as we know it, is not working. There are thousands of people within our cities that remain unsaved and there is very little being done to reach them. This perhaps is the greatest proof of our dysfunction. And, of course, our infighting and competition continues. Don't you think that it's time for a change? Time to pray, fast and seek God for revival and for His methods? Not just change for the sake of change; change by the leading of the Holy Spirit.

Dear leader, people resist new ways. Be gentle, teach them and lead them forward at a slow to moderate pace. In other words, don't make a sharp 90-degree turn or some will go over the edge. Keep a few things that are familiar and add the new. Jesus Himself instituted some traditions. Of course, these should not change. Even so, when all is said and done, you must obey God. He never changes but His methods do. Throughout church history, the Lord has given His people vision, guidance, and specific directions for implementing new strategies to reach the lost, to comfort the afflicted, to care for the poor and bring justice to the oppressed. Your challenge today: seek God. He will show you wonderful new ways, *which you do not know*. He will reveal the vision, the method and the timing. Don't forget: Revival begins with prevailing prayer. PRAY!

The Commandments of Men

"O foolish Galatians! Who has bewitched you that you should not obey the truth, before whose eyes Jesus Christ was clearly portrayed among you as crucified? This only I want to learn from you: Did you receive the Spirit by the works of the law, or by the hearing of faith? Are you so foolish? Having begun in the Spirit, are you now being made perfect by the flesh?" Galatians 3:1-3

Dear Christian, something on this short list of rules may offend you unless you have matured to freedom. The doctrines of men are not new; religious people from all backgrounds have burdened their followers with rules not found in the scriptures. In some cases, leaders being fearful of their own weaknesses have imposed their personal restraint upon all. In other instances, legalism and poor teaching have been handed down for generations. Some offer scriptural foundations for their unscriptural restrictions, but if the truth be known, their theological premise is quite shaky.

Disciple of Jesus, how the Church needs a fresh understanding of the ways of God. Religious rules have hindered the work of the Holy Spirit and caused the Church to appear as an exclusive religious club for holy people. This is not what the Lord intended.

- No fellowship with those of a different church
- No Holy Communion with those of differing doctrine
- No Bible translation except the *Authorized Version*
- No women allowed to do ministry
- No drums or other instruments except piano / organ
- No clapping or dancing in church
- No prophecy or speaking in tongues
- No makeup or jewelry
- No long hair or short hair
- No meat
- No alcohol
- No coffee
- No movies or TV
- No dancing
- No playing card games

Jesus said, *"Hear and understand: 'Not what goes into the mouth defiles a man; but what comes out of the mouth, this defiles a man'"* (Matt. 15:11). *"For it seemed good to the Holy Spirit, and to us, to lay upon you no greater burden than these necessary things: that you abstain from things offered to idols, from blood, from things strangled, and from sexual immorality. If you keep yourselves from these, you will do well"* (Acts 15:28-29).

What About Our Youth?

They need to be challenged; young people need a cause. Why not call them to a radical commitment to Jesus Christ? Not with "every eye closed and every head bowed," but to boldly acknowledge Jesus before all. Tell them of the many around the world who are suffering persecution for their faith. Challenge them to give up their life for the cause of Christ... even to be willing to die for Him. Call them to true discipleship and challenge them to give their *everything*. Oh, but before you do, you had better be living it yourself! Kids are very good at detecting hypocrisy.

197

The Open Church

"How is it then, brethren? Whenever you come together, each of you has a psalm, has a teaching, has a tongue, has a revelation, has an interpretation. Let all things be done for edification." 1Cor. 14:26

Christianity has followed its standard worship format for centuries. Services usually last from one to two hours and contain these basic elements: singing, prayer, preaching, an offering, and according to tradition, Holy Communion. Of course, they are all excellent things to do, but whoever said that all of these needed to be contained in your weekly service? There is certainly no scriptural mandate. Some people are so indoctrinated that they don't feel like they've attended church unless they do them all.

Week after week, churchgoers repeat the same things, the same way, and have become almost sinfully complacent. The minister or priest is up-front and does almost everything. Although some churches have given the laity a minimal role, for the most part, there is very little participation by the congregation. They have become mere spectators. Dear disciple, will you do something to change this?

Did you realize that the Hebraic style of "church meetings" found full expression during the time of Christ? Topics were openly discussed, and their preaching and teaching methods encouraged questions *during* the message. Paul told the Corinthians to each bring a song, a teaching, or a revelation. The meetings were designed to stimulate personal growth and bring mutual edification. Church members could pray for one another and practice the use of their spiritual gifts. You would come to church prepared to share something with the others. This is a far cry from the "feed me" mentality commonly seen in our churches today.

Can you imagine how marvelous it could be? Someone bursts forth in song, another in prayer, and then the song and prayer are somehow blended together in a crescendo of praise. A short teaching or revelation is expressed, and others who heard the Lord tell them the same thing give strong confirmation. A need is made known and the group gathers around to pray. Some practice their gifts of healings, or prophesy, or bring a word of knowledge and the congregation affirms them. Dear saint, this is a normal worship service. Now that you know the truth, ask the Spirit to help you implement it. Will you trust Him to direct your meetings?

Servant Leadership

"You call me Teacher and Lord, and you say well, for so I am. If I then, your Lord and Teacher, have washed your feet, you also ought to wash one another's feet. For I have given you an example, that you should do as I have done to you. Most assuredly, I say to you, a servant is not greater than his master; nor is he who is sent greater than he who sent him. If you know these things, blessed are you if you do them." John 13:13-17

Have you ever viewed a corporate management flow chart? You will note that the Chairman of the Board is placed at the top of the chart just above the officers and Board of Directors; from there it pyramids down to the middle management, department heads, and so on. If the profile were extended, it would finally flow to the factory worker and building maintenance. This is the way the world perceives leadership, beloved. Unfortunately, the Church is not much different.

The Teacher showed us a different way... the way of servanthood. *"And He said to them, 'The kings of the Gentiles exercise lordship over them, and those who exercise authority over them are called `benefactors.' But not so among you; on the contrary, he who is greatest among you, let him be as the younger, and he who governs as he who serves. For who is greater, he who sits at the table, or he who serves? Is it not he who sits at the table? Yet I am among you as the One who serves.'"* Luke 22:25-27

You must never forget this; the fruitfulness of your work depends upon it. Lead in this fashion and the Lord will bless you... the people will gladly go with you. Lord it over the people and you will have to strive, cajole, manipulate and do a "smoke and mirrors" routine to get them to follow.

Consider this: In God's kingdom, the management pyramid is inverted...with the leadership point on the bottom. The leader is holding the others up in prayer. He is lifting them up, building them up... serving, encouraging, giving, and washing feet. He becomes less; they become more... learning to do it better than he does. This is your goal, dear servant leader: Lay down your life for those whom you lead... become a rung in their ladder to success. The Kingdom would benefit from one like this! Will you be that one?

Revolutionaries

"Then Jesus said to His disciples, 'If anyone desires to come after Me, let him deny himself, and take up his cross, and follow Me.'" Matthew 16:24

"Revolutionaries," that is what the respected pollster George Barna is calling the new breed of *committed* Christians.... those who are dissatisfied with their experience in the local church. Barna's statistics show that a lot of Christians feel the need to attend additional meetings outside of their home church to receive spiritual nourishment. Many are leaving their church altogether – a total of about twenty million!

Yes, there are those who exit because of offense and other things ... backsliding, etc., but according to the polls, these revolutionaries are leaving because they want MORE of God, more than they can find in church! They are meeting in homes and other venues to pray and worship and seek the Lord. In this way they have the freedom to participate and practice the use of their spiritual gifts.

The face of Christianity is changing and the organized Church had better pay attention. It's too easy to label these "called out ones" *rebellious* or *overzealous*... and discount our responsibility in the matter. There are no two ways around it: The Church is falling asleep... and we had better wake up. We have been preaching and teaching a diluted form of Christianity and the people have become complacent and self-absorbed. We remain spiritually immature when we should be growing in the Lord. How will we accommodate those who are earnestly seeking more of God? How will we stir the others to shake off their lukewarm lethargy?

A Defibrillator Won't Help

"Will You not revive us again, that Your people may rejoice in You? Show us Your mercy, Lord, and grant us Your salvation."
Psalm 85:6-7

A recent radio broadcast mentioned that a particular congregation had purchased a defibrillator and was training their members to do CPR. Most of the congregation was over 65 years of age. Almost prophetic, isn't it? This group is in trouble. Church members are getting old and dying; soon the church will die too. Sorry, the defibrillator won't help.

Many churches have similar problems. They have grown comfortable and complacent. They offer great social activities for the flock, and of course, Sunday services; and for sure, the pastor is faithful to make home visits. Nice meetings, good fellowship, but no outreach! (Unless you consider the annual pancake supper an outreach.) Churches that don't reproduce new Christians will eventually cease to exist.

Dear Christian, the Master, without a doubt, gave you a mandate to reach the lost and to make disciples. Family, friends, neighbors, and co-workers all need to know that Jesus died for them. CPR is good, but how much better to teach Holy Spirit inspired methods of evangelism. Seek the Lord; He has an excellent strategy for your congregation to reach out to the neighborhood children, the unwed mothers, the chemically dependent, the rich, the poor, the many, the few. He will guide you. Please seek Him. Jesus wants to resuscitate your dying congregation.

Lord of the harvest, please revive my congregation and send laborers into your harvest fields. Cause us to love you above all things and give us Your strategies for reaching our community. I ask this, with resolve, in Jesus' precious name.

A First Line of Defense

"Blessed is he who considers the poor; the Lord will deliver him in time of trouble. The Lord will preserve him and keep him alive, and he will be blessed on the earth; You will not deliver him to the will of his enemies. The Lord will strengthen him on his bed of illness; You will sustain him on his sickbed." Psalm 41:1-3

There has been much written about spiritual warfare, but have you ever considered ministry to the weak and poor as a defensive weapon of war? Look at this passage again. God is telling us that if we help the poor, He will deliver us in time of trouble. (The word for *poor* can also be interpreted *weak*.) This is an awesome promise and one worth noting. But now see this: *"You will not deliver him to the will of his enemies."* Can you imagine the enemy of our soul, standing before the throne of God, presenting a plethora of accusations against us? We know that God and Satan conversed about Job, and we also know that Satan asked God for permission to sift Peter like wheat. Could it be possible that when the enemy comes before the Almighty and seeks to have his way with you, God will reply, "No, you can't touch this one. They have helped the weak / poor!"

In light of these scriptural promises, it would seem wise for any minister or ministry to bolster their spiritual defenses by giving generously to the poor and serving the weak.

Going to the Specialist

"For I have not shunned to declare to you the whole counsel of God. Therefore take heed to yourselves and to all the flock, among which the Holy Spirit has made you overseers, to shepherd the church of God which He purchased with His own blood." Acts 20:27-28

Consider the hour in which we live; knowledge increases exponentially. What physician could know it all, all of the diseases and malfunctions of the body systems, all of the medications and all of the treatments? This is the age of specialization: cardiologist, gastro-enterologist, neurologist, nutritionist. Dear Lord! Thank You for all of this knowledge and for all of their help. The Great Physician uses doctors to bring healing. (He also uses your prayers and faith!)

Likewise, within the Kingdom of God there are specialists, those who preach and teach about salvation, for example. On any given day you will find them presenting the same type of message; "You must be born-again." In addition, there are those who teach about faith, prayer, children's ministry, missions, works of mercy, and social justice. Need I say more? God has stirred their heart to teach and exhort the church to grow up and do what the scripture clearly states. Their lessons are usually not balanced; nor are they intended to be. God has called them to repeatedly preach or teach about one issue.

It is good to sit at the feet of a specialist. You can learn many things about a particular aspect of Christian life. However, know this: the Lord will keep you there only for a season. You will assimilate what you have learned and then you are to move on. Your diet must consist of more than one type of teaching. If you only hear the salvation message each week, no matter how anointed, you will starve.

Do you understand? This is not advisement to leave the ministry you are affiliated with. Remain faithful as long as God wants you to be there. Faithfulness and loyalty are very necessary elements of Christian maturity. But receive additional teaching, as led by the Holy Spirit. If you are following a specialist, realize that there is so much more to learn, and at some point in the future, God may lead you to another.

Dear specialist, even you must be well rounded in your personal spiritual development. If not, you may become an expert in your field, yet find yourself to be an immature Christian, narrow in understanding and lacking in character. Very interesting, how this Kingdom operates, isn't it?

Hell

"And I say to you, My friends, do not be afraid of those who kill the body, and after that have no more that they can do. But I will show you whom you should fear: Fear Him who, after He has killed, has power to cast into hell; yes, I say to you, fear Him!" Luke 12:4-5

No one likes to speak about hell anymore; not even the true Christian. It is not politically correct. At this writing, polls reveal that only about 32% of the US population believes in a literal hell. And among those who do believe in such a place, there are a multitude of understandings. "It's only for the very wicked." "Life here on earth is hell." At the same time, about 80% of the general public are quite confident that they are going to heaven. How can this be, at an hour when national morals are plummeting to an all time low? It was never more apparent that a huge number of people are deluded, and that upon their death, they will be in for a terrible, shocking surprise.

Do you realize that Jesus mentioned hell 12 times as recorded in the New Testament? Hell is described as a place of fire, torment and a place of outer darkness. Jesus, quoting the prophet Isaiah, compared hell (Gehenna) to the Jerusalem city dump, *"where their worm does not die, and the fire is not quenched"* (Mark 9:47).

Do you believe there is such a place? If you believe Jesus, then you must believe. Hell was prepared for the rebellious angels; God did not intend humans to go there. Unfortunately, by their own choice, some will enter hell. They choose to reject Jesus and choose to spurn His love. All who refuse Jesus as their Savior will enter into hell.

If you believe this, why won't you warn your friends and coworkers? Many, throughout our nation, have heard that God loves them, but they don't care about loving and obeying Him. They are perfectly content to go on in their sin. You know that this is true. Be kind and very gracious to them. I pray that your loving testimony will persuade them to turn to Jesus. But if not, will you warn them of their impending disaster? Very few Christians have the courage to warn of hell.

If you narrowly escaped the certain death of a bridge collapse, wouldn't you try to prevent other people from plunging to their death? If you noticed your neighbor's house afire, wouldn't you warn them, even waking them in the middle of the night? Wouldn't you shout, bang, or do whatever was necessary to rouse them. Isn't hell a far worse plight? Wake up, Christian! See that your neighborhood is ablaze with destruction. Won't you warn them? Warn them with love in your heart and tears in your eyes, your words filled with concern. Warn them not from the pedestal of self-righteousness, but as a sinner, yourself, who has barely eluded hell's tormenting flames. Warn them by the leading of the Holy Spirit. Please warn them. How the Church needs to revisit this teaching!

Beginning On The Outside?

"Wisdom strengthens the wise more than ten rulers of the city."
Ecclesiastes 7:19

Oh, the evil that lurks in the hearts of men: pride, unforgiveness, greed, lust, rebellion, covetousness, idolatry. Many who turn to Christ, struggle with some of these issues for several years after they have been "saved." Major strongholds such as lust or unforgiveness will hinder, and even obstruct, your spiritual growth.

The common mode of operation, when instructing the new believer, is to clean up the outside, not the inside: stop smoking, stop drinking, stop your foul language, wear this, don't wear that. The intellect is also fed with doctrines. Of course, doctrine is important, but not as important as the matters of the heart. You can fill the head with teaching and lose your people, because doctrines and church policies do not solve their internal problems.

Don't you think that we need a better strategy? As it has been said, we "major on the minors." Unforgiveness, for example, can cause every type of emotional and physical problem. The servant of God is frequently asked to minister to these needs over and over again, draining the time and resources of the church. Wouldn't it be better to teach the new convert about forgiveness at the beginning?

Dear Christian leader, would you please consider a weekend retreat for new believers, perhaps a semi-annual event? Strong encourage-ment should be given for every new Christian to attend. Teach and minister healing and deliverance. Several smaller churches could do this together.

The church has fumbled the ball in this respect, and we continue to do so. Our time is consumed with maintenance, dealing with personal issues that should have been resolved years ago. We never seem to have the reserve energy to seek God for a plan to advance His Kingdom. This is *not* normal.

Titles

"Do not call anyone on earth your father; for One is your Father, He who is in heaven. And do not be called teachers; for One is your Teacher, the Christ." Matthew 23:9-10

(You may be upset after reading this. Please bring it to the Lord.) There is no biblical foundation for the servant of God to carry a title. In fact, it appears from this scripture that you should not. It has often been taught in Bible schools and seminaries that the use of titles, i.e. Pastor, Evangelist, Doctor, Father, etc., teaches the people in the congregation to show respect. It is difficult to accept this as truth in light of reality. Respect given to a title is of little significance. Yes, respect must be shown for the office and for the person filling the office, but not because of the title, but because of their servanthood and God-given authority. Do you understand?

Praise God for all of His ministers. Thank Him for the gifts that are given *for the equipping of the saints for the work of ministry, for the edifying of the body of Christ.* Please take a moment right now to pray for your pastor and the leaders God has placed over you. It is very important to note, however, that the 'gifts' given to the body, as listed in Ephesians 4:11, are functions and offices, not titles. Paul, an apostle, not Apostle Paul, is how this great saint addressed himself.

Those of you, who do carry titles, examine your heart and be very honest. Does your title give you self-esteem? Take note of the word "self." Your worth is in Jesus alone. Each time you use your title as a means to build self-esteem, you are stimulating self-life. Remember that God is trying to puncture your flesh. Why would you want to build it up again?

Check your heart, Christian minister: Do you enjoy using your title amongst Christians, but you are a bit ashamed to use it while associating with those in the world? This should tell you something.

Tongues

"I thank my God I speak with tongues more than you all" 1Cor 14:18

Tongues are definitely not the most important spiritual gift and should not be magnified, but neither should it be ignored. About 20 years after his conversion, Paul told the Corinthians that he spoke in tongues more than all of them (1Cor 14:18), and he wished they all spoke in tongues (1Cor 14:5). It is obvious that his initial infilling of the Holy Spirit, and subsequent speaking in tongues was not simply a one-time, religious experience. Paul continued to use this gift throughout his ministry. Dear seeker of truth, perhaps you should reexamine this long debated subject.

Granted, some charismatic zealots have gone overboard espousing unscriptural doctrines regarding this gift. But that is no reason to throw the baby out with the bath water. Do you have a dogmatic stance against this topic? Why? Did you know recent statistics reveal that those who speak in tongues have established more than half of the churches that have been planted around the world, in this present day? Thank God for these workers in the harvest fields! Did you realize that many of the beautiful praise and worship songs that you sing, that have indeed stirred your heart to worship the Most High, were written by those who speak in tongues?

Yes, Christian, speaking in tongues is very strange, and offends the intellect of man. This may be precisely why God has ordained it. Ask the Lord to teach you; He has brought this to your attention for a reason. There are three types of supernatural tongues mentioned in scripture. Perhaps this is the crux of your confusion. Examine these scriptural references:

- Speaking in unknown languages, yet understood by the listeners. This occurred at Pentecost (Acts 2:4)
- A prayer language understood by God alone (1Cor.14:2)

- Speaking forth a prophetic message from God in an unknown language. This is to be done only when there is someone present with the gift of interpretation (1Cor. 14:27,28).

Of course, you can be filled with the Spirit and not speak in tongues. But why not ask for this gift? If Paul considered it worth doing, why shouldn't you? God is still pouring out His Spirit and empowering His servants just as in the Book of Acts. Every Christian can simply ask God to continually fill them with His Spirit, *"...how much more will your heavenly Father give the Holy Spirit to those who ask Him"* (Luke11:13). Ask Him to fill you to overflowing today!

If you already speak or pray in tongues, have you been exercising your gift? You have been given this unusual gift for a reason; use it! Pray daily in the Spirit.

Praise and Worship: the Difference

"Let them praise His name with the dance; Let them sing praises to Him with the timbrel and harp." Psalm 149:3 *"Oh come, let us worship and bow down; Let us kneel before the Lord our Maker."* Psalm 95:6

Do you realize that there is a difference between praise and worship? Many do not. They think that any type of spiritual singing is worship or vise versa. Here are some basics that may help you understand the difference.

Praise declares the attributes of God: His glory, power and strength, His love, kindness and goodness, His holiness, purity and beauty. Praise remembers His mighty deeds and proclaims and teaches the truth of Scripture. In short, praise is speaking or singing about God, all that He is and does. It is expressed before the Lord and proclaimed to others. Praise can be accompanied by fast or slow music.

Praise is meant to bless the heart of God much like children bragging about their parents. Praise is also meant to edify, teach, and strengthen. It may be sedate or vigorous according to culture and tradition. Even so, when expressed from a grateful heart, it cannot be contained. In some cultures, it is quite normal to praise God with loud singing and shouts of joy, using all of your strength. A variety of musical instruments are played with dancing, even twirling before the Lord. God is pleased when you use your gifts, talents and enthusiasm to express yourself to Him.

Worship, on the other hand, consists of acts of service and songs, spoken or sung directly to God. It is usually accompanied by slower music. Remember, praise speaks *about* God. Worship is sung directly *to* God, an expression of your love and gratitude. You are speaking and singing wholeheartedly to the awesome God of all creation; conveying your love to the Lover of your soul. Worship is not about you; although you are greatly blessed as His presence surrounds and fills you. Again, worship is not about others, it is about Him: to Him, for Him.

Songs of worship have become increasingly more intimate over the past few decades. God is preparing His bride. He is drawing you closer. Will you worship Him now? Sing Him a new song, from your heart. Tell Him that you love Him. Then praise Him: declaring His mighty power and goodness. This is your homework; this is *normal Christianity*. Ready to begin?

"But the hour is coming, and now is, when the true worshipers will worship the Father in spirit and truth; for the Father is seeking such to worship Him" (John 4:23).

Executing Justice

"The Lord executes righteousness and justice for all who are oppressed." Psalm 103:6

A very serious question for the Evangelical and Pentecostal Church: Who among you is executing justice? Dear Christian leader, when is the last time you encouraged your members to run for public office? The truth is, church leaders have instructed their flock not to become involved in politics; or at least have not recommended it; thinking public service to be too dirty a business. Perhaps this has been one of the greatest theological blunders of the 20th Century.

Born-again Christians in the United States have stood idly by while prayer was removed from public schools, abortion made legal, and the free exercise of religion trampled under foot. And those Christians who have stood for social justice are somehow considered less spiritual and delegated to the fringe. This should not be! Within a free society there are many opportunities. Thanks be to God. There are also many responsibilities. Prayer and voting, of course, but what about actually doing the work? Will you leave that to the non-believer and then complain because of the appalling decisions they make? Were you expecting different results?

It is time for you to consider this ministry. Yes, ministry! Stand for what is right; speak out! This is not about your rights. You are in the process of dying to self and surrendering your rights. This is about defending the rights of others: the poor, the widow, the orphan, the underprivileged, the handicapped, and the unborn. This is the work of the Christian. This is the will of the Lord.

It is time to prepare young men and women to lead with righteousness and justice. Instruct your children to know and love the Lord with all of their heart. Also prepare them to take positions on the school board or city counsel, as mayor, or judge. If not you or your children, then who? *"Is this not the fast that I have chosen: To loose the bonds of wickedness, to undo the heavy burdens, to let the oppressed go free, and that you break every yoke?"* Isaiah 58:6

Divine Healing

"And these signs will follow those who believe: ...they will lay hands on the sick, and they will recover." Mark 16:17-18

Some may question the authenticity of this section of the Gospel of Mark. Even so, there are several other scriptures that reveal God's proclivity to heal. He clearly promises to heal, and commands His servants to go and do likewise. Church history is filled with testimonies of God's miraculous healing power. Only the narrow-minded would dare refute this claim. Our God heals; sometimes sovereignly and other times using mere men as His instrument.

Having expressed the fact that God promises healing and that healing does occur, the following questions beg an answer: Why are so few healed? What is necessary to accomplish God's purposes? What method should be followed to obtain the optimum results? Is it *your* faith that is required, or the faith of the one in need of healing? Or, perhaps neither, but it is the faith of someone praying on the other side of the world. Do you anoint with oil and lay hands on? Do you pray quietly or loud? Must you confess sins first or can a sinning non-believer be healed? Must demons be cast out?

Minister of healing, there are many teachings about this subject, offering an abundance of information. They are well worth reading and may indeed increase your faith. Please put into practice all that you have learned. You may find, however, that certain techniques may not be applicable in every situation. Did you know that the Bible is very revealing in regard to the topic of divine healing? Will you search the scriptures and seek the Lord for His ways?

Apart from methodology, please know this foundational truth: *God's healing power is always flowing.* Healing is part of God's nature, much like His love and His forgiveness. He does not turn His love on and off, nor does He refuse forgiveness. Can you recall even one instance in the scriptures when Jesus refused to heal someone? If you desire to be healed, you may need to learn how to receive His healing power. If you are ministering to another, please learn how to deliver it to them. The world urgently needs someone who will carry this great gift to the workplace and to the neighborhood. Will you be that one? *"And these signs will follow those who believe... they will lay hands on the sick, and they will recover"* (Mark 16:17-18).

Speaking the Truth in Love

"but, speaking the truth in love, may grow up in all things into Him who is the head—Christ." Ephesians 4:15

Most certainly you have heard this scripture before. No doubt it can have multiple applications. Let's take a look. What does it mean to speak the truth in love? Of course, it does not mean for us to compromise the truth for the sake of maintaining fellowship or for any other reason. For example: when speaking with a Muslim, you wouldn't dilute the gospel for the sake of unity. So, let us establish the fact that you must maintain absolute truth. Agreed? But what about the *love* aspect of this verse; what is necessary to declare uncompromised truth in love?'

Recently there was a panel of five "Christian" clerics debating the exclusivity of the claims of Christ. A few of these religious leaders ascribed to a univeralist view of salvation, that is, all who believe in God will be saved, including Muslims and Hindus, etc. In response, the Bible-believing Christians quoted scripture and stood firmly on the Truth. Unfortunately they seemed very cold and methodical, even defensive... 1 point scored for truth, 0 for love. An undecided listener could hardly have been attracted to their loveless truth.

Dear Christian, no one needs to have doctrines and Bible verses shoved in their face. Having said that, Praise God for the truth of the Bible! But please, dear disciple, let the truth be expressed with *obvious* love. When you possess the truth, you can stand in confidence. There is no need to be intimidated or defensive. Would you get into a fight with someone who believed that the world is flat? Of course not! You would probably pity them. Herald of truth, you can proclaim Jesus with this same quiet assurance. Your face should clearly portray sincerity with a genuine smile. Love should be flowing from your eyes. Extend Christ's wisdom and grace with a firm, confident gentleness. Never compromise, always love. How many have been held back from receiving the truth because of unfriendly, unloving gospel messengers!

Legalism At It's Worst

"And though I have the gift of prophecy, and understand all myster- ies and all knowledge, and though I have all faith, so that I could remove mountains, but have not love, I am nothing." 1Cor. 13:2

Here is a very interesting problem for your consideration. Those in the industrialized countries will more than likely never have to deal with this issue. The ministers in some parts of Africa, however, find this occurring quite frequently. How would you respond? Your answer may reveal your heart.

The missionary, from where it does not matter, enters the village and lives among the people for a season, preaching the gospel in the power of the Holy Spirit. By the grace of God, many believe the truth and are gloriously saved; whole families come to Christ. Praise be to Jesus! Now here is the problem: several of the new Christians are polygamists. The man has three to five wives, according to his wealth; he also has many children. This is the cultural norm. What do you do now? Your choices: 1) Allow the man to keep His first wife and their children and send the others away. 2) Allow him to keep his first wife and all of the children and send the other wives away. 3) Allow him to keep all wives and children but only have sexual relations with the first wife. 4) Allow them to remain as they were.

What would you do, Christian leader? How do you maintain truth in this situation? Oh, here is another fact to throw into the mix: There are no jobs for women in this culture and no training available. If a woman is to survive, she must be married (which is unlikely if she already has children), or she could be a prostitute.

Regrettably, in many of these instances, legalistic religious groups have either split up families, forcing women into poverty and prostitution or have constrained these women to remain celibate, tempting them to commit adultery. Somehow, dear reader, this does not seem like the love of God. Doesn't godly wisdom and love clearly dictate that the families should stay together with all marital privileges? Of course, no additional wives should be taken. And the ways of monogamy would then be taught to the next generation. The polygamist must not become a church leader, however. *"A deacon must be the husband of but one wife and must manage his children and his household well."* 1Tim 3:12 (NIV)

Help me, Lord, to know your ways, for they are perfect.

Jerusalem, The Capital of the World

"Thus says the Lord of hosts: 'I am zealous for Zion with great zeal; with great fervor I am zealous for her.' Thus says the Lord: 'I will return to Zion, and dwell in the midst of Jerusalem. Jerusalem shall be called the City of Truth, The Mountain of the Lord of hosts, The Holy Mountain.'" Zechariah 8:2-3

Since its establishment by King David around 1000 B.C., this holy city has been captured, recaptured, and destroyed. Jerusalem has become a stumbling block for the whole world. What is it with this city? Why does the world focus here? There is no oil, great industries, or technological advancements that would warrant such attention. Why then, Jerusalem? Because **God loves Jerusalem!** God has spoken blessing to her and tells us to pray for her peace. The Faithful One has a plan for her!

During the past century, we have seen amazing prophetic fulfillment: In 1948, Israel became a nation once again by the mere signing of a piece of paper. Since then, cities have been built, a language and monetary system rebirthed, even the desert has been irrigated... fulfilling Amos' prophecy that the deserts would bloom. (Israel is one of the world's largest exporters of cut flowers ... grown in the desert!) There have been wars and terrorism, but in the midst of it all, those with only minimal spiritual discernment can see God's miraculous defense. He stood up and fought for her, repelling each attack and giving Israel more land, including the entire city of Jerusalem.

Jesus said, *"..Jerusalem will be trampled by Gentiles until the times of the Gentiles are fulfilled"* (Luke 21:24). Dear Christian, it would be wise to reset your prophetic clock. There has been a shift in the heavenlies. Jerusalem is no longer under Gentile rule. The *times of the Gentiles* (season of favor) is coming to an end. God will soon direct His redeeming love upon Jerusalem and the salvation of the Jew. He will soon graft them back into the olive tree (Rom. 11:24).

Open your eyes! The Holy One of Israel is doing a wonderful thing! The Almighty is faithful to fulfill every one of His promises. He has made an *everlasting* covenant with Israel. Keep your eyes on Jerusalem, my friend. The stage is being set for the final act of human history. Jesus will soon return to earth and will reign supreme. Jerusalem will become the capital of the world! *"Pray for the peace of Jerusalem: may those who love you be secure."* Ps.122:6

The Salvation of the Jews

Does God still have a plan for the Jews; or were they rejected after refusing salvation through Messiah, Jesus? These questions have perplexed Christians for nearly two thousand years. Frankly, I'm not quite sure why. Perhaps anti-Semitism or unbelief has influenced some of the doctrine. Either way, it is time to revisit these doctrines. Jehovah is about to do something amazing!

Scripture seems to have very clear information regarding this matter: *"Concerning the gospel they are enemies for your sake, but concerning the election **they are beloved for the sake of the fathers. For the gifts and the calling of God are irrevocable.** For as you were once disobedient to God, yet have now obtained mercy through their disobedience, even so these also have now been disobedient, that through the mercy shown you they also may obtain mercy. For God has committed them all to disobedience, that He might have mercy on all. Oh, the depth of the riches both of the wisdom and knowledge of God"* (Rom. 11:28-33)!

In this scripture, Paul obviously states: 1) At the present time, the Jews are enemies of the gospel. 2) Concerning their election (calling) they are beloved for the sake of Abraham, Isaac, Jacob. 3) Their calling is irrevocable. 4) Just as we (Gentiles) were disobedient and have now obtained mercy, God has committed all of the Jews to disobedience so *"He might have mercy on all."* 5) Paul marvels at the wisdom of God!

Exactly how this great salvation will occur is uncertain. Will it happen en masse, or individually? Perhaps, in one moment the truth will break forth. A revelation of Messiah will come like a veil being removed from their eyes. The prophet Zechariah wrote: *"And I will pour on the house of David and on the inhabitants of Jerusalem the Spirit of grace and supplication; then they will look on Me whom they pierced. Yes, they will mourn for Him as one mourns for his*

215

only son, and grieve for Him as one grieves for a firstborn" (Zech. 12:10)
We can only seek the Lord for the full meaning of this verse. But be sure of one thing: God is faithful. He has made an everlasting covenant with Abraham. Salvation will come to the Jews! See what God is doing in your very midst: He has reestablished the nation of Israel, drawing Jews from north, south, east and west - just as He said that He would. In His perfect time, after the harvest of Gentiles is complete, the Lord will cast out His net and Israel will be saved.

"For I do not desire, brethren, that you should be ignorant of this mystery, lest you should be wise in your own opinion, that blindness in part has happened to Israel until the fullness of the Gentiles has come in. And so all Israel will be saved..." (Rom. 11:25-27). Pray for the salvation of the Jews. This is God's perfect will!

There is a Difference

"Jesus said to him, 'I am the way, the truth, and the life. No one comes to the Father except through Me.'" John 14:6

It is truly amazing how some use excellent reasoning and logic to determine the best choices for their life (where to live, where to go to school, what job to accept); but when it comes to spiritual matters, many actually become quite dense. Haven't you heard the mantra "All religions are the same." or "All roads lead to heaven"?

Only a fool would believe that all roads lead to New York, or London, or Nairobi. Why would anyone assume that all roads lead to heaven? And, even casual observation reveals that all religions are not the same. For instance: one religion teaches that Jesus and Lucifer are brothers, another that you can become a god if you work hard enough. Yet another expounds that all who do not accept their beliefs should be killed. There is a common denominator, though; they all claim to be the only way. And all of them believe if you pray or meditate, work, or suffer enough in this life, then and only then, will you earn eternal peace. In other words, you must secure your own salvation. One religion is unique, however. Christianity admits man's inability to reach up to God. Rather, God has lovingly reached down to us through His only Son.

It seems to be in vogue these days to seek spiritual truth. Many are doing it. Years are spent exploring religious philosophy. Seeking seems to be an end unto itself. It appears, however, that no one really wants to *find*. Their spiritual hunger is appeased with the process of seeking and with mere intellectual crumbs. This is also the age of tolerance and openness. It is socially acceptable to believe whatever you please. But is that really wise when your eternal destiny is at stake? Consider the words of Jesus: *"No one comes to the Father except through Me."*

For all who seek the truth here is a brief synopsis: There are many religions, many beliefs, and many religious leaders. All teach a good works based righteousness except one. All claim to know the way to God, but only One claimed to be God, Himself. All of these leaders died. One rose from the dead and lives forever. His name is Jesus Christ.

Dear searcher, God is no longer a mystery. He has clearly revealed Himself through His Word; He is love! There is no one who has wholeheartedly sought God and not found Him. Why not seek Him now? *I want to know You, Lord. Please reveal Yourself to me.*

Blessed Assurance

"These things I have written to you who believe in the name of the Son of God, that you may know that you have eternal life..."
1John 5:13

John, the apostle, told the churches that they could be certain of their salvation. Do you see what he wrote? You can **know** that you have eternal life, if you believe in Jesus Christ. If you abide in Him, you can say with confidence, "I know that I'm going to Heaven."

A large segment of Christianity has a big problem with this. They consider it to be the utmost arrogance and pride to declare assurance. Why? because of a faulty concept called *works righteousness,* or maybe because of a false sense of humility. If you believe that you must somehow earn your salvation by doing good things, then of course, someone claiming to be sure of heaven would be saying, "I'm so good that I deserve to be in heaven."

In fact, they are saying the opposite. You see, salvation is the free gift of God; paid in full by the shed blood of Jesus. It is a gift to you because God offered His only Son to suffer and die in your place. Jesus earned your salvation. You must simply receive it. It is not arrogance, but humility, to say, "I can do nothing to save myself." Some would reply, "This is too easy. It can't be true." They feel that they must do something to merit the gift. Think about that for a minute. It would not be a gift if it was earned. It would be a payment. Wouldn't it? The Word of God clearly says: *"but the gift of God is eternal life in Christ Jesus our Lord"* (Rom. 6:23).

You can be sure of this: You are saved by grace, not works. There will be no boasting in heaven about your accomplishments. Perhaps you don't like that idea. You want credit for your good works. There will be rewards in heaven, but no one will enter because they deserved it. You will be there only because of Jesus, His sacrifice and His love. If you think otherwise, you have not understood what Paul wrote to the Ephesians: *"For by grace you have been saved through faith, and that not of yourselves; it is the gift of God, not of works, lest anyone should boast"* (Eph. 2:8-9).

Assurance of salvation brings you peace. Your good deeds then spring forth from a heart of thanksgiving rather than from striving to be good enough. Striving is bondage, my friend, working day after day to somehow attain heaven. You have been saved by Jesus, saved to the uttermost. Receive Him, believe in Him, and rejoice with full assurance. *"Blessed assurance, Jesus is mine. O what a foretaste of glory divine.'"*

Santa Claus

"The father shall make known Your truth to the children." Isa 38:19

How western civilization loves Santa Claus. Jolly old Saint Nick circumnavigates the globe in his flying sleigh bringing presents to good little boys and girls. This nice story stimulates the imagination of millions of children. It also enhances retail sales to the tune of billions of dollars. Seems all very harmless, doesn't it?

Dear parents, fantasy is wonderful; and pretending is a necessary part of a child's development, but please understand, teaching your children to believe in Santa Claus is neither fantasy nor pretending. You tell your children something that is not true and then reinforce this non-truth with "evidence" - like a letter from the North Pole or a half eaten snack that was left for Santa. Your child believes you with all of their heart. Regrettably, you are deceiving them. Can this be good? This may be difficult for you to accept because it is so deeply ingrained within the culture.

What about the disappointment that ensues after your child discovers that Santa is not real. Some children are extremely upset. They quickly cover their hurt because they don't want to be a baby. Nonetheless, the whole process has taken its toll. Deep within, truth has been eroded and trust diminished. Millions suffer from depression during the Christmas season for a variety of reasons, no doubt. But the manifestation of an unresolved emotional wound cannot be ruled out. Little hopes and dreams have been crushed.

Does this mean that you should deprive your children of the fun and excitement generated by Santa? Absolutely not. Simply tell them that he is pretend. Of course, you want their focus to be on Jesus anyway, don't you? His Christmas story is filled with awesome wonder and excitement too. And the best part of all: It is TRUTH!

Lord, please heal my deeply buried emotional wounds, whatever their cause. And help me to fully enjoy the celebration of the birth of Jesus. Forgive me for deceiving the children.

Building The Ministry

You are well aware that Jesus chose mostly unlearned men to lay the foundation of His earth-shattering, world encompassing ministry. He used the least likely of vessels to carry His Father's glory. Paul reiterated this principle when writing to the Corinthian church: *"But God has chosen the foolish things of the world to put to shame the wise, and God has chosen the weak things of the world to put to shame the things which are mighty; and the base things of the world and the things which are despised God has chosen, and the things which are not, to bring to nothing the things that are, that no flesh should glory in His presence"* (1Cor. 1:27).

Disciple, how often the Church of Jesus has suffered from the use of worldly wisdom! If you are in the process of building a work of God, do not look for the most qualified according to the standards of men. How many ministries are top-heavy with those holding doctorates and masters degrees! But where is the power of God? Where are the mighty men and women of God who do exploits? Who carries the anointing that breaks the yoke of bondage? Don't you want someone like this to help you build... someone who is more anointed than you! (Think about it!)

You must follow the leading of the Spirit, as the Lord builds His Church. Please don't be concerned with academic credentials; look at their heart. Is this person humble and broken? Are they completely abandoned to the purposes of God? Will they go anywhere and do anything that the Lord tells them? Can they live by faith as well as by salary? Are they givers? Do they have courage? Are they loyal and teachable? Do they have a servant's heart? The meek and lowly, the weak and foolish, the humble and the broken, these are the most likely candidates to carry God's anointing to this generation. You know this to be true; Church history is full of examples. Surely you don't want to merely look impressive by presenting a letterhead full of PhDs. You want to be effective, don't you... seeing lives changed by the power of God?

In saying these things, let it be perfectly clear that knowledge is a very good thing; Paul was a highly gifted and educated man. But Paul was also completely surrendered to the will of God. Knowledge can be obtained in a variety of ways, formal education being only one method. (After all, who is a better Teacher than the Holy Spirit?) Know this too: Gifts and talents come directly from God, but they must be exercised. There are many diamonds in the rough that have yet to be polished.

If you must choose between the educated and the broken, choose the broken. In fact, surround yourself with weak, foolish, obedient lovers of God. Surely this is the fertile seedbed for revival!

Welcome to Our Church

… Oh, not our church, we mean Jesus' church

"For if there should come into your assembly a man with gold rings, in fine apparel, and there should also come in a poor man in filthy clothes" James 2:2

Have you ever entered a church building only to be greeted by an instructive sign? *No Food in the Sanctuary, No Chewing Gum, No Talking,, No something or other.* Do you realize what type of image you are presenting? It brings to mind a sign on the border of Bhutan and Tibet: **Welcome, No Admittance.** Very uninviting, don't you think?

There certainly is a place for rules and boundaries, but perhaps there is also a better way of presenting them. Visitors need to feel welcome, not restricted. The first thing hurting people want to see is a sincere non-judgmental look on the face of an open-armed greeter; not another worldly "posted" sign. This is common sense.

Dear Christian leader, please know that the time is soon coming when the unclean, uncouth, unsociable folk will be gracing the doorstep of the church. Will your members be ready? Not only to accept them as they are, but also to give them a lifetime to be conformed to the image of Jesus? They will not be prepared unless you prepare them. If they are now complaining about those who smoke on the front steps of the church or leave gum under the seats, just think of the upset when the drunken, foul smelling homeless come in and sit beside them... and then take months, if not years, to maintain sobriety. May God bless your congregation with such an opportunity. *Lord, please prepare us to truly welcome those in need. Anoint us to love the unlovable... without complaining.*

Doctrine Supreme?

"Then Peter opened his mouth and said: 'In truth I perceive that God shows no partiality. But in every nation whoever fears Him and works righteousness is accepted by Him.'" Acts 10: 34-35

Methodists, Lutherans, Catholics, Pentecostals, Baptists, and Seventh Day Adventists are all operating in the gifts of the Holy Spirit? How can this be? Members from diverse doctrinal backgrounds have been experiencing signs and wonders. It should be obvious that God is pouring out His Spirit on all flesh. Some of the sons and daughters that are prophesying and flowing in the Spirit have doctrines that may be quite different from yours. When you observe God doing these things logic should certainly dictate that God is no respecter of persons.

The Pharisees considered doctrine to be supreme; and so do religious people of today. But Jesus rebuked the Pharisees for their dogmatic approach. Be careful that you don't make the same blunder. There will be no rewards handed out for the one with the best doctrine. The Lord is far more interested in your heart.

Maybe you will be surprised to see those in heaven whose beliefs you did not agree with. Yes, they embraced Jesus' death and resurrection but, "Those other things are complete heresy," you say. Surprise! The blood of Jesus even covers inaccurate doctrines. And that's not all! Their position of honor and responsibility in heaven may be greater than the ones with the "perfect" doctrine and the "correct" order of service. While they were busy searching the scriptures to prove the so-called heretics wrong, criticizing their doctrines and practices, these imperfect ones were pouring out their heart… giving, serving and loving.

Any doctrine that denies Salvation through the shed blood of Jesus, or tolerates sin, is heresy; make no mistake about that! The Apostle's Creed is an excellent criterion for sound doctrine and has been the foundational standard for nearly 2000 years... Lord, please forgive me for my judgmental heart. Help me to lovingly receive all of my brothers and sisters in Christ. By Your grace, as You give opportunity, I will serve them and serve with them.

New Members

"Blessed are the peacemakers, for they shall be called sons of God." Matthew 5:9

Dear Pastor and church leaders, how do you receive new members? I mean do you make it easy or difficult for those coming from another congregation to join your church? Throughout Christendom, there is an alarming trend run rampant. Statistics verify that most church growth numbers don't reflect the addition of new converts but are merely church transfers. This means that while one church is gaining members, another is loosing them. How could this be good for the overall well being of the Church in any region?

There are a variety of reasons why people leave one church and flee to another, and one ministry principle cannot apply to every situation; this is for sure. But how many pastors are happy to receive new members "no questions asked." They welcome the new people without considering any of the harmful consequences. This should not be. Of course, we are not implying that they are simply after the tithe or offering. God forbid that this would be true. But be very honest; is it partially true? Wouldn't it be better to sit with those interested in joining your church and find out why they are leaving their former congregation. Did God call them out of their church home and tell them to become a member here; or was it due to an offense or some other negative thing that needs to be addressed?

Some of these folks should be strongly urged to return to their previous congregation and seek reconciliation and healing. Perhaps you could even help in this process. Surely you are not so interested in gaining new members that you would not be willing to help reinstate them in their former place of worship. Having said these things let it be perfectly clear that pastors should never "possess" their flock. Members should be free to leave at any time without feeling condemned. But they should only leave by the leading of the Spirit.

The Confessional Booth

"Confess your trespasses to one another, and pray for one another, that you may be healed..." James 5:16

A grave disservice was rendered to all of Christendom when the reformers dismantled the confessional booth. If you are a Protestant, this statement may be a bit shocking. Let me be perfectly clear: When you confess your sins to God He forgives you. You need no intermediary. There is no suggestion being made that the presence of a minister or priest is necessary for the forgiveness of sins. This is not the issue. But, have you considered the emotional, and consequently, the physical benefits of unburdening one's conscience? Even after confessing their sin directly to God, many people feel the need to tell someone else. This can bring reassurance of forgiveness and a measure of correction and encouragement. Regrettably, the opportunity is unavailable to a large segment of the faithful. In lieu of the confessional, thousands of Christians flock to counselors and psychiatrists for relief of guilt.

Did you know that John and Charles Wesley, the great 19th century revivalists, met weekly with a small group of men to confess their sins to one another? We too should reconsider the value of confession, even going as far as reinstituting the anonymous confessional (a curtain or room divider), making a way for those who are fearful. And why not facilitate groups like Wesley's where accountability would be fostered. What freedom and growth could be experienced! Not by law or compulsion, but a tool for healing and holiness. Is this too radical? Jesus is very radical. Don't be too proud to confess your sins to another.

The Sin of Murder

"Keep yourself far from a false matter; do not kill the innocent and righteous. For I will not justify the wicked." Exodus 23:7

Who could possibly justify the murder of a baby? What lie is sufficient to cause an entire culture to abort their young with impunity? Dear reader, who will stand for righteousness? Who will cry out? It has long been stated it is not good to bring an unwanted child into the world, leaving them vulnerable to abuse and neglect. In the United States alone there are currently 1.3 million abortions per year. But if the truth be known, there are 2 million parents searching for a child to adopt. No baby would be unwanted. Others contend that a woman has a right to choose because "it is my body." Medical evidence clearly refutes this. The baby is a totally separate person with his or her own blood supply, heart, and brain. Yes, dependant upon the mother, but unequivocally distinct.

Another point that is often made: What about victims of incest and rape; should they be forced to have the baby? The truth remains that less than 2% of all abortions are performed as a result of rape and incest. In the Old Testament, God instructed the people to kill the rapist. In our society, we often set the rapist free with only minimal punishment and instead kill the innocent baby. This is an unbelievable perversion of justice! During an abortion, defenseless babies have their arms and legs torn off as well as their skull crushed; others are burned to death with caustic saline. The media has shown every type of brutal, violent murder, including the atrocities of the holocaust, but they refuse to show an abortion. I wonder why. If the world could see the barbarity of this abomination, perhaps then, there would be an outcry in the land.

Are you disturbed by these facts? Do they revolt you to the point of nausea? Or are you merely sick of hearing about it? Check your heart, Christian. Will you stand for righteousness? Will you cry?

Perhaps you have performed or received an abortion; know that God is merciful. Please do not attempt to justify yourself. It is only when you admit your sin that you can be forgiven and healed. God loves you. Turn to Him now.

Feminism

"The Lord executes righteousness and justice for all who are oppressed." Psalm 103:6

Definition: "A doctrine that advocates equal rights for women, the movement aimed at equal rights for women, the women's liberation movement." Guard you heart, dear woman. Truth is powerful; it is also offensive at times. There are few who dare to venture into this minefield of discussion. But, by the grace of God, we will proceed.

The original *women's movement* legitimately fought for women's rights in our society: the right to equal pay for equal work, the right for equal opportunity for job consideration and advancement, and justice for those who were raped and abused. Thank God for their efforts. However, feminism as we now know it has moved far beyond these basic civil rights, and many bruised and angry women have fallen prey to their agenda. In the process they have trampled God's laws and have sought to redefine the very fiber of society. God help us.

Among the various feminist groups, certain philosophies have been espoused claiming that there is no difference between a man and a woman (except for the obvious biological ones)... "A woman can and should do everything a man does!" There has even been an attempt to change God's identity from Father to "mother," to suite their purposes. How absurd! Dear daughter of God, your heavenly Father has made you different from a man for a reason. Your body and your emotional makeup is no better or worse, just different. What a wonderful gift your femininity is!

Women are also taught that they have the right to discard the baby that the Creator has placed within their womb. As a result, abortion has been legalized and many women now suffer the serious spiritual, emotional, and sometimes physical, consequences of this choice. Lesbianism is also promoted through this "liberation" agenda, a clear violation of God's natural law.

A great scourge has inflicted its wounds upon the women of the western culture... and many scarcely recognize it. Women are exploited under the guise of equal rights. Stress, anxiety, fear and depression have accompanied the loss of a woman's God ordained identity and purposes. Physical maladies abound as a result.

Can you imagine the deception? Within this generation, God has raised up a men's movement to encourage husbands to fulfill the promises they have made to their wife: to love, honor and care for them and be truthful to them... to nurture their giftings with support and encouragement. What could be more woman friendly? What teaching could be more family supportive? And yet, the feminist stand vehemently opposed to them. Who can comprehend this?!

Be careful, servant of God. It is easy to sympathize with the cause of exploited, downtrodden women. Of course, you should seek justice for all who are oppressed, but understand that this package contains much more than equal rights.

Jesus as Savior, Jesus as Lord

"He who loves father or mother more than Me is not worthy of Me. And he who loves son or daughter more than Me is not worthy of Me. And he who does not take his cross and follow after Me is not worthy of Me. He who finds his life will lose it, and he who loses his life for My sake will find it." Matthew 10:37-39

Is there really a difference, beloved... Jesus as Savior vs. Jesus as Lord? In this present diluted understanding of Christianity, we have heard it stated that someone can be "saved" without making Jesus the Lord of their life. They can accept His great sacrifice for their sin but not completely surrender to His authority. Is this true? Was Jesus' call to radical obedient discipleship a second level of Christianity, another step in the process of sanctification, or was it merely the entry level, a call to salvation. Where does the scripture make a clear distinction between the two?

The gospel of Jesus Christ, as presented during the 20th century, has been candy-coated almost to the point of heresy. It was not this way in previous generations. Seekers were well aware of the commitment they were making before they surrendered all to become a Christian. The biblical concepts of obedience to the Word of God, including a turning away from sin... have been obscured by the "salvation made simple" practice of saying, "With every head bowed and every eye closed, just raise your hand if you want to invite Jesus into your life." Do you really think that this method of evangelism affords a true and lasting salvation? Perhaps, but consider this:

An affluent western culture wants everything to be easy... no need to be embarrassed or uncomfortable. "Jesus loves you; just believe in Him and you will be saved." What about those in China, or India, or the Middle East... a decision to accept Christ as Savior most certainly incurs the wrath of family and friends, not to mention the threat of imprisonment, torture, or even death. Do you think that these precious saints don't count the cost before they accept the Lord? Should there be less of a commitment for those in the west? Let's get real. If a doctrine doesn't work everywhere in the world... in every culture, it is not truth.

Jesus Christ died for the sins of all mankind. He invites everyone to follow Him, everyone to be saved. Have you decided to follow Jesus? Did you examine the fine print of the New Covenant? It reads something like this: "Jesus suffered and died for the remission of your sins. He redeemed you from the curse of the law and the works of the devil. If you will believe in Him, have trusting faith in Him, He freely offers you forgiveness of your sins and the matchless gift of eternal life... by grace not by works." But read on: "You were purchased by the shedding of His precious blood, the blood of the only begotten son of the Father. *You do not belong to yourself any longer.* You have been bought with a great price. You now belong to God and He has sovereign rights to your life... He will lead you and guide you and bless you. He will also correct and discipline you. You must love Him above all things... and if you do love Him, you will obey Him." Does this sound familiar?

Having said this, let it be perfectly clear that even true followers of Jesus experience failure; a disciple may occasionally succumb to temptation; the flesh is weak. We sometimes respond incorrectly; our thoughts, words, and actions are imperfect. It will take an entire lifetime to be conformed to the image of Christ. But what we are speaking of here is not the process of sanctification. Rather, a necessary attitude of heart when deciding to become a Christian: turning away from sin, a surrendered will, holding nothing back. Isn't this the way to become a Christian? Beloved, make no mistake : obedient surrender to the sovereign lordship of Christ is an intricate part of Salvation. Shouldn't this be taught?

Bring Them To Christ Or Bring Christ To Them?

"And He said, 'The kingdom of God is as if a man should scatter seed on the ground, and should sleep by night and rise by day, and the seed should sprout and grow, he himself does not know how. For the earth yields crops by itself: first the blade, then the head, after that the full grain in the head. But when the grain ripens, immediately he puts in the sickle, because the harvest has come.'"
Mark 4:26-29

Evangelism is such a touchy subject, isn't it? Everyone agrees that we should be doing it, and yet few actually do. Most of the time Christians feel so inadequate and uncomfortable that they can barely say, "God bless you." How do you overcome such an obstacle? Perhaps, beloved, you have been seeing it all wrong. It has often been taught that you are to "lead them to Christ." This may include an agenda driven witness that presents the gospel in abbreviated form and follows with the *prayer,* a decision to accept Christ as Savior. Isn't it time to reexamine this timeworn method?

In saying this, let it be perfectly clear that there are many who have had a measure of success with this approach; let's thank God for their faithful work. Certainly this way is far better than doing nothing; but dear disciple, some people feel pressured when this method is applied. They may even acquiesce to the point of saying the sinner's prayer, but this does not mean that they are truly saved. Salvation comes by faith in Jesus, not by simply mouthing a prayer.

Surveys have revealed that most born again believers have received a positive Christian witness from between five and fifteen individuals before they made the decision to accept Christ's sacrifice for the forgiveness of their sins. Take another look at Mark 4:26-29; Jesus is speaking of the Kingdom of God being likened to a man who sows seeds. He sleeps and rises, the seeds sprout and grow, he doesn't know how. But finally, when the grain ripens, it is harvested.

This explains the process of evangelism, dear one. After the soil of the heart is broken, seeds of the gospel are sown, and the rain of

Christian witness will water them. When the soul is fully ripe, you put in the sickle. If indeed this *is* a true picture of the process, how foolish it would be to harvest a seedling soul before it had come to true faith... And yet, so many well-meaning "evangelists," attempt to do this very thing.

Usually the fruit of evangelism does not grow overnight. Do not feel compelled to close the deal with every person you witness to. Someone will plant the seed, others will water it, and another will harvest. If you could see yourself as part of that process, you may feel a bit more at ease. Surely, you can *bring Jesus to them* through love, and concern, and your practical help. Yes, be ready and willing to give a reason for your hope. Learn how to share the personal testimonies of God's loving intervention in your life. Learn a few scriptures, and apply them when appropriate. Nevertheless, you do not need to do all of these things... all of the time. Be a friend, show kindness, offer Godly counsel, offer to pray for their needs. You can do this; you can bring Jesus to them! Remember, true evangelism is the work of the Holy Spirit; follow His leading!

"Then I looked, and behold, a white cloud, and on the cloud sat One like the Son of Man, having on His head a golden crown, and in His hand a sharp sickle. And another angel came out of the temple, crying with a loud voice to Him who sat on the cloud, 'Thrust in Your sickle and reap, for the time has come for You to reap, for the harvest of the earth is ripe.' So He who sat on the cloud thrust in His sickle on the earth, and the earth was reaped." Rev. 14:14-16

Holy Communion

"And as they were eating, Jesus took bread, blessed and broke it, and gave it to them and said, 'Take, eat; this is My body.' Then He took the cup, and when He had given thanks He gave it to them, and they all drank from it. And He said to them, 'This is My blood of the new covenant, which is shed for many.'" Mark 14:22-24

There is so much controversy regarding this precious gift of God. Some would even fight about it. Catholics believe that the bread and wine actually becomes the body and blood of Christ (transubstantiation). Other liturgical churches believe the bread and wine/juice are the body and blood of Christ in a spiritual or mystical way (consubstantiation). Another large segment of Christianity considers the elements to be only a remembrance. Can we not debate these issues again, and again?

Regardless of your doctrinal beliefs I think we can agree that by partaking of this wondrous mystery, we are obeying Jesus' command to *"do this in remembrance of Me."* We should also agree that Holy Communion is far more than a mere ceremony. God forgive us for regressing to such a low point.

Dear lover of God, Communion is a way of experiencing intimacy with God. The bread and wine/juice becomes a point of contact, a means of grace. Too much time is wasted debating the meaning of the elements, when the emphasis should be placed upon the meal itself. Do you understand?

As we partake, we choose to eat and drink the *Life* of Jesus in a spiritual sense. In this way, Holy Communion becomes spiritual nourishment... offering physical and spiritual strength and healing to those who partake of this life-giving blessing. And, of course, we find strength in the unity of communing with one another.

There is a resurgence in progress. The Lord is bringing to the forefront the importance of receiving Holy Communion, The Table of the Lord, as it were. Please see what He is doing in this hour and reap the maximum benefit. If you are a leader, be sure to minister this heavenly meal often... that the people will be blessed. Many have begun the practice of daily communion... personally or corporately. Don't allow your preconceived ideas to rob you of the richness of this great blessing.

Make the time to be alone with the One who suffered and died for you, and remember what He has done. Prepare the portion of bread and wine/juice according to your custom. Examine yourself thoroughly, yielding to the gentle promptings of the Holy Spirit. As He reveals your sins, simply repent. Enjoy God's forgiveness as you partake of the bread and the cup. Do this regularly, perhaps, every day for thirty days... maybe every day for the rest of your life. Breakthroughs are awaiting you!

In an Unworthy Manner

"For as often as you eat this bread and drink this cup, you proclaim the Lord's death till He comes. Therefore whoever eats this bread or drinks this cup of the Lord in an unworthy manner will be guilty of the body and blood of the Lord. But let a man examine himself, and so let him eat of the bread and drink of the cup. For he who eats and drinks in an unworthy manner eats and drinks judgment to himself, not discerning the Lord's body. For this reason many are weak and sick among you, and many sleep. For if we would judge ourselves, we would not be judged." 1Cor 11:26-31

Is it merely a ceremony, the Lord's Supper? Has it become matter of fact, casual, just another religious thing to do? Dear one, be careful! Please reread this passage. *"For this reason many are weak and sick among you, and many sleep."* Paul exhorts the Corinthian church to seriously consider what they are doing. Do not partake of the bread and drink of the cup in an unworthy manner. Discern the Lord's body and examine yourself; yes, judge yourself so that you will not be judged.

The Bread of Life

"And she brought forth her firstborn Son, and wrapped Him in swaddling cloths, and laid Him in a manger, because there was no room for them in the inn." Luke 2:7

Have you ever seen this verse? Of course you have, a hundred times. But did you ever see this? Jesus called Himself *the Bread of Life* (John 6:48). He was born in Bethlehem, which means: *house of bread.* And where did Mary lay Jesus? In a manger... a feeding trough!

How fitting for the Bread of Life to be born in the house of bread and laid in a feeding trough! What a perfect picture of God's intended purposes! What a perfect God we have! Eat and drink deeply, beloved. *"I am the living bread which came down from heaven. If anyone eats of this bread, he will live forever."* (John 6:51).

Homosexuality

"If a man lies with a male as he lies with a woman, both of them have committed an abomination..." Leviticus 20:13 *"Therefore God also gave them up to uncleanness, in the lusts of their hearts, to dishonor their bodies among themselves, who exchanged the truth of God for the lie, and worshiped and served the creature rather than the Creator, who is blessed forever. Amen. For this reason God gave them up to vile passions. For even their women exchanged the natural use for what is against nature. Likewise also the men, leaving the natural use of the woman, burned in their lust for one another, men with men committing what is shameful, and receiving in themselves the penalty of their error which was due."* Romans 1:24

Is there any question that homosexuality is a sin? Nonetheless, western culture is embracing this "alternate" lifestyle, just as we have already embraced adultery and divorce. The family is disintegrating before our very eyes; our society is in grave danger. Servant of God, will you have the courage to take a stand for righteousness?

The sinner is never to be hated or mistreated; after all, where would *you* be if God did not love the sinner. But do not be deceived, this sin must be seen for what it is. The proliferation of homosexuality is an affront to God and a serious threat to our culture. Do you know, that because of sexually transmitted disease and other factors, the average life expectancy of the homosexual male is well below that of heterosexuals? During their lifetime, the average homosexual male can have more than one hundred sexual partners. Even if the scripture did not condemn this way of life, should this really be considered a viable lifestyle?

Unfortunately, even some churches have accepted the practice of homosexuality and have ordained clergy who are openly gay. Throughout history, the Church has frequently disagreed on various aspects of doctrine and practice, this is nothing new. But for a denomination to endorse a lifestyle that the Lord clearly declares to be a sin... this renders those churches apostate. Wrong is being said to be right, in direct contradiction to God's Word. This can never be justified.

Please love the homosexual and the lesbian; be compassionate and understanding; offer wise counsel and God's truth, with much love. They should feel very welcome in your church. But dear one, homosexual sin is sin indeed. It must be repented of... with a turning away from that way of life. How can it be stated any more clearly than this: *"Do you not know that the unrighteous will not inherit the kingdom of God? Do not be deceived. Neither fornicators, nor idolaters, nor adulterers, nor homosexuals, nor sodomites, nor thieves, nor covetous, nor drunkards, nor revilers, nor extortioners will inherit the kingdom of God"* (1Cor. 6:9).

If you are a fornicator, or a thief, or a drunkard, obviously, this passage also applies to you. However, it is one thing to admit that you have sinned and to struggle with that sin; it is completely another thing to refuse to admit your sin and to willingly misinterpret God's Word to facilitate your sinfulness. The former will be forgiven; the later will be adjudged unrighteous.

Exchanging the Truth

"Now before they lay down, the men of the city, the men of Sodom, both old and young, all the people from every quarter, surrounded the house. And they called to Lot and said to him, 'Where are the men who came to you tonight? Bring them out to us that we may know them.'" Genesis 19:4-5

The homosexual community has long taught that Sodom was not destroyed because of deviant sexual promiscuity but because the inhabitants were unjust and inhospitable. The foundation of this belief seems to center on the Hebrew word "yada" (to know) found in Genesis 19. They claim that the men of Sodom merely wanted to become acquainted with the messengers of God. The word "yada" however, has been used in several Old Testament passages as a euphemism for intercourse. It is highly unlikely that it's meaning would be different here. Gays would have us believe they have received new revelation regarding this scripture...

The agony of repressed sexual desire can cause a variety of things to occur, including discouragement and depression. Desperate for relief, one's mindset may begin to change...even their beliefs and doctrines. It is easier for a Christian to modify their beliefs to accommodate their sin, than to outright disobey God. The person with homosexual tendencies who relieves the pressure in this way will have to spend the rest of their life defending their new beliefs and may eventually become angry, bitter and even feeling hatred toward anyone who challenges him. Is this happening to you, beloved? Please be aware of your self-deception. Exchanging God's truth for a lie will only lead to more pain.

Someone's sexual orientation can be formed in a variety of ways, sometimes in ways that are beyond their control. Nevertheless, we do know that God has permitted whatever situation one finds themselves in. (Obviously, He is in control of everything!) People struggle with all types of difficulty, adversity and pain. God knows exactly what to allow into each life and then supplies the grace to deal with it. Whether it is a life-long infirmity or handicap, obesity, poverty, persecution, difficult relationship, sexual temptation... in their deepest depths, each one feels that their situation is the absolute worst place to be. We know that our God is a God of peace, healing and deliverance and He will surely deliver us. But even if He does not, we will praise Him and seek to obey Him.

You are a lover of God who wants to do God's will. Stand! Do not take the easy way. The Master has helped you until this very day and He will continue to help you. He has been with you in your darkest hours and His good plan for you is still unfolding. He loves you! How glorious it will be in that Day for those who overcome.

What If There Was No Christ?

"Jesus said to him, 'You shall love the Lord your God with all your heart, with all your soul, and with all your mind. This is the first and great commandment. And the second is like it: You shall love your neighbor as yourself.'" Matthew 22:37-39

Throughout history, Christianity has been maligned for its hypocrisy and self-righteous, religious ways. It has been accused of bigotry, judgmentalism, tyranny, and of even starting wars. Guilty? Yes, unfortunately it is true... because the unparalleled Word of

Life was entrusted to mere men. But dear believer, what would the world be like if there was no Christ and there were no Christians? At the time of Jesus' birth, people were being brutalized in the Roman arenas, torn to shreds by gladiators, eaten by wild animals... all for the purpose of entertainment. The rise of Christianity put a stop to that. In fact, over the next two millennium, as Christians went out into the world, these types of practices were abated. There was (and still is) no end to the list of cruelties and atrocities perpetrated upon the weak and helpless: Women were abused (cattle were treated better); children were discarded in garbage dumps, the sick were left to die. But, Christians intervened! Unwanted babies were taken into homes and orphanages, the sick were cared for, and hospitals were established, the widow was sustained, and the uneducated have been taught. Christian generosity has feed millions of starving people all over the world and women have been given dignity and a sense of worth... not by feminists, but by Jesus Christ!

Every type of loving concern began to emerge as the message of Salvation transformed the hearts and minds of those who would believe. The words of Christ, *"You shall love your neighbor as yourself"* were engraved upon their hearts. Over the years, charities were formed, disaster relief given, and slavery was abolished... all by Christians. Even the founding documents of some of the greatest nations on earth were based on biblical principles. And the just laws that govern these prosperous countries were based upon the Ten Commandments. Beloved, you can be very proud of your Christian heritage. The brothers and sisters that went before you have accomplished mighty things. By the grace of God, they have worked tirelessly to fulfill their scriptural mandate. Many have even paid the ultimate price.

In contrast, look at the "achievements" of the atheists: hundreds of millions of people have been tortured and murdered; hopes and aspirations were crushed under the iron fist of Communism and other totalitarian regimes. The track record of the nations influenced by Hinduism, Buddhism, and Islam fare little better: poverty, sickness, and social injustice abound. Dear reader, make no mistake about it. This world would be much more bleak... a harder, more fearful place if Jesus had never come.

As you continue your journey of introspection for the purpose of being conformed to His image, it is wise to occasionally look at the progress that has been made. The same is true for the Church. We often point to her failings and faults, but one cannot help but marvel at what has been accomplished! Give God praise and honor now!

All praise, and glory, and honor to You, King of Kings and the Lord of Lords, the Only One True God. And unto You Jesus Christ, the Savior of the world, be praise forever! You have used Your mighty power to demonstrate Your awesome love!

Spiritual Gifts

"Now concerning spiritual gifts, brethren, I do not want you to be ignorant" 1Corinthians 12:1

Dear saint, it would seem that most Christians need to learn a bit more about the gifts of the Holy Spirit, as mentioned in 1Corinthians 12-14. Please review them again... and let's not get sectarian as we discuss these things; this is not Pentecostalism; this is the Word of God. There is clear evidence that the gifts of the Spirit were given by God for the purpose of building His Church. Are they not needed today? How foolish to think that they have ceased from operating.

Have you been blinded by denominational bias? Open your eyes, dear disciple; see what God has been doing. The gifts of the Spirit are alive and well! Millions of believers from every Christian background are using these gifts today. Shouldn't you also? Seek the Lord in this matter. If you are a dedicated servant of the Most High, you need the power of the Holy Spirit to accomplish His purposes... and His gifts. You most definitely need supernatural knowledge, wisdom, insights and spiritual power to bring healing, deliverance, and true miracles. Look around you, beloved; do you really think that your training, your intellect and your good programs will transform your city? Even with all diligence and perseverance? Come now, let us reason together! You need every tool that God has to offer. The master has been giving the Holy Spirit and His gifts to all who will ask - why not ask?

Yes, there has been foolishness, and abuse and downright heresy when it comes to the subject of spiritual gifts, nevertheless are you willing to discount entire sections of scripture because you are afraid of them? It may be a little scary to first learn to drive a car, but how foolish it would be to continue to ride your bicycle for the rest of your life, when you could be driving. You who pride yourself on your knowledge of God's Word: There is still so much for you to learn! *Lord, I want everything that you have for me. Please fill me afresh with your Holy Spirit and give me every spiritual gift that I may need. Please fill me now!*

Foods, Festivals and Sabbaths

"So let no one judge you in food or in drink, or regarding a festival or a new moon or sabbaths, which are a shadow of things to come, but the substance is of Christ." Colossians 2:16,17

It has become popular these days to revisit the Jewish roots of Christianity. Messianic congregations are springing up here and there with increased emphasis on Old Testament biblical truths... in addition to the beloved New Testament. This is good and helpful. What a rich heritage we have; how much depth of understanding can be obtained. Study, and learn well. Remember, dear Gentile, you have been grafted in (Rom. 11:17-18).

Nevertheless, be careful. In your zeal to go deeper don't become entangled in the law, especially regarding dietary restrictions and the observance of festivals and Sabbaths. In today's passage Paul is clearly telling the Colossians not to be concerned with such regulations. If you choose to observe, this may enrich your worship experience, but don't judge those who choose not to or think them to be lesser Christians. Observing festivals and Sabbaths won't make anyone more pleasing to God. Jesus' blood is sufficient!

If you are zealous to please God: forgive those who have offended you, give to the poor, champion justice for the oppressed, be light and salt to this hurting generation.

The Goodness and Severity of God

"You will say then, 'Branches were broken off that I might be grafted in.' Well said. Because of unbelief they were broken off, and you stand by faith. Do not be haughty, but fear. For if God did not spare the natural branches, He may not spare you either. Therefore consider the goodness and severity of God: on those who fell, severity; but toward you, goodness, if you continue in His goodness. Otherwise you also will be cut off. And they also, if they do not continue in unbelief, will be grafted in, for God is able to graft them in again." Romans 11:19-23

Obviously this scripture speaks of Israel's unbelief and the consequences, but it also reveals something that perhaps you would rather not see... *"Do not be haughty, but fear. For if God did not spare the natural branches, He may not spare you either."* Imagine that; the apostle of grace is telling the Roman, gentile believers not to be haughty, but to fear God... continue in His goodness and stand by faith *"otherwise you also will be cut off."* This is very disconcerting, especially if you believe in eternal security - once saved, always saved. It is quite similar to the theological conundrum posed by Luther's *faith alone* doctrine. James 2:24 boldly declares the direct opposite: *"You see then that a man is justified by works, and not by faith only."*

What do you do with these apparent contradictions? Beloved, they are only contradictory if you have chosen to believe the opposite of what is clearly stated. Dear believer, a pointed recommendation: believe exactly what is written! (Of course, you must also consider the context and recognize figures of speech - i.e. *"He shall cover you with His feathers..."* but please don't manipulate the Scripture if it does not concur with your doctrine.)

The Holy One is loving, kind, merciful, gracious, and slow to anger. You can trust Him with every aspect of your life; He is trustworthy and faithful. We could fill volumes ascribing to His marvelous attributes. But know this too: Paul tells you to consider both the goodness AND the severity of God. The Almighty is a consuming fire...a righteous judge. He covered the earth with a great deluge; He annihilated Sodom and Gomorrah; He brought plagues upon Egypt; and struck Uzza dead. Lest you be tempted to discount this as Old Testament theology, don't forget Ananias and Sapphira! Stand by faith and continue in His goodness *"otherwise you also will be cut off."* If you feel it necessary to debate the meaning of "cut off," first check your lexicon. Nevertheless, do you really want to be in such a state, regardless of what you think it means?

The Doctrine of Dying

"We are hard pressed on every side, yet not crushed; we are perplexed, but not in despair; persecuted, but not forsaken; struck down, but not destroyed-- always carrying about in the body the dying of the Lord Jesus, that the life of Jesus also may be manifested in our body. For we who live are always delivered to death for Jesus' sake, that the life of Jesus also may be manifested in our mortal flesh. So then death is working in us, but life in you."
2Corinthians 4:8-12

Paul was notified when our Lord first called him, that he would suffer greatly; and surely this came to pass: *"We are hard pressed on every side...we are perplexed... persecuted... struck down.... -- always carrying about in the body the dying of the Lord Jesus..."* What a difficult ministry: Whipped, beaten with rods, stoned, shipwrecked, with various perils, weariness and toils, sleeplessness, hunger and thirst, cold and nakedness... Absolutely incredible!

But read on; this next line is extremely revealing. Perhaps we are so taken back by Paul's suffering that we miss the reason for it... the key principle of fruitful ministry and the foundation of the doctrine of *dying to self*. Paul goes on to explain why he was hard pressed, perplexed, persecuted and struck down. The reason: *" ... **that the life of Jesus also may be manifested in our body.** For we who live are always delivered to death for Jesus' sake, **that the life of Jesus also may be manifested in our mortal flesh.** So then death is working in us, but life in you."* Do you understand? Paul's life was crushed; he was made weak, always delivered to death... so that the life of Jesus may be made manifest in his mortal body! *"Therefore most gladly I will rather boast in my infirmities, that the power of Christ may rest upon me. Therefore I take pleasure in infirmities,*

240

in reproaches, in needs, in persecutions, in distresses, for Christ's sake. For when I am weak, then I am strong" (2Cor.12: 9,10). Do you see? *Death* was working in Paul so that *life* could flow from him to others.

This is not only true for Paul, but a biographical sketch of any fruitful servant of God (contemporary or historical) always reveals trials, sufferings, frailties and failures... death being at work in their mortal bodies, making them strong and powerful in the spirit. Watchman Nee said, "It is through your wounds that the Holy Spirit flows out from you." I know many a saint who minister out of their woundedness, their weakness and brokenness: They struggle and wrestle, but Spirit-life flows out from them and many are blessed. Conversely, there are those who have it "all together" and act like they are moving in power, but actually demonstrate very little - lives are not being transformed. They are strong, relying upon themselves.

The pride of one's life does not have to be blatantly obvious... with haughtiness and arrogance. Surely Paul was not that way. Nonetheless, because of his great revelations, a "messenger of Satan" was sent to buffet him, to prevent him from becoming prideful. And although we do not know what this thorn was, you can be sure that it was quite troublesome... causing him to literally plead with the Lord more than once. *"And lest I should be exalted above measure by the abundance of the revelations, a thorn in the flesh was given to me, a messenger of Satan to buffet me, lest I be exalted above measure. Concerning this thing I pleaded with the Lord three times that it might depart from me. And He said to me, 'My grace is sufficient for you, for My strength is made perfect in weakness...'" (2Cor. 12:7-9).*

Paul gives us another reason for the intense trials that work death in us: *"Yes, we had the sentence of death in ourselves, **that we should not trust in ourselves but in God** who raises the dead..."* (2Cor. 1:9). We are to be totally dependant upon God. Most Christians pledge allegiance to this concept but few actually live this way. Complete dependency is a place where faith is grown and power made manifest. How awesome is our God; how glorious are His ways! Have you ever wondered why Jesus told the twelve (when

He sent them to the towns and villages of Israel) *"Provide neither gold nor silver nor copper in your money belts, nor bag for your journey, nor two tunics, nor sandals, nor staffs..."* (Matt. 10:9,10). Yes, a workman is worthy of his hire, but the state of total dependency is an incubator for faith... and the subsequent release of spiritual power!

Remember, beloved, the dying process is a work of God. He allowed, or perhaps even arranged, the circumstances that worked *death* in Paul. He is doing the same for you. No need to bring it upon yourself. Who would want to? (Although some religious zealots do.) The Lord has seasons for refining, pruning and breaking, to a lesser or greater degree, according to His plans and purpose for you. He will perform it and bring it to completion... to the glory of His name, for the blessing of others.

Miracle power can be released through proud, sinful vessels... for the sake of the hurting masses. Thank the Lord for His grace and mercy. Nonetheless, personal strength, self-reliance, and pride are major hindrances to the work of God. Transforming, Holy Spirit power flows best through the weak and foolish, the lowly. God will resist, and may eventually reject the proud. History clearly reveals these things.

Extravagant Worship

"... as He sat at the table, a woman came having an alabaster flask of very costly oil of spikenard. Then she broke the flask and poured it on His head. But there were some who were indignant among themselves, and said, 'Why was this fragrant oil wasted? For it might have been sold for more than three hundred denarii and given to the poor.' And they criticized her sharply." Mark 14:3,4

What an awesome passage - one of my favorites. There is another similar to it (Luke 7:37), in which a woman spills her tears upon Jesus' feet and wipes them with her hair... kissing His feet and anointing them with fragrant oil. How beautiful and precious. There is no concern of what others will think; dignity is not an issue. No cost is too great; there is complete abandonment of self.

The onlooker's reaction, however, was far less than admirable. Michal made the same error when she observed King David dancing before his God with complete abandonment. You see, beloved, true worship can expose the lukewarmness in the hearts of others. The response is usually one of self-righteousness... as they try to conceal their backslidden state... especially from themselves! And the unsaved? They can't even begin to comprehend why anyone would "waste" their time, their money, their life on such foolishness.

Dear worshipper, be extravagant! Pour out all that you have, all that you are. Give Him your very best. He will be pleased and you will be richly blessed. Our Master was so taken with this woman's extraordinary act of worship that He prophetically declared, *"Assuredly, I say to you, wherever this gospel is preached in the whole world, what this woman has done will also be told as a memorial to her."*

Isn't this *Normal Christianity*? Bride of Jesus Christ, how could you offer Him anything less? It's time to make yourself ready.